The Hope of Glory

A "Connections" Book

The Hope of Glory

Honor Discourse and New Testament Interpretation

David A. deSilva

WIPF & STOCK · Eugene, Oregon

Wipf and Stock Publishers
199 W 8th Ave, Suite 3
Eugene, OR 97401

The Hope of Glory
Honor Discourse and New Testament Interpretation
By deSilva, David A.
Copyright©1999 by deSilva, David A.
ISBN 13: 978-1-60608-412-0
Publication date 7/1/2009
Previously published by The Liturgical Press, 1999

Unless indicated otherwise the Scripture quotations in this book are from the Revised Standard Version of the Bible, © 1946, 1952, and 1971 by the Division of Christian Education of the National Council of the Churches of Christ in the USA or from the New Revised Standard Version of the Bible, © 1989 by the Division of Christian Education of the National Council of the Churches of Christ in the USA. All rights reserved. Used by permission.

To James Adrian, John Austin, and Justin Alexander

The father of righteous children has great joy;

he who has wise sons delights in them.

—*Proverbs 23:24*

Contents

Abbreviations ... ix

Preface ... xi

Introduction: Reading the New Testament in Cultural Context ... xiii

1 Honor Discourse, Classical Rhetoric, and Social Engineering ... 1

2 Honor Discourse in Matthew ... 34

3 Honor Discourse in the Fourth Gospel ... 70

4 Honor Discourse in 1 and 2 Thessalonians ... 91

5 Honor Discourse in the Corinthian Correspondence ... 118

6 Honor Discourse in the Epistle to the Hebrews ... 144

7 Honor Discourse in the Apocalypse of John ... 178

Conclusion: Honor Discourse, Exegesis, and the Church ... 203

Bibliography of Modern Authors ... 210

Index of Texts Cited ... 216

Index of Modern Authors ... 227

Abbreviations

AB	The Anchor Bible
AJT	*American Journal of Theology*
AUSS	Andrews University Seminary Studies
BTB	*Biblical Theology Bulletin*
CBQ	*Catholic Biblical Quarterly*
HThR	Harvard Theological Review
ICC	International Critical Commentary
JBL	*Journal of Biblical Literature*
JSNT	*Journal for the Study of the New Testament*
JSNT.S	Journal for the Study of the New Testament Supplement Series
JSP	*Journal for the Study of the Pseudepigrapha*
LCL	Loeb Classical Library (London: Heinemann, and Cambridge, Mass.: Harvard University Press)
NCBC	New Century Bible Commentary
NICNT	New International Commentary on the New Testament
NIGTC	New International Greek Testament Commentary
NPNF[1]	A Select Library of the Nicene and Post-Nicene Fathers of the Christian Church, First Series (edited by Philip Schaff and H. Wace; 14 vols.; Grand Rapids: Eerdmans, 1956)

NovT	*Novum Testamentum*
NTS	*New Testament Studies*
PG	Patrologiae Graeca (edited by J. P. Migne; 162 vols.; Paris, 1857–1866)
SBL.DS	Society of Biblical Literature Dissertation Series
SBLSP	*Society of Biblical Literature Seminar Papers*
SP	Sacra Pagina
TDNT	*Theological Dictionary of the New Testament* (edited by Gerhard Kittel and Gerhard Friedrich; 10 vols.; translated by Geoffrey Bromiley; Grand Rapids: Eerdmans, 1964–1976)
WBC	Word Biblical Commentary
WTJ	*Westminster Theological Journal*

Abbreviations of classical literature follow the Oxford Classical Dictionary wherever possible.

Preface

During the past twenty years interest in the cultural context of the New Testament writings has soared. We have seen a proliferation of articles and books that speak about honor and shame in the pages of the New Testament and claim to free the reader from ethnocentric readings of these ancient Mediterranean documents. These studies are frequently eye-opening and always stimulating. They have been met, however, with suspicion from many scholars working in more traditional exegetical disciplines. The cause for this, it appears, is that the model has grown out of the work of twentieth-century cultural anthropologists studying various cultures in the modern Mediterranean, which is then imposed upon ancient texts. A second critique is that the model, while it may assist in illuminating certain interactions between characters in the biblical story or help us recognize when a topic of honor is being introduced, does not aid us in understanding the rhetorical impact of the language or discerning its social effects within the body of Christians reading the text.

The present study, while grateful to earlier authors for bringing the attention of biblical scholars back to the importance of honor and dishonor in the first-century world, seeks to address this dual criticism of earlier work. Native informants from the ancient world such as the authors of ethical and rhetorical handbooks emerge as our best instructors on how honor is conceived and how the social power of shaming and honoring works to maintain the values of a particular culture. These informants help us discern how an author like Paul or John may use honor discourse as part of a larger, orchestrated strategy of persuasion and as a tool for forming and maintaining communities of people committed to the Christian way of life in the midst of competing groups with very different ideas about what is noble and what disgraceful.

This volume is the product of several years not merely of private study and reflection but also of fruitful conversation. I wish to thank Luke T. Johnson, Vernon K. Robbins, Carl R. Holladay, and Arthur Wainwright for their generous guidance during the years of my dissertation research, where the foundations for my understanding of the rhetorical and social use of honor discourse were poured, and for their ongoing encouragement since that initial statement. The present volume has also benefited from conversations with Duane F. Watson, Gail R. O'Day, and Ben Witherington III, as well as many students at Ashland Theological Seminary who wrestled alongside me with the task of discerning honor discourse in the New Testament and sorting out its place in the larger program of exegesis.

As this book comes at the end of a long line of studies, many of its pages have appeared scattered about in journal articles or other academic publications. Chapters 1 and 4 of the present volume incorporate material from "Worthy of His Kingdom: Honor Discourse and Social Engineering in 1 Thessalonians," *JSNT* 64 (1996) 49–79. Chapter 7 was published in a slightly fuller version as "Honor Discourse and the Rhetorical Strategy of the Apocalypse of John," *JSNT* 71 (1998) 79–110. Chapters 1 and 6 incorporate substantial portions of "Investigating Honor Discourse: Guidelines from Classical Rhetoricians" (*SBLSP* 36 [1997] 491–525), "Despising Shame: A Cultural-Anthropological Investigation of the Epistle to the Hebrews" (*JBL* 113 [1994] 459–481), and "Exchanging Favor for Wrath: Apostasy in Hebrews and Patron-Client Relations" (*JBL* 115 [1996] 91–116). Parts of chapter 5 appeared previously in *The Credentials of an Apostle: Paul's Gospel in 2 Corinthians 1–7* (N. Richland Hills, Tex.: BIBAL Press, 1998) and in "Let the One Who Claims Honor, Establish That Claim in the Lord" (*BTB* 28 [1998] 61–74). My appreciation is extended to the editors and publishers of these journals and monographs for their kind permission to reprint that material here.

Introduction: Reading the New Testament in Cultural Context

Students of biblical exegesis are accustomed to looking at a passage within a number of contexts as a means of gaining a richer and more accurate understanding of what the passage meant to its first hearers. A passage is regularly viewed in its historical context, that is, how it is shaped by and responds to a particular historical situation or pastoral need within the community it addresses. A passage is necessarily studied with regard to its literary context, that is, how its meaning is informed by the text that has preceded it and that follows it. This may include narrative analysis and rhetorical analysis of how the passage is situated within an emerging plot or argument. A passage is examined against the background of theological, philosophical, and ethical traditions that are invoked directly or indirectly by the language of the text. The list could be multiplied to include careful analysis of the passage's linguistic, social, and ideological contexts, not to mention many other fruitful areas of investigation that are part of a standard course in exegesis or hermeneutics.

This book seeks to introduce the reader to yet another context for reading texts from the Greco-Roman Period, particularly the texts contained in the New Testament—one not in competition with the foregoing contexts but complementary to them. This is the cultural context of the ancient Mediterranean world, particularly the role of the social value of honor and dishonor. Part of the task of becoming a more sensitive reader of the New Testament involves entering into the cultural world shared by its authors, readers, and protagonists. "Culture" is a very broad term, taken here to signify the web of relationships, mutual expectations, customs, and understanding of the world that is shared by a group of people and makes true communication possible. Culture is the prerequisite to communication. Anyone who reads the New Testament assuming that the culture he or she takes for granted was shared by its authors will surely misread it or at least read it without proper sensitivity. Fortunately, with the help of cultural anthropologists, sociologists, and some important ancient authors who reflected on their culture at first hand we may let ourselves into that world and hear the Scriptures in a fresh and illuminating way.

Several classicists and cultural anthropologists have contributed to the understanding of the first-century Mediterranean world as an honor-shame culture. In his *Merit and Responsibility,* a foundational investigation of honor and shame in the Greek world, A.W.H. Adkins develops a picture of the Homeric world as a culture highly sensitive to, and competitive for, honor.[1] Honor as a pivotal value, he argues, persists into the world of fourth-century Athens (as seen especially in the tragedies of Aeschylus, Euripides, and Sophocles). Adkins shows also how the definition of honorable action changes in situations in which cooperation (e.g., between host and guest) is called for rather than competition. Adkins acknowledges the importance of other values but stresses forcefully that the evaluation of some act as honorable or dishonorable is a final verdict.[2] Other classicists, such as E. R. Dodds and Bernard Williams, have extended and refined Adkins' study.[3]

Students of cultural anthropology like Julian Pitt-Rivers have also provided essential foundations for reflection on honor and shame in the Mediterranean. In an important essay[4] Pitt-Rivers describes the culture of modern Mediterranean villages as an honor culture, testifying to the persistence of this social value from Homeric to modern times (although, of course, not without constant evolution). His insights have been used by students of the New Testament such as Bruce Malina and Jerome Neyrey and applied directly to the interpretation of social interactions between characters in the gospels.[5]

The present book builds on the insights already gleaned from classical and cultural-anthropological studies, but with a special interest in how attention to honor discourse opens up a text's meaning for and impact upon a first-century audience. The choice of the term "honor discourse" highlights the rhetorical interest of this book, the aim of which is to push beyond using texts merely as documents that illustrate the social value of honor at work to show how analysis of honor language affords a deeper understanding of how the author has shaped a text to elicit specific responses from the original audience. The close reading of texts, particularly within the framework of exegesis, calls us to develop a model for discerning how an author uses honor discourse as part of an orchestrated strategy of persuasion, as a tool for forming and maintaining a social body (i.e., the Church) in the midst of competing cultures. Such a model will then be a useful tool alongside the many other contexts of reading that make up the larger enterprise of biblical exegesis.

To accomplish this we will rely heavily on native informants from the Greek and Roman periods, specifically the authors of handbooks on rhetoric (e.g., Aristotle's *Art of Rhetoric*, the *Rhetorica ad Herennium*, and Quintilian's *Institutes*).[6] Since these are books about the art of persuasion—how to win over one's audience to a particular course of action, set of values, or decision—what they say about honor language will be of primary importance in discerning what New Testament authors hoped to effect in their audience through the use of honor language. Further, their detailed advice will provide many clues concerning how honor or dishonor are being invoked by an author.

The first chapter will discuss the role of the social values of honor and dishonor within ancient Mediterranean societies, particularly as they relate to the maintenance of group values and boundaries. This will be followed by an examination of how first-century authors would use honor discourse within the art of persuasion, with a view to recognizing these appeals to honor in New Testament texts (i.e., how will considerations related to honor affect the evaluations and ambitions of the hearers?). A final step will be to connect the use of honor discourse in a text with the social-engineering program of its author for his or her audience (i.e., how does the text seek to influence the behaviors and boundaries of the group it addresses?).

The larger part of the book will be devoted to providing examples or models of how this approach may bear fruit in the study of the rhetorical strategy of the narrative, epistolary, and visionary literature in the New Testament. Reflecting on honor discourse in the Gospels and Revelation is particularly helpful as a means for uncovering the rhetorical effect of these texts, which belong to genres particularly resistant to classical rhetorical criticism. With regard to the epistles attention to honor discourse frequently supplements and may even lead classical rhetorical analysis.

In our concluding chapter we will explore the integration of this area of investigation into the larger task of exegesis and the interpretation of ancient texts. We will find that attention to honor discourse in a text interacts with many of the more traditional contexts for developing an exegesis of a passage, especially lexical, literary, philosophical, rhetorical, and social contexts. Interest in a richly textured reading of a passage that takes into consideration multiple contexts has perhaps been shown nowhere more than in the recent work of Vernon Robbins,[7] whose formulation of a socio-rhetorical method of interpretation may become the best framework for conversations between analysis of honor discourse and other areas of investigation.

NOTES: INTRODUCTION

[1] Aristotle himself thus characterizes the society of the Homeric epics (*Nicomachean Ethics* 3.8.1-3 [LCL]): "Those races appear to be the bravest among which cowards are degraded and brave men held in honour. It is this citizen courage which inspires the heroes portrayed by Homer, like Diomedes and Hector . . . . This type of courage . . . is prompted by a virtue, namely the sense of shame, and by the desire for something noble, namely honour, and the wish to avoid the disgrace of being reproached."

[2] A.W.H. Adkins, *Merit and Responsibility: A Study in Greek Values* (Oxford: Oxford University Press, 1960) 185.

[3] E. R. Dodds (*The Greeks and the Irrational* [Berkeley: University of California Press, 1966]) traces the emergence of a guilt culture during the Classical age alongside the older honor culture of the Homeric age, resisting the temptation to collapse concern for pollution and atonement into concern for honor. Bernard Williams (*Shame and Necessity* [Berkeley: University of California Press, 1993]) balances the picture developed by Adkins of a strongly agonistic culture in which people regularly challenged the honor of others in an attempt to win honor for themselves with an emphasis on the importance of respect for the honor of others lest one incur nemesis, divine or human vengeance.

[4] Julian Pitt-Rivers, "Honour and Social Status," in *Honour and Shame: The Values of Mediterranean Society*, ed. J. G. Peristiany (Chicago: University of Chicago Press, 1966) 21–77.

[5] Bruce J. Malina, *The New Testament World: Insights from Cultural Anthropology* (Louisville: Westminster/John Knox, 1993); Bruce J. Malina and Jerome H. Neyrey, "Honor and Shame in Luke-Acts: Pivotal Values of the Mediterranean World," in Jerome H. Neyrey, ed., *The Social World of Luke-Acts: Models for Interpretation* (Peabody, Mass.: Hendrickson, 1991) 26–65; Bruce J. Malina and Richard Rohrbaugh, *Social-Science Commentary on the Synoptic Gospels* (Minneapolis: Fortress, 1992). Also noteworthy is the work of Halvor

Moxnes, whose studies of Romans take analysis of honor discourse forward in a number of important respects, not least of which is an analysis of the way honor discourse reinforces group boundaries and preserves a group's culture within a dominant culture (see Halvor Moxnes, "Honor and Shame: A Reader's Guide," *BTB* 23 [1993] 167–176; idem, "Honor, Shame, and the Outside World in Paul's Letter to the Romans," in Jacob Neusner, Peder Borgen, E. S. Frerichs, and Richard Horsley, eds., *The Social World of Formative Christianity and Judaism* [Philadelphia: Fortress, 1988]; idem, "Honour and Righteousness in Romans," *JSNT* 32 [1988] 61–77).

[6] Malina and Neyrey have recently used aspects of these same sources fruitfully in a study of ancient personality (*Portraits of Paul: An Archaeology of Ancient Personality* [Louisville: Westminster/John Knox, 1996), anchoring their discussions of honor and personality in the specificity and reliability of rhetorical handbooks as primary sources.

[7] Vernon K. Robbins, *The Tapestry of Early Christian Discourse: Rhetoric, Society and Ideology* (London: Routledge, 1996); *Exploring the Texture of Texts* (Valley Forge, Pa.: Trinity Press International, 1996).

1

Honor Discourse, Classical Rhetoric, and Social Engineering

*W*hat does it mean to say that the authors and audiences of the New Testament texts were members of an honor culture? How would concern for honor guide the choices and actions of such people? Before we can approach New Testament texts directly, we will need to explore the dynamics of living within an honor culture. We will need to reflect on the relationship between personal concern for honor and the maintenance of the values of the group—the honor-bestowing body—to which the individual belongs. We will need, further, to consider the complexities of the first-century Greco-Roman world, in which numerous cultures coexisted and often competed for the loyalty of their members. What was honorable for one group might not be honorable for another group within this mixed society,[1] and so we will need to explore the strategies developed by groups to insulate their own members from the opinion of outsiders and maintain their commitment to the group's definition of honorable behavior. Finally, we must learn to recognize the vocabulary of honor—the words, symbols, patterns, and exchanges that would be heard by first-century people as related to the concern for honor—and the rhetorical impact of this vocabulary. The insights of earlier pioneers in the study of the honor culture of the ancient Mediterranean, together with the testimony and guidance of classical informants, will provide the necessary material to lay an adequate foundation.

HONOR AND THE IMPLANTATION OF CULTURAL VALUES

A person born into the first-century Mediterranean world, whether Gentile or Jewish, was trained from childhood to desire honor and avoid disgrace.[2] These two coordinates—honor and disgrace—are central social values for people living around the Mediterranean from the time of Homer, extending even into the present day in the less urbanized areas. The definitions of what is honorable and what is disgraceful change from culture to culture and from century to century, but honor remains an abiding concern however one's society defines it.

What does it mean to seek honor and avoid disgrace? It means that a person will be oriented toward the approval of society and will engage those behaviors and seek to reflect those virtues that society regards as honorable so as to be regarded as an honorable person. Since honor and dishonor are granted by the larger group they represent the primary means of social control in the ancient Mediterranean world. A society upholds its values by rewarding with greater degrees of honor those who embody those values in greater degrees. Dishonor represents a group's disapproval of a member based on his or her lack of conformity with those values deemed essential for the group's continued existence. Since people are raised in a world where honor is of great importance to a person's sense of worth and for a person's access to and interaction with other honorable people, the social group is in a strong position to motivate conformity among its individual members. An individual has self-respect on the basis of his or her perception of how fully he or she has embodied the culture's ideals; that individual has honor on the basis of the society's recognition of that person's conformity with essential values.

The threat of dishonor supports a society's prohibitions of socially disruptive behavior. For example, adultery—the violation of the sanctity and peace of the marriage bond that is foundational to society—carries with it the promise of disgrace (cf. Prov 6:32-33). Agreement and unity, essential values for the orderly life of the Greek city, are lauded as honorable, while dissensions and strife bring the threat of disgrace for the city (cf. Dio, *Or.* 48.5-6). Similarly, courage in battle, necessary especially during the pre-Hellenistic period for a city's survival, wins honor and lasting remembrance (cf. Pericles' Funeral Oration in Thucydides, *Hist.* 2.35-42). In a society that had as its basic building block the patron-client relationship (Seneca, *Ben.* 1.4.2; see "Recognizing Honor Scripts" below), the threat of irrevocable dishonor, and therefore exclusion from future patronage, supports the value of showing gratitude to one's patron (or a city's benefactors: Dio, *Oration* 31).

"Honor" becomes the umbrella that extends over the set of behaviors, commitments, and attitudes that preserve a given culture and society; individuals raised with a desire for honor will seek the good of the larger group, willingly embodying the group's values as the path to self-fulfillment. Ancient collections of advice, whether Greek or the more familiar Jewish collection of Proverbs, label actions either with the positive sanction "noble" or "honorable" or with the negative sanction "disgraceful." By such means the author sets before the reader a model of existence that acts always in the best interest of the public trust, that honors the established authorities on which the state rests (gods, parents, laws), and restrains the expenditure of resources on what brings pleasure only to the self and not benefit to others as well. Similarly, memorial services and other public, civic occasions were opportunities for orations that would reinforce the society's values by holding up as praiseworthy those people who have exemplified those values (e.g., in a eulogy). Hearing others praised for living out virtues the larger group valued and honored would lead the members of the audience to recommit themselves to the virtue or behavior that led to praise (see "Honor and Persuasion" below). Those who follow such models will be rewarded with society's approval and affirmation, that is, honor.[3]

HONOR AND COMPETING CULTURES

A person in an honor culture is oriented from birth toward seeking the approval of the significant others: this is how the culture maintains its essential identity and values across generational lines. In a simple society (wherein one culture, one set of values is shared by all the group members) this process results in a fairly consistent method of social control and predictable adherence to the society's values. Where all the people one encounters from birth value life to the extent that they sweep the sidewalk in front of them lest they trample an insect it will be difficult for one to start killing insects, let alone rabbits or deer. Such a person would be disgraced: shamed in an attempt both to rehabilitate the offender and to dissuade others from following his or her irrational and offensive behavior. Those who continue to sweep the sidewalk in front of them, on the other hand, will be affirmed by their peers as honorable and valuable members of the society.

The situation becomes more interesting in a complex society in which one finds competing cultures, or at least alternative cultures within a dominant culture. When it becomes known to members of this life-loving, bug-saving society that not everyone everywhere has such regard for all life, people within that culture may begin to question the value of the life of an insect. When it becomes known that some people in another culture make their living exterminating insects, the practice of sweeping the sidewalk in front of you to save insects comes into question. How can this strange, life-honoring culture survive in the face of other available cultures that do not share its values? First it must find ways of reaffirming its own values to its own members as the only divinely-ordained way of life; it must find ways of demonstrating to its members that the way of life of the bug-killing cultures is opposed to the divine order. If the bug-killing cultures start making their contempt for the sidewalk sweepers known the sidewalk sweepers must find some way to assure each other that the opinion of bug killers is meaningless or depraved, and no reflection of the sidewalk sweepers' true honor, which consists in remaining faithful to the ancestral culture's way of life. God will vindicate the sidewalk sweepers' honor and way of life and bring dishonor upon the heads of the bug killers!

Defining the "Court of Reputation"

I have chosen this rather bizarre example so as to focus us on the process rather than the content of how a culture might begin to develop survival techniques when it ceases to be the sole culture available to its members, when rival cultures rise up casting doubt on the formerly unquestioned practices of the group.[4] This process is very important for cultures in the first-century Mediterranean world, for that world was quite complex. It was a world dominated by the culture of Hellenism. This is what we can call the "dominant culture" because it was the culture shared by those in power. It also happened to be the "majority culture," as most of the people in the Mediterranean world had lived under the influence of Hellenism since Alexander the Great and had accepted much of its thought, its values, and its way of life.[5] What did the dominant culture value? It valued piety, the expression of due reverence and allegiance to the gods, the rulers, the city, and the family—all of this surrounded by the trappings of idolatry. It valued civic unity and harmony; it valued the display of gratitude and honor toward benefactors; it valued youth, beauty of appearance, and strength. Within this dominant culture Jews struggled to maintain their culture. We can call this an "ethnic subculture": it is defined by race and it shares many of the values of the dominant culture but believes that it fulfills those values better. Members of this Jewish subculture would claim to know what true piety is all about, for they serve the one and only God, the sole benefactor of the human race. They share with the Greco-Roman culture the value of piety but fulfill it differently and, in their own opinion, better.

It was not easy during the Hellenistic and Greco-Roman periods, however, to remain completely dedicated to the Jewish way of life. The Torah, the way of life inherited from the ancestors, was no longer the unquestionable way of life. Another way of life, the "Greek way," was always present nearby, full of promise for the Jew who desired to enter the larger world, to reap the benefits of profitable contacts with powerful Gentiles, to seek honor in a larger arena. The problem, of course, was that "honor" is no longer simply and only the result of obedience to Torah. The dominant (Gentile) culture actually regarded following Torah as a mark against one's honor. Following Torah was the equivalent of atheism in the eyes of many Greeks, for their gods were denied the services due them; following Torah was a serious breach in civic unity, for Jews who observed Torah tended to remain within closely-knit groups and engage in the life of the larger city in limited ways;[6] Jews would also have appeared ungrateful, in the eyes of many, to the chief patrons of the Greco-Roman world, namely the emperors, for they refused them the worship in which all other people in the Eastern provinces willingly engaged. The Jew was thus confronted by a dilemma: following Torah might lead to honor in the sight of other observant Jews, but it appeared to lead away from honor and even to bring on contempt in the sight of the dominant culture.[7] How could a Jew remain a loyal Jew in such a world?

In such a setting the definition of who comprise one's group of significant others becomes essential. If one seeks status in the eyes of the larger society one will seek to maintain the values and fulfill the expectations of the dominant or majority culture. If one has been brought into a minority culture (e.g., a philosophical school or a voluntary association like the early Christian community) or has been born into an ethnic subculture (such as Judaism), then one's adherence to the group's values and ideals will only remain strong if one redefines the constituency of one's circle of significant others. The "court of reputation" must be limited to group members, who will support the group values in their grants of honor and censure.[8] Including some supra-social entity in this group (e.g., God, Reason, or Nature) offsets the minority (and therefore "deviant") status of the group's opinion. The opinion of one's fellow group members is thus fortified by, anchored in, and legitimated by a "higher" court of reputation whose judgments are of greater importance and more lasting consequence than the opinion of the disapproving majority or the dominant culture. Both Greco-Roman philosophers and Jewish authors routinely pointed to the opinion of God as a support for the minority culture's values: both admonished group members to remain committed to the group's values, for that is what God looks for and honors in a person.[9]

Where the values and commitments of a minority culture differ from those of a dominant (or other alternative) culture, members of that minority culture must be moved to disregard the opinion of non-members about their behavior. All groups will seek to use honor and disgrace to enforce the values of their particular culture, so each group must insulate its members from the influence of the opinion of non-members. Those who do not hold to the values and construals of reality embodied in the group are excluded from the "court of reputation" as shameless or errant: approval or disapproval in their eyes must count for nothing because it rests on error, and the representative of the minority culture can look forward to his or her vindication when the extent of that error is revealed.[10] When the dominant, Greco-Roman culture held a group like the Jews in contempt the effect was a constant pressure on individual Jews to give up their Jewishness and join in those behaviors that would be greeted as honorable by the members of the dominant culture. Jewish authors would urge their fellow Jews to set their hearts on the opinion of the congregation and the opinion of God and so be able to resist the pull of the Gentile world.

Members of this clearly-defined court of reputation must have frequent and meaningful interaction within the group. They must encourage one another to pursue group values and ideals, and honor one another on that basis. Those who begin to show signs of slackening in their commitment to the values of the group out of a growing regard for the opinion of outsiders must be made to feel ashamed by the members of the group and thus pulled back from assimilation. Such people will need reminders that the realm "outside" the group is also "outside" the sphere of God's approval.

In a complex society where other sets of values are available and where other views of the world are formed to support those values each culture is always in danger of being disconfirmed by the availability of other cultures. It becomes all the more necessary, therefore, and particularly within minority cultures, for the members to reflect back to one another the reality of the group's definitions of the world (e.g., the reality of Christ's return and the coming judgment). Maintenance of the group culture calls for the investment of energy, time, and resources. The minority worldview is rendered ever firmer and more real by the degree of one's participation in it and through the member's continually being held accountable by his or her significant others to the ethos created by that worldview.

Encouragement within the group, in short, must outweigh the discouragement that comes to the individual from outside the group. Relationships within the group—the sense of connectedness and belonging so essential to the social being—must offset the sense of disconnectedness and alienation from the larger society (particularly if, as in the case of the convent, it formerly provided one's primary reference group).

Reinterpreting the Opinion of Outsiders

A society's displays of disapproval (whether in the form of insult, abuse, shunning, or more severe marginalization, e.g., martyrdom) seek to "shame" those whom society regards as deviants into falling back in line with society's values. Dishonor and persecution are, in the first place, attempts to rehabilitate deviant members and to prevent similar transgressions of the group's values. This social pressure carries tremendous weight, especially as it continues over time. How might a minority group insulate itself from these negative sanctions, these attempts to erode group commitment and promote a return to the values and ideals of the dominant or majority culture?

The attack on the larger society's ability to form a reliable opinion about the group members is, of course, the first step in this direction. Jews and Christians will routinely point out that unbelievers do not have all the facts, as it were. They are ignorant that the Judeo-Christian God is the one who will judge the world and assign eternal honor or disgrace. They are ignorant of the ways in which this God has made known the behaviors and commitments God will reward with honor. How, then, can outsiders form an intelligent opinion about group members? The outsiders' contempt for the Jew or the Christian is really a sign of the outsiders' ignorance of what God values, really a sign of the outsiders' lack of honor, and no true reflection upon the honor of the believer.

We find, however, that minority cultures were able to develop an even more durable insulation against the effects of society's assaults. Those very actions by which society hoped to shame the deviants back into conformity become a source of honor within the group. We see this particularly in the use of athletic and military imagery by writers from first-century minority cultures.[11] The athletic competitions and the battlefield were two arenas in which honor could be regularly won from the dominant, majority culture. The virtues of courage and endurance—essential to the dominant culture's very survival when tested by war or the reflection of war in the athletic games—are now claimed for members of minority cultures who bravely face the opposition of the larger society and endure in their commitments despite abuse, insult, and hardship.

Since athletes are known for their endurance of pain and hardship in order to win at the games the metaphor of the athletic contest becomes a natural one for all minority cultures that suffer pain or hardship at the hands of the host society. The use of contest or athletic imagery leads to the minority culture's appropriation of topics of courage or endurance, which are now made to serve minority cultural values. Courage is defined as "the reaching for great things and contempt for what is mean; also the endurance of hardship in expectation of profit" (*Rhet. ad Her.* 3.2.3). Hardship is thus no longer a sign of society's rejection and the group member's deviance and dishonor, but merely what must be endured in order to gain a greater goal.[12] Similarly, military imagery achieves the same end, as the language of conquering in Revelation attests (cf. Rev 2:7, 11, 17, 26; 3:5, 12, 21; 12:11; 15:2).

Another strategy in minority cultural rhetoric focuses on society's abuse as a form of educative discipline by which God fits the individual for the prize of virtue, or immortality, or holiness. This is especially frequent in the Jewish subcultural tradition (cf. Wis 3:5; Heb 12:4-12), where the disgrace suffered at the dominant culture's hands becomes a sign of acceptance by God, and endurance of those hardships becomes the process by which God forms the believer's character even as an earthly parent might use strict means to cultivate his or her young. The impact of such rhetoric is that society's attempts at reclaiming the members of what society regards as deviant groups (like the Christians) are now read as signs of divine approval. Not only do they fail to have their desired impact, they actually serve to confirm the deviants in their new loyalties and commitments.

RECOGNIZING HONOR SCRIPTS

In the investigation of the use of honor discourse within a text one may start with a basic inventory of places in which the vocabulary of honor and dishonor are used. This would include words for "reputation" or "opinion" *(doxa)*, "honor" *(timē* or *doxa)*, "dishonor" *(aischunē)*, "reproach" *(oneidismos)*, "outrage" *(hybris)*, "worthy" *(axios)*, "noble" *(kalos)*, "praise" *(aineō)*, "scorn" *(kataphroneō)*, and the like. This list could be expanded by considering synonyms and by looking for other forms (e.g., verbs, adjectives, etc.) built on the same roots as the words above.[13] Considerations of honor, however, may certainly be present even where such vocabulary items are not explicitly used. Recognition of these depends on acquiring an awareness of how honor was symbolized and achieved. The discussion of honor discourse in classical rhetoric (see "Honor and Persuasion" below) will provide further assistance to the modern reader's attempt to discover honor language at work within a text.

Ascribed and Achieved Honor

A person could receive honor passively or actively. Honor could thus be ascribed to a person from sources external to that person or achieved by a person's own action.[14] Ascriptions of honor center on the honor one has by virtue of one's birth into a particular family or race and on the honor bestowed on one by a greater person through, for example, adoption into a noble family or appointment to a prominent office. A person's honor begins with the honor of his or her family. Belonging to the family of Augustus would give one greater honor than birth into the family of a peasant or a slave. Descent from David would give one greater honor by birth than descent from a less noble ancestor. Within cities and villages there were always more distinguished and less distinguished families, and one's birth into a family determined one's starting place, as it were, in the field of honor.

Genealogies or briefer notices of descent (the name of the father or tribe), therefore, have implications for the honor of the person being described: the honor gained or lost by the members of one's family would reflect on the honor of the individual member. Belonging to a certain race or people, moreover, would have general consequences for one's honor in the sight of people of the same or other races, depending on the history of the interaction between those races. Thus "Samaritan" or "Edomite" become marks against one's honor in the eyes of Judeans given the hostilities in the history of the relationships of these ethnic groups. In Alexandria, being a native "Egyptian" is generally a mark of dishonor in the eyes of both the Greek dominant culture and the Jewish subculture.

Honor may also be ascribed after one's birth by a grant from a more powerful person. This might happen through adoption into a more noble family. Being adopted as the son of a noble and powerful person (a practice common among Romans), for example, would bestow the honor of the parent upon the adopted child. A ruler might bestow honor upon an individual by appointing him or her[15] to a prestigious office. When we read, therefore, about such topics as adoption into the household of God or Abraham, or appointment to priesthood or judgeship, we are looking at topics of ascribed honor.

Honor is achieved as an individual embodies in specific actions and habits the virtues prized by the group. An individual may acquire honor by enacting courage in battle, or by acts that embody generosity. A person who fulfills obligations toward the gods, the state, patrons, clients, and family will gain honor as a just or pious individual. The commemorative addresses (eulogies) of the period especially testify to each ancient Mediterranean society's tendency to promote its values by honoring those who embody them in specific ways.[16]

Cultural anthropologists have also discovered a common form of gaining honor in modern Mediterranean villages that appears to have deep roots in Mediterranean culture. Honor may be gained when a person offers a challenge to another person of equal social status and the challenged one fails to respond effectively in defense of his or her honor. This form of social interaction has been labeled the "challenge-riposte" or the "challenge-response."[17] The exchange must be public so that the group may bear witness to any honor lost or won. The challenge may take many shapes, some of which may be overtly hostile (such as a slap across the face) and some of which may appear quite innocent (such as a question). Even requests for help or benefactions may in some cases be read as challenges to the honor of the one being asked for favor, since his or her reputation for generosity may be at stake.[18] The witnesses will be looking for the response of the one challenged, and will adjudicate whether or not the response meets the challenge. In the words of Julian Pitt-Rivers, "the victor in any competition for honour finds his reputation enhanced by the humiliation of the vanquished."[19] We will find such exchanges to be common in the gospels, for example the frequent exchanges between Pharisees or legal experts and Jesus, but competition for honor also appears "behind the scenes" of numerous epistles as well (e.g., the challenges aimed by rival teachers at Paul and vice versa).

Honor in Patron-Client Relationships

The potential for challenges and contests for honor between social equals needs to be balanced by some attention to the cooperation among "friends" and the unequal partnership among patrons and clients. The institution of patronage touched the lives of many in the ancient world and, since honor plays an important role in patron-client relations, merits development within a book on honor discourse.

The Greco-Roman world was a "patronal" society supported by an infrastructure of networks of favor and loyalty.[20] Between social equals this relationship was called "friendship" and the members in such relationships exchanged favors as needed, with neither party being in an inferior, dependent role. In relationships between social unequals, who were unable to exchange like benefits, one party was the patron of the other (although the language of friendship might still be used out of sensitivity to the person in the inferior role; cf. John 19:12). Since most of the wealth, land, and access to power was concentrated into the hands of a very small percentage of the population most people found themselves in need of assistance in one form or another, and therefore sought out better-endowed individuals as patrons. Patrons provided money, grain, employment, land, or even professional or social advancement. The recipient of such favors became a client to the patron, which meant accepting certain specific obligations to the patron. Since the system did not lend itself to precise evaluations of favors, mutual commitment tended to be long-term.

The obligation of the client was "gratitude," one of the three possible translations of *charis* in the context of patronage (the other two being the "favor" of the patron and the "gift" itself). The triple use of this single Greek word illustrates the reciprocity and obligation inherent in the relationship. A person who received "grace" (a patron's favor) knew also that "grace" (gratitude) of proportional magnitude must be returned. This was a sacred obligation, and the client who failed to show gratitude appropriately was considered base and impious (Dio, *Or.* 31.37). Gratitude in the ancient world involved in the first instance honoring the benefactor by publicizing the favor and one's gratitude for it,[21] offering the patron one's respect in demeanor and action, and certainly avoiding any course of action that would bring the patron into disrepute. A client who showed disregard for a patron would exchange favor for wrath.

Gratitude also involved both obedience and intense personal loyalty to the patron even if that loyalty should lead one to lose one's place in one's homeland, one's physical well-being, one's wealth, and one's reputation (Seneca, *Ep. Mor.* 81.27). To show disloyalty or disobedience, or to show distrust in the patron's ability to provide any benefits he or she promised, would be to dishonor the patron. In such an event the patron would not respond as an equal (in the challenge-riposte scheme) but as a superior, bringing punishment on the client and gaining satisfaction for the patron's affronted honor. The honorable person, however, would embody the virtues of justice and loyalty ("faith") by giving one's patron his or her due.

Representations of Honor

A person's honor could be symbolized in numerous ways among ancient Mediterranean societies. One prominent way of speaking about a person's honor was reference to that person's "name." Thus one finds the psalmist urging the congregation to exalt the "name" of the Lord (Pss 29:2; 34:3) or speaking of the blotting out of the "name" of the ungodly (Ps 9:5), or Jesus teaching his disciples to have regard for revering the "name" of God (Matt 6:9), or Isaiah warning about disobedience to God's commandments among Jews as a blemish on the "name" of God among the Gentiles (Isa 52:5; Rom 2:24). The name of a person or the name of a family represents the honor of that person or family. Malina and Neyrey suggest that a "good name" in the first century was rather like "good credit" in the twentieth-century Western world: an honorable name or reputation opened doors to partnerships and access to opportunities from which a dishonorable name would exclude one.[22] This topic is, of course, closely related to the earlier discussion of honor ascribed by birth into a particular family or people. Attention, then, to concern for a "name" belongs to an investigation of honor discourse.

A more complex system of symbolizing the honor of a person is to be located in the treatment of the physical body, for there existed an "intimate relation between honour and the physical person."[23] The head and face of a person are physical representations of the person's honor, hence "rituals by which honour is formally bestowed involve a ceremony which commonly centres upon the head of the protagonist." Crowning or anointing are physical representations of the honor being conferred upon the recipient of the action. Conversely, slapping, striking, or, in the extreme, beheading are tokens of dishonor. The right hand of a person is a symbol of the individual's power, and thereby of honor. To be seated at the right hand of a person of worth becomes a grant of honor to the one so seated. Similarly, to be placed at the feet of another or to prostrate oneself before another are physical representations of the relative honor of the two parties (cf., for example, the expectation that Christ's enemies will be made a footstool in Heb 1:13). Corporeal punishment, such as flagellation or crucifixion, is an act of degradation imposed upon a body, a token of the lack of esteem in which criminals, who are so punished, are held. Such observations should lead us, then, to pay careful attention to details touching the physical person and the treatment of that person by others as indications of honor exchanges.

Honor and Gender

Just as definitions of honorable behavior vary between different groups, so definitions of honorable behavior may vary between genders. In the ancient Mediterranean world women and men tended to express their concern for honor and the opinion of others differently. For women, honor was closely linked to sexuality and visibility.[24] The woman who was sexually exclusive (the virgin daughter or the faithful wife of one husband) was recognized as honorable, while the honor of the divorced or widowed woman, whose sexual purity had no champion and defender, might be in danger as far as public opinion was concerned. Women tended to be located within the home (indeed, only the more private areas of the home), while men tended to be found outside the home.

This is not to say, however, that women and men could not aspire to the same virtues. Both women and men could be praised for courage or endurance, or for showing piety and duty toward the gods and family.[25] Indeed, the sexual exclusiveness of the honorable woman was also expected of the honorable man, who should exhibit temperance with regard to sexual desire and justice with regard to the marital bond.[26] There did remain, however, a heavier emphasis on certain private spaces within which it was most appropriate for a woman to maintain her good name, and on the particular virtue of chastity in singleness and fidelity in marriage.

An investigation of honor discourse in a text, then, involves not only a search for vocabulary items connected with honor, dishonor, and the like, but also a close inspection of the ways in which an author may be indicating the honor ascribed to an individual by the group (through birth, race, appointment) or achieved by an individual (through acts of virtue; successful challenges or ripostes), or the ways in which honor or dishonor are being represented in the "name" of the person or in the treatment of the physical body of a person. The reader should observe whether or not persons are acting honorably in light of certain mutual obligations, such as friendship or patronage. In addition, the reader must be attentive to potential differences between genders in the way honor is preserved or lost.

Honor and Persuasion

The foregoing considerations help to orient us generally toward identifying honor discourse in texts. We are truly fortunate, however, to have access to firsthand information concerning how authors and speakers might use considerations of honor in order to move an audience to a particular course of action. These handbooks will also provide us with many specific pointers concerning how we might discover honor language at work in a text. Turning to handbooks such as Aristotle's *Art of Rhetoric*, the *Rhetorica ad Herennium*, and Quintilian's *Institutes*[27] for the present investigation is more than an intuitive choice. These are books about how to persuade, and as such they operate on a meta-level, one step removed from, or one level of abstraction above "normal" communication. They reflect on how taken-for-granted values may be harnessed for the task of persuasion. They will not explain why honor is an important consideration, but they will provide guidance for how a Greco-Roman communicator might effectively tap into the hearers' concern for their own honor and the honor due others to impel them to choose one course of action over another.

Aristotle organizes rhetorical appeals into three types: *logos*, *ethos*, and *pathos*. Appeals to *logos* ("reason") attempted to persuade the hearer through syllogistic reasoning or examples and analogies. Appeals to *ethos* sought to persuade by demonstrating (generally indirectly) the credibility and authority of the speaker. Appeals to *pathos* ("emotion" or "passion") sought to assist persuasion by putting the hearers in that disposition (anger, fear, shame, or the like) that would make them more likely to move in the direction desired by the orator.

We will take up these types of appeal in turn, examining how honor discourse could surface within each appeal.

1. Honor and Appeals to Logos

Classical rhetoricians discerned three genres of oratory related to three basic institutions of the Greek city (the council hall, the courtroom, the public forum) and their functions. The first genre is called "deliberative" rhetoric, which is appropriate to the council chamber where decisions must be made about a course of action to be taken in the future. The second genre is called "forensic" or "judicial" rhetoric, which is appropriate to the courtroom where verdicts must be rendered concerning the guilt or innocence of individuals allegedly involved in some past actions. The third genre is called "epideictic" rhetoric, which is appropriate to the public forum where the lives of the fallen are honored in funeral speeches. Epideictic rhetoric became a sort of catchall category and came to include philosophical demonstrations, speeches promoting a certain way of life, as well as the formal eulogies of the dead.[28]

Considerations of honor are central to deliberative as well as epideictic rhetoric. Both Aristotle and Quintilian bear witness to the intimate relationship between these two genres:

> Praise and counsels have a common aspect; for what you might suggest in counselling becomes encomium by a change in the phrase. . . . Accordingly, if you desire to praise, look what you would suggest; if you desire to suggest, look what you would praise (Aristotle, *Rhet.* 1.9.35-36).

> But panegyric is akin to deliberative oratory inasmuch as the same things are usually praised in the former as are advised in the latter (Quintilian, *Inst.* 3.7.28).

Aristotle speaks of the scope of deliberative rhetoric as the "expedient" or the "harmful" (*Rhet.* 1.3.5), recognizing that a number of considerations move people to take action.[29] He later specifically points the counselor, however, to considerations of honor when pondering what advice should be offered. Since the orator's addressees would desire what was praiseworthy, the successful advisor should point to the honorable course: precisely the course that would be praised in retrospect.[30]

The *Rhetorica ad Herennium*, in keeping with Aristotle's classification of deliberative oratory as concerned with the "expedient," speaks of the aim of deliberative rhetoric as "advantage." Here as well, however, the textbook writer depicts the intimate relationship of "advantage" and honor by considering "advantage" as being comprised of two subcategories: security and honor (*Rhet. ad Her.* 3.2.3). Security, or safety, is also a central value, to be sure, but even in cases where considerations of safety outweigh considerations of honor the orator could never admit that the proposed course is dishonorable (*Rhet. ad Her.* 3.5.8-9).

The task of the appeal to *logos* in a deliberative speech was to demonstrate by reason or analogy that the course of action proposed by the speaker would lead to advantage (honor and/or security). Seeing how the promise of honor would undergird an exhortation to a specific course of action, how would the orator bring topics of honor into the speech? We have already seen that honor discourse is present even when words related to honor or dishonor are not explicit. A primary means of demonstrating that a course is honorable would be to show how such a course embodied an essential virtue of the group—frequently one of the four cardinal virtues of wisdom, justice, temperance, and courage (since the possession of these virtues is a component of honor: *Rhet. ad Her.* 3.2.3). While these may be considered values of the "dominant culture" it is noteworthy that the philosophical and Jewish cultures also embraced them as essential virtues, merely defining them in terms of their groups' specific definitions of reality.

The *Rhetorica ad Herennium* also provides definitions of the realms of discourse belonging to each of these virtues, and hence to honor discourse more broadly:

> We shall be using the topics of Wisdom in our discourse if we compare advantages and disadvantages, counselling the pursuit of the one and the avoidance of the other;[31] . . . or if we recommend some policy in a matter whose history we can recall either from direct experience or hearsay—in this instance we can easily persuade our hearers to the course we wish by adducing the precedent (3.3.4).

> We shall be using the topics of Justice . . . if we show that it is proper to repay the well-deserving with gratitude; . . . if we urge that faith (*fidem*) ought zealously to be kept; . . . if we contend that alliances and friendships should scrupulously be honored; if we make it clear that the duty imposed by nature towards parents, gods, and the fatherland (*in parentes, deos, patriam*) must be religiously observed; if we maintain that ties of hospitality, clientage,[32] kinship, and relationship by marriage must inviolably be cherished; if we show that neither reward nor favour nor peril nor animosity ought to lead us astray from the right path (3.3.4).

> When we invoke as motive for a course of action steadfastness in Courage, we shall make it clear that . . . from an honorable act no peril or toil, however great, should divert us; death ought to be preferred to disgrace; no pain should force abandonment of duty; . . . for country *(patria)*, for parents, guest-friends, intimates, and for the things justice commands us to respect, it behooves us to brave any peril and endure any toil (3.3.5).
>
> We shall be using the topics of Temperance if we censure the inordinate desire for office, money, or the like (3.3.5).

These virtues, popularized by Plato and by Stoic ethical philosophy, were the subject and cause of praise; those who displayed them were recognized by their peers as honorable people, and the thought of gaining honor made the pursuit of these virtues desirable.[33] Where we find a course of action being described as just, courageous, or pious, the author is harnessing strong sanctions of the "noble" in favor of that course.

This discussion of the topics associated with the cardinal virtues opens up the ways in which New Testament authors may be appealing to these same virtues, and hence demonstrating that the course they recommend is the course that leads to honor (advantage). The list of topics in *Rhetorica ad Herennium* shows that an author may never mention these four virtues by name and yet still be introducing them into the discourse through these associated topics. The author of Hebrews, for example, uses topics associated with all four virtues. He urges temperance in 13:4-6, where he cautions against the love of money. He uses topics of wisdom in numerous ways. First he himself compares advantages and disadvantages, concluding that loyalty to Christ, despite temporary disadvantages, is ultimately more advantageous than desertion. Thus, for example, enduring "discipline" (12:7) is more advantageous than rejecting God's gift of adoption (10:26-31). He supports this by "adducing the precedent," particularly in his discussion of the disadvantages that accrued to the wilderness generation (3:7–4:11) and the foolish evaluation of advantage and disadvantage conducted by Esau (12:16-17), and in his inclusion of positive precedents (Abraham in 6:15; the community's own past decisions in 10:32-34; the correct evaluations of advantage by Abraham, Moses, and Christ in 11:13-16, 25-27; 12:1-2).

The author of Hebrews is especially fond of topics of justice and courage. He instructs the members of the community to maintain the obligations of kinship toward one another (13:1, 3)—obligations they assumed when they became part of the "household of God" (10:21; cf. 3:6).

Similarly he urges the continued fulfillment of the obligations of hospitality (13:2) and the marital covenant (13:4). The primary obligation that must be maintained, however, is that of clientage. Jesus has been presented as the believers' patron (2:9-18) who has given them among other gifts access to God as their personal Patron (4:14-16; 10:19-21). It would be unjust to show disloyalty, dishonoring this selfless benefactor and spurning his gifts—an injustice not without severe consequences (disadvantage) for the addressees (6:4-8; 10:24-31). He urges rather that steadfastness and gratitude be preserved toward the community's Benefactor (10:23; 12:28). Moreover, since perils await the one who would remain faithful the author uses topics of courage to urge them not to allow the threats of temporary hardship and pain to divert them from the honorable course. They are not to be cowards who shrink back from the contest, but are to persevere in loyalty (10:36-39), just as their benefactor did not shrink from shame and pain on their behalf (12:1-3). They are to match his loyalty and courage with their own (13:12-14).

The overall effect of his discourse, then, will be to affirm the honor of the Christian group based on their dedication to these virtues. Their continuation in their Christian walk is not a strike against their honor, as their neighbors would have them believe, but is in fact the only way they can preserve their honor and gain the greater honor God has promised them. Most strongly, the author urges that desertion from the community amounts to disloyalty to God—a base show of ingratitude, which is an injustice leading to everlasting disgrace.

The *Rhetorica ad Herennium* also highlights the "praiseworthy" as a component of honor, not because it is different from the "right" (the virtues) but because it often happens that the results of pursuing the "right" have to be underscored. The promise of praise and an honorable remembrance, that is, must often be made directly. Epideictic rhetoric—the praise or blame of individuals or groups on the basis of their adherence to essential group values—may here take on a helping role in the task of persuasion.[34] Figures of past or present history may be held up as exemplifying a particular virtue or praiseworthy accomplishment. The accumulation of such figures in example lists may be used to reinforce the impression that an honorable and long-lasting remembrance does indeed attach to the sort of action or virtuous behavior that is being advised. This would motivate the hearers to emulate the exemplar in an attempt to attain similar recognition for themselves. Such lists of honorable examples appear in Sir 44:1–50:24; 4 Macc 16:18-23; and Heb 11:1–12:3. These passages show the readers/hearers what course of action gains a lasting, honorable reputation, and so recommends that course strongly for their consideration.

Honor discourse feeds the rhetorical strategy of a text, then, where authors seek to demonstrate that a certain course is indeed the path to preserving or augmenting the honor of the addressees, often in terms of exemplifying a mutually-recognized virtue. We may look for indications that a particular course of action is linked to the expression of a particular virtue by enthymematic reasoning. Dio Chrysostom affords us examples of this strategy at work, as in his appeal for civic unity on the occasion of the new governor's arrival:

> If ever a quarrel arises and your adversaries taunt you with having wicked citizens, with dissension, are you not put to shame? . . . Is it not disgraceful that bees are of one mind and no one has ever seen a swarm that is factious and fights against itself, but, on the contrary, they both work and live together. . . . Is it not disgraceful, then, that human beings should be more unintelligent than wild creatures which are so tiny and unintelligent? (*Or.* 48.5, 15-16).

In the first argument Dio reasons from common experience: civic disunity does indeed lead to rival cities' taunts and jeers. In the second Dio uses an enthymeme to drive his case home (the unstated premise being that human beings are superior to insects).

We may also look for indications that an author is commending a course as honorable by holding up an honored figure of the recent or distant past who achieved good repute (a "good name") by following a similar course, or warning against a course by holding up examples of those who have come to dishonor and lasting disrepute by following a similar course. The use of examples in the New Testament frequently serves the purpose of recommending pursuit of the group's values as the way to greater honor, and guarding against neglect of these pursuits as the way to lasting disgrace. Even where "visionary rhetoric" is the medium of argumentative texture one can still find these basic forms of persuasion at work. In Rev 14:9-11, for example, the course of action involving participation in the imperial cult (advantageous from the point of view of relieving the tension between Church and society) is sternly cautioned against as the path leading specifically to degradation "in the presence of the holy angels and in the presence of the Lamb." The public nature of the torment reveals that dishonor is a key factor in motivating the hearers to shun the course of action that leads to such eternal shame.

2. Honor and Appeals to Ethos

Of critical importance was the appeal to *ethos,* or the character of the speaker. The speech itself and not merely prior impressions of the speaker had to give evidence of the speaker's credibility and noble character. According to Aristotle this "constitutes the most effective [or leading, *kuriōtatēn*] means of proof" (*Rhet.* 1.2.4).[35] For persuasion to be effected the audience had to regard the speaker as reasonable and honorable.[36] How could a speaker demonstrate nobility when direct self-praise was impossible, or at least dangerous? Aristotle provides the following guidelines:

> We will next speak of virtue and vice, of the noble and the disgraceful, since they constitute the aim of one who praises and of one who blames; for, when speaking of these, we shall incidentally bring to light the means of making us appear of such and such a character, which, as we have said, is a second method of proof; for it is by the same means that we shall be able to inspire confidence in ourselves or others in regard to virtue (*Rhet.* 1.9.1).

By urging the hearers to pursue the virtuous course or avoid a vicious course the orator would be recognized as honorable himself or herself, and hence possessing a voice worth considering by those who were themselves concerned about honor. Thus the author of Hebrews, for example, when using the topics of wisdom shows himself to be a reasonable person, and when urging the strict maintenance of loyalty even in the face of hardship shows himself to be a virtuous and honorable person worthy of the hearers' attention and trust.

One might also find honor discourse at work negatively here, as part of an attempt to undermine the *ethos* of rival speakers. By demonstrating that they are motivated by vice, or are actually urging the audience to do what would compromise their own virtue and honor, a speaker can create prejudice against rivals. That this may be an important part of a speaker's establishment of *ethos* is evident in such texts as Galatians, 2 Corinthians, and Revelation.

3. Honor and Appeals to Pathos

Aristotle's discussion of the third mode of proof, the appeal to the emotions (*pathē*) of the hearer,[37] shows how considerations of honor may be used to arouse strategic emotional responses in the audience. These passages are not adduced to suggest that honor is always involved in the rousing of these emotions, but to help us ask whether or not considerations of honor might be part of an author's appeal to certain emotions. As such it continues our inventory of the ways in which honor discourse may be present in a text.

The first emotion Aristotle treats is anger. While anger can be provoked by many things Aristotle highlights its relationship to honor in his definition: "Let us then define anger *(orgē)* as a longing, accompanied by pain, for a real or apparent revenge for a real or apparent slight" (*Rhet.* 2.2.1). Orators could therefore expect to move their audience to anger by making the audience feel that it had been slighted or dishonored.[38] Aristotle's definition of slighting *(oligōria)* leads us to watch carefully in a text for mention of disdain or insult, or for regarding something or someone as less valuable or less worthy of respect than is proper (*Rhet.* 2.2.3). This would move the addressees to anger if the slight is directed against them, or to indignation if they are observing a slight offered to someone or something worthy of greater respect,[39] or to fear if they have slighted, or are in danger of slighting, someone worthy of respect with the power to gain satisfaction.

Aristotle's discussion of anger takes us back into the world of patron-client relationships, pointing out specifically that people "are angry at slights from those by whom they think they have a right to expect to be well treated; such are those on whom they have conferred or are conferring benefits . . . and all those whom they desire, or did desire, to benefit" (*Rhet.* 2.2.8). Within the patron-client relationship it is expected that those who have benefited will repay their benefactors in part by honoring them. Repaying "grace" with dishonor was a slight that would certainly arouse anger.

Aristotle presents fear as a sort of reciprocal emotion to anger. Where the experience of being slighted leads to anger the act of slighting or dishonoring another may lead to fear if the prospect of revenge is sufficiently daunting:

> Let fear be defined as a painful or troubled feeling caused by the impression of an imminent evil that causes destruction or pain. . . . Such signs are the enmity and anger of those able to injure us in any way . . . and outraged virtue when it has power, for it . . . always desires satisfaction (*Rhet.* 2.5.1, 3, 5).

The fear aroused in the hearers is proportionate to the honor and power of the one who has been slighted. An orator might arouse fear by augmenting the picture of the honor and virtue of the slighted figure through encomiastic embellishment.

At this point it may be helpful to turn to a text in which one can see how attention to the strategic use of honor discourse to rouse emotions in the hearers can contribute to the student's analysis of the meaning and impact of a given passage. The Epistle to the Hebrews contains several striking appeals to *pathos*, none stronger than 10:26-31:

> If we sin intentionally after receiving knowledge of the truth, there remains no longer a sacrifice for sin but a certain fearful expectation of judgment and passion of fire which is prepared to consume the enemies. Anyone setting aside a law of Moses dies without mercy upon the witness of two or three: how much worse punishment do you think the one who tramples upon the Son of God, who regards as profane the blood of the covenant by which he or she was sanctified, and who insults the Spirit of favor deserves? For we know the One who said "vengeance is mine; I will repay." And again, "the Lord judges his people." Fearful it is to fall into the hands of the living God!

The repetition of the word "fearful" (Heb 10:27, 31), and the author's depiction of these fearful consequences as potentially close to the addressees (an impending injury; see Aristotle, *Rhet.* 2.5.1), show this to be an attempt to move the addressees to fear, hence an appeal to *pathos*. The author has identified a certain course of action, namely shrinking away from loyalty to Jesus and its consequences, as an affront to the divine Benefactor. Preferring the benefits that peaceful reassimilation into society would provide over the benefits Jesus gained for the believers at the cost of his own blood amounts to a crass slighting of the latter. The author portrays such a course as a violation of the patron-client relationship, returning not gratitude but insult to the divine Benefactor. This affront is painted in the most striking of terms: the apostate tramples the Son of God, the one who will one day subject all his enemies under his own feet (Heb 1:13; 10:13); the one who trades the promised inheritance for peace with the world shows contempt for the cost at which the former was purchased, namely the blood of the mediator of the new covenant; finally, the apostate counters divine favor with insult (a shameful act of impiety).[40]

We recognize thus in this passage a script that is essentially the same as that articulated by Aristotle (*Rhet.* 2.5.1) in his definition of fear as "a painful or troubled feeling caused by the impression of an imminent evil that causes destruction or pain." The author has provided the prerequisite for fear in his depiction of the coming of God as Judge and Avenger. In showing contempt for the Son of God one knowingly incurs the anger of God, as anger is the expected response to a slight (all the more when one is slighted by those whom one desired to benefit; see Aristotle, *Rhet.* 2.2.8). The apostate has outraged the embodiment of the virtue of favor and generosity in insulting the Spirit of grace, and so can expect to be visited by an act of God's power seeking satisfaction. This fear is heightened by a comparison with the infraction of the Mosaic covenant (a "lesser to greater" argument based on legal precedent). Just as the dignity of Jesus exceeds that of Moses (see Heb 3:1-6), so violations of that dignity will incur a greater punishment than even the "death without mercy" that fell upon those who disregarded Torah. Fear is also heightened by the declaration of the impossibility of restoration (10:26), for after one has rejected the brokerage of Jesus there remains no mediator who can regain God's favor for the transgressor.[41]

Returning from our example to the theoretical discussion we find two other emotions aroused directly through considerations related to honor—shame *(aischunē)* and emulation *(zēlos)*. Aristotle defines shame as "a kind of pain or uneasiness in respect of misdeeds, past, present, or future, which seem to tend to bring dishonour; and shamelessness as contempt and indifference in regard to these same things" (*Rhet.* 2.6.2). Orators sought to motivate audiences to adopt or discontinue certain courses of action by causing them to feel that their reputation was at stake, or that their reputation had already been marred and must be repaired quickly. Similarly, shaming the audience may aim at motivating them to pursue some good they ought to have attained but have for some reason or other failed to secure (*Rhet.* 2.6.12).

Once again Dio Chrysostom provides a fine illustration of this strategy at work. The Rhodian assembly was in the habit of honoring benefactors through erecting statues to them. After the city was overrun with monuments they hit upon the space-saving and money-saving practice of simply striking out the names of benefactors long since dead and rededicating the statue to a more recent benefactor. Part of Dio's strategy in urging them to cease this practice is to shame them for being willing to dishonor the memory of noble people for the sake of money (*Or.* 31.100). He further shames them by pointing to their past history, when, in worse conditions, they willingly incurred civic debt in order not to incur a blot on their civic honor. Their past commitment to nobility stands in stark contrast to the present, when there has been no disaster to threaten the economy but for the sake of conserving public funds this disgrace is being perpetrated on the statues designated for the honor of past benefactors. Throughout the speech he appeals to the powerful sanction of the *aischron*, the "shameful," in order to turn them away from a course of action and toward its remedy.

The appeal to the emotion of shame also appears in the New Testament documents. Hebrews 5:11-14, for example, chides the addressees for not attaining the status of "teachers" when they ought, in the author's opinion, to have done so by this time (the good they ought to have attained but have failed to secure). He hopes by such means to move them to cease questioning their own commitment to the Christian way of life and devote themselves rather to reinforcing this commitment in others.

The positive counterpart of "shame" is "emulation" *(zēlos)*. Emulation resembles ambition, particularly the ambition to maintain one's status among one's peers:

> Let us assume that emulation is a feeling of pain at the evident presence of highly valued goods, which are possible for us to attain, in the possession of those who naturally resemble us—pain not due to the fact that another possesses them, but to the fact that we ourselves do not. Emulation therefore is virtuous and characteristic of virtuous men, whereas envy is base and characteristic of base men; for the one, owing to emulation, fits himself to obtain such goods, while the object of the other, owing to envy, is to prevent his neighbour possessing them (*Rhet.* 2.11.1).

Again epideictic rhetoric may serve deliberative goals, as orators bring in praiseworthy examples or heighten the desirability of a good that others have attained in order to stir up the hearers to desire that good themselves and take the course necessary to attain it.

At this point we should turn our attention to another of the three genres of oratory, namely epideictic rhetoric. It is fitting to look briefly at this genre under the heading of "emulation," for this appears to be a primary goal of the public praise of some figure or virtue. In Thucydides' *History* (2.35) Pericles is given the honor of delivering a funeral oration that is somewhat self-reflective on the Greek practice of giving and hearing such a speech. Pericles approaches the task of praising the fallen soldiers with some caution: "Praise of other people is tolerable only up to a certain point, the point where one still believes that one could do oneself some of the things one is hearing about. Once you get beyond this point, you will find people becoming jealous and incredulous" (2.35.2).

This comment provides important insights into the way epideictic speeches—especially speeches that praised some individual or group—

were heard. The audience responded by being roused to emulation at the praise of others, affirming their own nobility by telling themselves that they too could act in a similarly praiseworthy manner when the situation called for it. If the audience began to distance themselves from emulating the subjects of the encomium they would become unfavorably disposed toward the speaker. Public praise of figures such as these soldiers appealed to the hearers' own desire for honor, moving them to desire the same opportunity for praise. It encouraged them to reaffirm their belief that adherence to the civic virtues would lead to the fulfillment of their desire for honor. They might not exhibit the virtue of, say, courage in the same manner, but in some field of life they would have some opportunity.[42]

Such emulation would also be the response of readers of the written encomiastic biography. Plutarch explains that part of his purpose in compiling the *Parallel Lives* and in dwelling on figures like Pericles is the rousing of his hearers' emulation such that they will seek to imitate the virtues of such great men of the past (*Per.* 3). The New Testament gospels have been fruitfully compared with the genre of the *bios,* and this opens up some avenues for investigating the way in which a gospel inculcates values through portraying them in action in the person of Jesus.[43]

Once more we find this strategy at work in Jewish and Christian rhetoric. Ben Sira concludes his collection of wisdom instructions with a lengthy "hymn to the ancestors." This catalogue is meant not as a history lesson but as an attempt to demonstrate through example that the way of obedience to Torah is the way that leads to honor and a praiseworthy remembrance. The readers of his books will be moved to emulate Abraham (Sir 44:20), Phineas (45:23), and those who kept the covenant (46:10-12) by the success of such figures in gaining lasting honor, and to avoid the emulation of those who soiled or lost their honor (Solomon; most of the kings of Judah and Israel: 47:20-21; 49:4-5) through apostasy from strict loyalty to the One God and God's Law. Hebrews similarly supports the exhortation to remain loyal to the Divine Patron and focused on that patron's promised favors by recalling especially the model of Jesus, who endured temporary dishonor and pain in order to gain the place of greatest honor: a seat at the right hand of God (Heb 12:1-2). The addressees are called to "consider" Jesus much as the audience of Pericles' funeral oration (Thucydides, *Hist.* 2.43.1-4) are called to "consider" the fallen soldiers whose courage gained them immortal fame in the city. Such "consideration" is calculated to arouse emulation of these figures, making their path to honor the desirable choice.

Summary

These observations lead us back into the New Testament texts armed with a new sensitivity to the rhetorical impact of honor discourse. When we understand that the addressees are people who are concerned about honor and who wish to be regarded as honorable people, appeals relevant to that concern become highly significant. What actions or attitudes lead to honor, according to the author? Are behaviors specifically suited to maintaining the life and values of the group (in this case a minority group existing among competing cultures within a frequently unsupportive dominant culture) now being vested with the sanctions of the "just," the "courageous," and so forth?[44] How does the author use examples to elevate a course of action as honorable (since praiseworthy), or warn against a course of action as censurable? How does the author's speech reveal the author to be an honorable person? How does the author seek to move the hearers to fear, shame, anger, indignation, or emulation by means of considerations of honor, and to what end? How does awareness of cultural scripts like patronage or kinship help us to discover where these considerations are woven into the argument? Such lines of inquiry, informed also by the foregoing discussion of the vocabulary, symbolization, ascription, and achievement of honor, will open up the rhetorical strategy of a given text in new and informative ways that will certainly supplement the insights gained through other avenues of exegesis.

CONCLUSION: A MODEL FOR INVESTIGATING HONOR DISCOURSE

Investigating the rhetorical impact of honor discourse in a text requires much more than attention to occurrences of the words "honor" or "dishonor." It requires reflection on the many ways in which honor is described and represented, as well as the many ways in which authors might use considerations related to honor as part of a strategy of persuasion. We must also remember, however, the connection between definitions of the "honorable" and the delineation of the social group that shares such definitions (the "court of reputation"). The way in which a text mirrors or constructs a court of reputation (that is, either reflects the realities of the social situation or seeks to shape it) is part of a full investigation of honor discourse. It may be useful to synthesize these observations into a model that, it is hoped, will be equally useful in investigating honor discourse in narratives and in epistolary and visionary rhetoric.

What topics or rhetorical tactics are relevant to the investigation of the relationship of argumentative and socio-cultural texture in the early Christian documents (or, indeed, those of any minority culture in the Hellenistic or Greco-Roman period)? What sorts of language or concepts should jump out at us as signals of an author's concern for the group's endurance in commitment to the community and its values in the face of another group's disapproval of its new loyalties? Our desire to discover the mutual shaping between text and social setting leads us to look closely at the following:

1. Language that establishes or reinforces the constituency of the court of reputation (the boundaries of the group) by: (a) explicitly naming those persons (and/or supra-social entities) for whose opinion and approval one should have regard; (b) stressing the differences in lifestyle, proximity to truth, *ethos,* and even ontology or origin between group members and outsiders (topics of encomia, such as origin and character, are used here negatively to heighten awareness of incompatibility); (c) censuring outsiders as unreliable guides to conduct, as shameless or dishonorable, as influences that ultimately jeopardize the well-being of individuals (again a place for epideictic rhetoric); (d) affirming the character of group members, particularly group leaders, strengthening the group's inner-directed focus on such people as reliable, honorable guides to right knowledge and conduct, bolstering the leaders' authority to delineate the group's norms and to grant honor or ascribe blame within the group.

2. Language that establishes or affirms the honor of the group or its members before the alternate court of reputation by: (a) detailing the honor the individual now possesses and the basis for this honor as defined by the group's world-construction; (b) praising the group for its adherence to the minority culture's values and giving expression to their honor and reputation within the larger body of significant others (a place for epideictic oratory); (c) reinterpreting the group's experience of dishonor or disapproval at society's hands, defusing the dominant culture's deviancy-control techniques or even turning them to advantage vis-à-vis group honor and commitment; (d) promising future honor and vindication for the group and dishonor for the group's opponents,

advising individuals to follow as the path to their own honor and security the course that will promote the survival of the group and preserve the group's distinctive world-construction and values (a place for deliberative rhetorical strategies, including the strategic use of epideictic rhetoric—examples—to support the promise of honor or disgrace).

Keeping these questions in the forefront of our minds will provide a useful framework for the investigation of New Testament texts. Within this framework we may use the preceding inventory of honor discourse to recognize honor scripts at work, but then to move on to inquire into their rhetorical function or social goal. For example, now that we may recognize a challenge-riposte scenario, or expressions of the physical replications of honor, or the expectations of honor within the patron-client relationship, what can we say about the author's purpose[s] in writing this information into the text? How does it serve the rhetorical goal of the author and support the maintenance of the social group? In the chapters that follow we will explore how this avenue of investigation opens up the New Testament texts and helps us to read them with a greater degree of cultural and exegetical sensitivity.

NOTES: CHAPTER ONE

[1] An insight noted by Julian Pitt-Rivers ("Honour and Social Status," in J. G. Peristiany, ed., *Honour and Shame: The Values of Mediterranean Society* [London: Weidenfeld and Nicolson, 1965] 22) with regard to modern Mediterranean cultures, but equally applicable to the first-century Mediterranean.

[2] The instruction manuals on living from both the Gentile and Jewish societies, commonly called wisdom or ethical literature, provide evidence for this. Proverbs, Ben Sira (Sirach), and the *Advice to Demonicus* of Pseudo-Isocrates, for example, all seek to shape the way of life of their readers by depicting certain actions as leading to honor or its components and others as leading to disgrace. Moreover, the success of such manuals depends on the student's prior acknowledgment of honor as desirable and its opposite as undesirable.

[3] For a fuller discussion of how honor and dishonor are used as sanctions for and against particular courses of action see David A. deSilva, *Despising Shame: Honor Discourse and Community Maintenance in the Epistle to the Hebrews*. SBL.DS 152 (Atlanta: Scholars, 1995) 49–79.

[4] For a fuller discussion of these group-maintaining techniques as they appear specifically in Greco-Roman philosophical cultures and the Jewish subculture see deSilva, *Despising Shame* 80–144.

⁵ The taxonomy of dominant culture, subcultures, and countercultures is developed and discussed in greater detail in Vernon Robbins, *The Tapestry of Early Christian Discourse: Rhetoric, Society and Ideology* (London: Routledge, 1996) 168–170; *Exploring the Texture of Texts* (Valley Forge, Pa.: Trinity Press International, 1996) 86–89. The term "majority culture" derives from a discussion I enjoyed with Dr. Robbins concerning the precise definition of "dominant" culture as the culture of the empowered: those who can maintain and propagate their culture through the exercise of power and other resources. The dominant elite, however, do not always speak for the majority. One finds in Aristotle, who as tutor to Alexander speaks with the voice of the dominant culture, repeated attempts to distinguish between the values of the cultivated elite and the "masses." Indications such as these point to the existence of a majority culture alongside a dominant culture, perhaps with the latter reinforcing their elite status specifically through drawing distinctions between themselves and the "many."

⁶ The Jewish community of Rome would be rather exceptional, having left evidence of widespread participation in the life of the city. See Harry J. Leon, *The Jews of Ancient Rome* (Philadelphia: JPS, 1960; reprint Peabody, Mass.: Hendrickson, 1994).

⁷ For some sample criticisms leveled against Jews by non-Jewish authors see Diodorus of Sicily *Bib. Hist.* 34.1-4; 40.3.4; Tacitus, *Hist.* 5.5; Juvenal, *Sat.* 14.100-104; cf. also Josephus's record of anti-Jewish attitudes (*Ap.* 2.121, 258). On ancient anti-Judaism see John Gager, *The Origins of Anti-Semitism: Attitudes Toward Judaism in Pagan and Christian Antiquity* (New York and Oxford: Oxford University Press, 1983) 35–112.

⁸ This may include the supra-local group culture (e.g., "the churches of God in every place") or supra-temporal group culture (e.g., the ancestors in the faith; cf. 4 Macc 13:17).

⁹ Plato thus speaks of living so as to achieve honor in the sight of God's court (Plato, *Gorgias* 526D-527D), as does Epictetus: "When you come into the presence of some prominent man, remember that Another looks from above on what is taking place, and that you must please Him rather than this man" (*Diss.* 1.30.1). This is a familiar device in the Jewish subcultural literature as well (cf. Sir 23:18-19).

¹⁰ This is a frequent device found among Greco-Roman philosophers. Plato, for example, frequently contrasts the unworthy opinion of the many, who are not guided by a commitment to philosophical inquiry, and the opinion of those few who do examine reality in the light of philosophical truth (*Crito* 44C; 46C-47A; cf. Seneca, *Const.* 13.2, 5; Epictetus, *Diss.* 1.29.50-54).

¹¹ The classic study of athletic imagery in the Greco-Roman world and in the New Testament is V. C. Pfitzner, *Paul and the Agon Motif: Traditional Athletic Imagery in the Pauline Literature* (Leiden: Brill, 1967).

¹² Some of the more striking uses of athletic imagery to ennoble the pursuit of the philosopher or the member of the Jewish subculture can be found in Dio Chrysostom, *Or.* 8.15-16; Epictetus, *Diss.* 3.22.56; 1.18.21; 1.24.1-2; 4 Macc 6:9-10; 11:20; 16:16; 17:11-16; Philo, *Omn. prob. lib.* 26-27. Discussion of these appears in deSilva, *Despising Shame*, ch. 3; idem, *4 Maccabees* (Sheffield: Sheffield Academic Press, 1998) ch. 4.

¹³ For another, English list see Bruce J. Malina and Jerome H. Neyrey, "Honor and Shame," in Jerome H. Neyrey, ed., *The Social World of Luke-Acts: Models for Interpretation* (Peabody, Mass.: Hendrickson, 1991) 46.

¹⁴ The instructions found in rhetorical handbooks and *progymnasmata* for writing the encomium demonstrate that a person was honored or praised for both virtuous deeds or successful competition and for those aspects of a person's life that were not under the control of the individual, such as accidents of birth and its concomitant opportunities and advantages. This has been discussed at some length in Bruce J. Malina and Jerome H. Neyrey, *Portraits of Paul: An Archaeology of Ancient Personality* (Louisville: Westminster/John Knox, 1996) 23–33. For an earlier discussion of ascribed and achieved honor, without the benefits of the use of ancient rhetorical handbooks, see Malina and Neyrey, "Honor and Shame," 27–38.

¹⁵ Opportunities for females to hold such offices were, of course, extremely few and were usually limited to religious offices.

¹⁶ Cf. Pericles' funeral oration for the fallen Athenian soldiers in Thucydides, *Hist.* 2.35-44; Dio Chrysostom, *Or.* 29; Ben Sira's hymn to the illustrious ancestors (Sirach 44–51); 4 Maccabees. Teachers of rhetoric also taught this as the appropriate way to honor the dead (cf. Quintilian, *Inst.* 3.7.10-18).

¹⁷ Malina and Neyrey, "Honor and Shame," 30.

¹⁸ This is notably the case in the opening scene of Sophocles' *Oedipus Tyrannus*, where the value of Oedipus' past act of delivering the city from the Sphinx, and hence the honor he has enjoyed for that act, are publicly threatened unless he should deliver the city from the new menace of the plague.

¹⁹ Pitt-Rivers, "Honour and Social Status," 27.

²⁰ According to Seneca it was the "chief bond of human society" (*Ben.* 1.4.2). Perhaps the most important studies of the phenomenon of patronage are R. P. Saller, *Personal Patronage under the Early Empire* (Cambridge: Cambridge University Press, 1982) and Frederick W. Danker, *Benefactor: Epigraphic Study of a Graeco-Roman and New Testament Semantic Field* (St. Louis: Clayton Publishing House, 1982). For a detailed study of how attention to patron-client scripts can unlock a New Testament text see David A. deSilva, "Exchanging Favor for Wrath: Apostasy in Hebrews and Patron-Client Relations," *JBL* 115 (1996) 91–116. The following classical sources are priceless as firsthand witnesses to the practice: Seneca, *De beneficiis;* Dio Chrysostom,

Oration 31 (To the Rhodian Assembly); Pliny's *Letters,* X (requests for favors addressed to the emperor Trajan on behalf of Pliny's clients).

[21] Cf. Seneca, *Ben.* 2.22.1; 2.24.2.

[22] Malina and Neyrey, "Honor and Shame," 33.

[23] Pitt-Rivers, "Honour and Social Status," 25.

[24] A number of striking examples of this may be found in 4 Macc 18:6-9; Sir 26:10-18; 42:9-14; and Thucydides, *Hist.* 2.45.2.

[25] See, for example, the praise of the mother of seven Jewish martyrs in 4 Macc 14:11–17:6, the heroic exploits of Judith, or the praise of numerous exemplars of courage among Greek women in Plutarch, "On the Bravery of Women."

[26] Maintaining the bond of matrimony as inviolable was held to be a topic of "justice" by the author of the *Rhetorica ad Herennium* (3.3.4). The abundance of material in Jewish and Christian literature concerning the disgrace of adultery and necessity of chastity and marital fidelity among both males and females, together with the witnesses of Aristotle or later ethical philosophers, should lead to some refinement of the discussion of male and female "honor" in Malina and Neyrey ("Honor and Shame," 41–44), in which it appears that the male acts honorably by acting beyond sexual exclusivity and only the female's honor is connected to chastity.

[27] All quotations in the following discussion come from the Loeb Classical Library editions of these works.

[28] For further discussions of the genres of rhetoric, and rhetorical criticism in general, see G. A. Kennedy, *New Testament Interpretation through Rhetorical Criticism* (Chapel Hill: University of North Carolina Press, 1984); Burton L. Mack, *Rhetoric and the New Testament* (Minneapolis: Fortress, 1990).

[29] "Motives of choice are the noble, beneficial, and pleasant *(kalou, sympherontos, hēdeos);* motives of avoidance are the shameful, harmful, and painful *(aischrou, blaberou, lupērou),*" *Nic. Eth.* 2.3.7; these motives are reduced to two in *Nic. Eth.* 3.1.11: "Pleasure and nobility *(ta hēdea kai ta kala)* between them supply the motives of all actions whatsoever."

[30] Quintilian even goes so far as to limit the province of deliberative rhetoric to the "honorable," since nothing dishonorable could be truly expedient *(Inst.* 3.8.1).

[31] It is at this juncture that an orator might place his considerations of security within the guise of considerations of honor, thus giving his advice the respectability needed for persuasion *(Rhet. ad Her.* 3.3.5-9).

[32] Cf. *Rhet. ad Alex.* 1421b36-40, which also includes honoring of parents, benefiting one's friends, and returning good to one's benefactors as topics of justice.

33 Cf. Aristotle, *On Virtue and Vice* 1.1-2: "The virtues are objects of praise, and also the causes of the virtues are objects of praise, and the things that accompany the virtues and that result from them, and their works, while the opposite are the objects of blame." Aristotle shows that the four cardinal virtues were just representative of the sorts of characteristics and manners of action that would lead to praise (adding such virtues as gentleness, great-spiritedness, and liberality to the list himself).

34 Cf. *Rhet. ad Her.* 3.8.15: "And if epideictic is only seldom employed by itself independently, still in judicial and deliberative causes extensive sections are often devoted to praise or censure"; cf. Quintilian, *Inst.* 3.4.16.

35 Cf. also Quintilian, *Inst.* 3.8.13: "But what really carries greatest weight in deliberative speeches is the authority of the speaker. For he, who would have all men trust his judgement as to what is expedient and honourable, should both possess and be regarded as possessing genuine wisdom and excellence of character."

36 The topics listed in the *Rhetorica ad Alexandrinus* reinforce these two key aspects of the advisor: "He who persuades must show that those things to which he exhorts are just, lawful, expedient, honourable, pleasant, and easy of accomplishment. Failing that, when he is exhorting to that which is difficult, he must show that it is practicable and that its execution is necessary" (*Rhet. ad Alex.* 1.1, 1421b23-27). The "lawful" and the "just" are subsets of the "honorable," and the other considerations (expedient, pleasant, easy or at least possible, and necessary) all contribute to the impression of the speaker as a "reasonable" counselor.

37 Aristotle, *Rhet.* 1.2.5: "The orator persuades by means of his hearers, when they are roused to emotion by his speech; for the judgements we deliver are not the same when we are influenced by joy or sorrow, love or hate." Cf. also *Rhet.* 2.1.8-9: "The emotions *(pathē)* are all those affections which cause men to change their opinion in regard to their judgements, and are accompanied by pleasure and pain; such are anger, pity, fear, and all similar emotions and their contraries"; Quintilian *Inst.* 3.8.12.

38 The reason for arousing anger relates to the particular situation: if the orator is seeking to prejudice a jury against a defendant or a counselor is urging the declaration of war, arousing anger might be part of that strategy. In the New Testament anger appears to be aroused but rarely, although enmity (another, related *pathos*) is more frequently roused in order to reinforce social boundaries.

39 This emotion is covered in Aristotle, *Rhet.* 2.9. Especially relevant is 2.9.11: "If a virtuous person does not obtain what is suitable to him, we feel indignant. Similarly, if the inferior contends with the superior."

40 Cf. Dio, *Or.* 31.14: "But to commit an outrage against good men who have been the benefactors of the state *(euergetas hybrizein)*, to annul the honours

given them and to blot out their remembrance, I for my part do not see how that could be otherwise termed."

[41] Cf. Aristotle, *Rhet.* 2.5.12: Fear is aroused "also when there is no possibility of help or it is not easy to obtain."

[42] Plutarch provides more evidence that hearing others praised for the attainment of some goal within the grasp of the hearers would motivate the hearers to pursue that goal with zeal. He suggests that praise of self could be excused if the aim was "to exhort hearers and inspire them with emulation and ambition *(ei protropēs heneka kai zēlou kai philotimias),* as Nestor by recounting his own exploits and battles incited Patroclus and roused the nine champions to offer themselves for the single combat" (*On Inoffensive Self-Praise* 15 [*Mor.* 544D]).

[43] See Ben Witherington III, "Principles for Interpreting the Gospels and Acts," *Ashland Theological Journal* 19 (1987) 35–70, at 35–37; R. S. Bauckham, ed., *The Gospels for all Christians* (Grand Rapids: Eerdmans, 1998) 27–30.

[44] Most often the labels "just" or "courageous" or "temperate" will not be explicitly used, hence the value of lists of examples of "topics" that fall under the category of justice, such as *Rhetorica ad Herennium* provides (3.3.4–3.3.5).

2

Honor Discourse in Matthew

Scholars have generally found it easier to probe the historical and social setting of epistles, with their firsthand information about the concerns and challenges facing a particular body, than gospels. It has also been easier to assess the purpose or intent of epistles and to explore their rhetorical strategy. Gospels, which tell a story for a potentially wide range of audiences and seek to inspire members of the Christian movement in a variety of settings to recommit themselves to the values promoted in those gospels are more elusive in this regard. Scholars rely heavily, and rightly, on redaction analysis to discover the distinctive emphases of an evangelist and the ways he/she has selected and redacted the traditions in order to discern the evangelist's interests in shaping the response of the readers to one another and the outside world. Information about the concerns and questions of the early Church known from other New Testament texts (largely epistles) has also been used to consider what needs the evangelist might be addressing. Investigation of honor discourse now opens up new avenues for examining the rhetorical effect of the gospels.[1]

By looking closely at how the gospel material leads the hearers to formulate their "court of reputation" (i.e., whose opinion is excluded and whose is important) the investigator can gain insights into the nature of the relationship the evangelist seeks to maintain or shape between the Christian group and other groups (or society). Moreover, attention to the way in which gospel traditions might shape behavior and connections within the group (activating the court of reputation, as it were) also provides useful material for analyzing the type of community the evangelist is attempting to form. Noting how the traditions posit honor or dishonor as the result of certain actions or attitudes also helps the interpreter discern the behaviors promoted and discouraged by the gospel. While such investigation will hardly help us decide whether or not a gospel was composed at Antioch or Ephesus, it will nevertheless help us fill out in a more general way the rhetorical and social impact of the gospel on its first hearers—information that can supplement insights from other avenues of study.

The four gospels have already been used as witnesses to the cultural phenomenon of honor and analyzed at the level of interactions within the narrative world itself (for example, reading the confrontations between Jesus and the Pharisees as challenge-riposte scenarios).[2] In this study we will press further beyond the identification of honor scripts in the story to show how honor and shame language in a narrative or story might be expected to shape the responses of the individuals and communities that read those narratives. We are looking here for connections between occurrences of honor discourse in the story and the social and cultural identity of the readers, specifically ways in which the former are designed to shape or reinforce the latter.

With regard to Matthew our exploration will focus first on the gospel's construction of Jesus' honor. The scandal of the cross—the dishonorable death *par excellence*—and the ongoing labeling of Jesus as sorcerer and deceiver among non-Christian Jews invited a presentation in defense of Jesus' noble and God-approved character for the benefit of Christians. In effect we will be exploring how honor discourse in Matthew constitutes an indirect appeal to *ethos*,[3] defending Jesus' credibility as a teacher of the "way of God in truth" (Matt 22:16), and hence an affirmation of Christian discipleship as the way to stand approved and honored by God. The second part of this chapter will analyze how Matthew's gospel would contribute to the maintenance of the Christian group in the face of contrary pressures from non-Christian Jews and Gentiles. This involves an examination of how the sayings and stories selected and shaped by Matthew would reinforce the definition of the believers' court of reputation so as to nullify the force of non-Christians' criticisms and attempts at shaming believers, together with a survey of those attitudes and behaviors that are proposed as the path to honor before the court of reputation that matters most.

THE SETTING OF MATTHEW'S AUDIENCE

The concept of an evangelist's "community" has risen to the status of a "given" in modern scholarship. It is virtually axiomatic that an evangelist is shaping the material in light of the needs, concerns, and history of a particular community or circle of communities, such that the story of Jesus is frequently read as the story of the community as well.[4] This has recently come under strong fire from Richard Bauckham, Michael Thompson, Stephen Barton, and others.[5] Bauckham argues that the gospels were written, like the other examples of their literary genre (the "life"), for a wide and general audience.[6] The fact that Christian congregations were not isolated communities, but rather developed networks of connection with one another and even wrote letters to one another, and the further circumstance that the leaders of the movement tended to be itinerant, also suggest a wide readership for each gospel.[7] This is indirectly supported by the hypothesis that Matthew and Luke knew Mark's gospel: if that work had circulated so widely, should they suppose that their gospels would be more limited in their reception?[8] Bauckham would have the modern scholar reconsider the wisdom of identifying the audience for whom the gospel was written with the local community within which the evangelist wrote it.[9]

This well-supported and cogently-presented assault on the concept of the "Matthean community" (for example) has several significant corollaries, the most important of which is the questioning of the previously unassailed "reflective" nature of the gospels. With the emphasis placed on reconstructing the Matthean community from the Matthean gospel, Matthew has been treated as a window or mirror for the community. The critique of this view calls us to consider the probability that for many readers Matthew raises a number of concerns rather than answering preexisting ones, and that this gospel presents in many respects a model for the audience rather than a mere reflection of a particular community.

This brings us back to the rhetorical character of the gospels, and for the study of this character we will continue to rely on the insights of redaction critics and their compatriots (whose work will not have been in vain even if this group calling the scholarly assumption into question should prove correct).[10] These investigations still provide important insights into the ways in which the evangelists shaped their material and the goals they had for their audiences (however broadly conceived). What is at stake in the discussion is not the rhetorical nature of the gospels as documents that seek to promote a certain *ethos*, evoke certain responses, and, in short, shape the audiences' interaction with the larger world and one another. Investigation of honor discourse can prove a rich resource for understanding the rhetorical effect of the gospel on its readership, whether this is construed in the narrow sense of the first circle that received the gospel or the broader sense of Christians in vastly different regions and settings.

We can approach some of the distinctive interests of Matthew through the recent work of Donald Hagner. Hagner has noted the importance of two marked tensions within the gospel: one between an exclusive mission to Israel (10:5-6, 23; 15:24) and a strong emphasis on Gentile inclusion (1:5; 2:1-12; 8:5-13; 12:21; 13:38; 15:21-28; 21:33-43; 22:1-10; 24:14; 27:54; 28:19-20), and another between the very Jewish tone of the gospel and the strong polemic against the representatives of the parent body of Judaism (11:20-24; 22:8; 23:1-39; 27:25).[11] He rightly stresses that one side of each tension cannot be elevated as "relevant" while the other side is ignored as a fossilized part of the tradition (e.g., stressing the "great commission" while downplaying the meaningfulness of the statements about an exclusive mission to Israel).

Hagner suggests that Matthew addresses a primarily Jewish-Christian readership, something that has frequently been averred on the basis of the omission of explanations of Jewish customs (15:1-2; 23:5, 24) and the emphasis on the ongoing validity of Torah (much more at home among Jewish Christians than, say, in Paul's predominantly Gentile congregation in Galatia). We should not rule out, both in light of Bauckham's critique and in view of the mixed character of many early Christian communities, the greater probability of a mixed audience of Jewish and Gentile Christians. Hagner understands Matthew's gospel to be first of all an inner-directed defense against non-Christian Judaism. It seeks to assure the community of its continuity with the revelation of God and God's will toward and through the people of Israel, particularly by portraying Jesus as the fulfillment of scriptural paradigms and models. It also deflects the charges leveled by non-Christian Jews at Jesus (specifically that he was a "deceiver" and "sorcerer"). Finally, it affirms them in their conviction that Jesus was the true teacher of the way to do God's will as revealed in Torah (against accusations from the parent body to the contrary), and thus of the community's own approval in God's sight.[12] Matthew's gospel was thus vitally concerned with insulating the Jewish Christian from the rejection and hostility of his or her non-Christian family, friends, and neighbors. These issues would of course be of equal interest to both Jewish and Gentile Christians: the desire of the latter group to know that they are "doing Torah" correctly and are fully joined to Israel is evident from the crisis addressed by Paul in Galatia.

Hagner also suggests that Matthew helps the audience to come to terms with the growing dominance of Gentile Christianity, the place of Christian Jews in the scheme of God's new acts of salvation, and the ongoing importance of Torah in an increasingly Gentile movement. First, the community must be assured that the overwhelming number of Gentiles in the *ekklēsia* does not prove its discontinuity with Israel, but rather just the opposite, namely that this is the realization of God's purposes all along. Second, the Gentile believers may be showing a distinct lack of regard for the Jewishness of Jewish-Christians, pressuring them to minimize their Jewishness, questioning the ongoing validity of Torah and all those practices that were a threat to the Gentile believer's sense of "equality" within the body. This is a not-unknown problem in the early Church, as Romans amply demonstrates. There both Jews and Gentiles need to be reminded of each other's importance and equality in the plan of God: Jewish privilege cannot be countenanced, but the holiness of the root and natural branches cannot be ignored either, and the essential fulfillment of God's Law remains a lasting goal and value. Once more, however, the rationale for restricting Matthew's "audience" to Jewish Christians crumbles. Gentile Christians would also be appropriate for Matthew to target with his message both about continuity with Israel and about the importance of respecting the contribution of their Jewish Christian brothers and sisters.

Investigation of honor discourse in Matthew provides considerable support for the first of Hagner's suggestions. Matthew certainly presents a narrative that insulates the readers from the reproaches and shaming techniques of the non-Christian Jewish body. Matthew also vindicates Jesus as the teacher whose instruction about Torah observance is affirmed by the highest court of all, namely God. Finally, Matthew offers many indications of the paths that lead to honor or dishonor before God, thus contributing to the formation of the distinctive *ethos* of the Christian group in whatever places his gospel was read.

JESUS AS THE HONORABLE TEACHER OF GOD'S WAY

Evidence within Matthew's gospel and several other Jewish and Christian texts attests to the negative evaluation of Jesus among non-

Christian Jews. Specifically, Jesus is frequently labeled a "sorcerer"—one who worked magic through association with demonic powers (Matt 9:34; 10:25; 12:24, 27; Justin, *Dial.* 69; Origen, *C. Celsum* 1.6; *b. Sanh.* 43a; 107b)—and a "deceiver"—one who sought to lead Israel away from covenant loyalty (Matt 27:63-64; cf. Luke 23:2, 5, 14; *T. Levi* 16.3). These labels were meant to nullify Jesus' appeal, to set him apart as a dangerous deviant whose ways led to disgrace and whose teaching was contrary to the way approved by God.[13]

The potential impact of these charges on Jewish-Christian believers was, of course, negative. Their Christian commitment would be jeopardized if they were to entertain the possibility that Jesus was not the one appointed by God to bring the definitive interpretation of Torah, and if they were to accept the parent body's labeling of them as deviant followers of a deviant teacher. The impact on Gentile believers who accepted the Jewish Scriptures as the oracles of God would be no less forceful. Part of Matthew's strategy for insulating the congregation from the shaming techniques of the parent body, therefore, naturally included a reaffirmation of Jesus as the true teacher of God's way. Returning to our paradigm for investigating honor discourse, we are presently viewing the gospel as affirming the character particularly of group leaders, "strengthening the group's inner-directed focus on such people as reliable, honorable guides to right knowledge and conduct, bolstering the leaders' authority to delineate the group's norms and to grant honor or ascribe blame within the group." In rhetorical-critical terms Matthew's demonstration of Jesus' honor serves as an overarching appeal to ethos, the counterpart of which is, of course, Matthew's preservation of traditions that undermine the credibility of Jesus' opponents (and hence the ongoing leadership of the non-Christian Jewish body).

The Honor of Jesus: Gospel as Encomiastic Biography

While a gospel is not an encomium *per se* it does resemble in certain important respects the ancient genre of the *bios,* or "life," in which an author recounted the deeds and words of some great figure of the recent or distant past with much the same end as the encomium proper, namely the promotion of central cultural values. The subject matter of Matthew, moreover, overlaps in many respects with the encomium: in comparison with Mark, Matthew brings the gospel genre even closer to the encomium by including information about Jesus' origins, an important heading within the standard encomium. A person's nobility was demonstrated, in the first instance, from the nobility of his or her ancestors, parents, race, city, and the circumstances of his or her birth (such as cosmological signs or supernatural occurrences). These will be recognized as sources of "ascribed" honor (cf. Aristotle, *Rhet.* 1.5.5).

Like Mark, Matthew also devotes considerable attention to Jesus' "achieved" honor, mainly through his deeds of virtue and his death (two other topics of encomia). Jesus' death as a dishonored criminal merited special attention in the early Church, and Matthew provides a fine witness to the transformation of a shameful death into a noble death: one that was, on the one hand, suffered unjustly as a result of the envy and craft of Jesus' rivals, and that was, on the other hand, endured voluntarily for the benefit of others (hence a most noble end). Another source of "achieved" honor is Jesus' victory in numerous challenge-riposte exchanges with hostile representatives of Jewish leadership, that, together with the other elements showing God's affirmation of Jesus' life and teaching, effectively affirms the believers in their commitment to discipleship and insulates them from the negative pressure of the synagogue.

1. Origins and Nurture

Matthew begins his gospel with a genealogy in order to set forth Jesus' illustrious ancestry, emphasizing his connection with Abraham, the founder of the Jewish race, and David, the founder of the monarchy and noble head of the leading house of the race. The genealogy of Jesus shows that he descends not from some obscure branch of the Davidic household, but rather directly through the line of reigning monarchs from David through Solomon down to Jeconiah and even extending to Zerubbabel in the post-exilic period. Jesus is thus presented as a legitimate "Son of David," a title that points not only to his ancestry but to his messianic appointment. This title, further, will recur throughout the gospel as an important testimony to the people's recognition of Jesus' ascribed honor as God's anointed (9:33; 12:22; 20:30-31; 21:9, 15).

The story of Jesus' birth contributes a number of details to the honorable origins of Jesus. Most explicitly it deals with the question of Jesus' legitimacy by claiming for Jesus an even more illustrious descent, namely from God. The affirmation that Joseph had no marital relations with Mary before the birth of Jesus (1:24-25)—an ironic defense of the virginity, hence honor, of a pregnant woman—becomes an affirmation of Jesus' legitimacy as Son of God. Matthew thus claims at the outset a doubly noble lineage for Jesus. Moreover, the birth is surrounded by visions and cosmological signs (the appearance of an uncommonly bright star) that would be understood as presages of Jesus' uncommon honor and noble destiny. This destiny is specified in the giving of the name Jesus (*Yᵊshua*). This otherwise rather common name was not selected by his parents but rather appointed for the child by God, delivered through an angel; it is the name that would encapsulate the meaning of his life and work: "he will save his people from their sins" (1:21 NRSV). The honorable nature of Jesus' death is already prepared for in the infancy narrative, for it is through the voluntary death of this righteous one that the sinners are spared.

It is also at this moment of naming that Matthew begins to bring in his formulaic citations of the Jewish Scriptures, which also would be heard as signs of Jesus' honor. Quintilian, for example, includes as part of the encomium any mention of "omens or prophecies foretelling future greatness" (*Inst.* 3.10.12). These references to the Jewish Scriptures, then, not only demonstrate for the audience that despite the claims of its opponents the Christian community is in true continuity with the ancient revelations of God to God's people, but also speak of the honor and nobility of Jesus, who fulfills divine oracles spoken long ago. In this first prophecy Jesus is given a second name that encapsulates his significance as the one who mediates God's presence to God's people ("Emmanuel," "God with us"), a theme that will be sounded throughout the gospel: "whoever receives you receives me, and whoever receives me receives him who sent me" (10:40); "all things have been handed over to me by my Father; and no one knows the Son except the Father, and no one knows the Father except the Son and any one to whom the Son chooses to reveal him" (11:27 NRSV). Great honor is claimed for Jesus (comparable to the gift he brings) as the mediator of access to God (a patron who gives access to a greater patron).

Chapter 2 continues to bring in topics that resonate with the encomium. The appearance of a new star signaled the birth of a noble ruler, and the adoration of the magi (note the physical representation of honor in their act of prostration) confirms this interpretation of the cosmic sign. The nobility of Jesus' city of origin, Bethlehem, is confirmed by the testimony of Micah (Matt 2:5-6). More visions aiming at the preservation of Jesus and further notice of prophetic oracles being fulfilled in his earliest years complete a picture of Jesus' origins that would be wholly understandable in terms of encomiastic praise of Jesus' ascribed honor.

A related part of an encomium dealt with the education and nurture of the subject of praise. Matthew provides none of this information directly, but the baptism and temptation scenes may offer an equivalent. After Jesus' baptism God speaks for the first of two times in the entire gospel: "This is my beloved Son, in whom I take delight" (3:17; NRSV: "with whom I am well pleased"). At the outset of Jesus' adult life and activity in the field of honor, as it were, the audience is told of God's witness to Jesus' character and formation to that point. He is explicitly approved by God. Further, the temptation scene portrays three challenge-ripostes between Satan and Jesus in which Jesus three times bests the opponent. His responses, however, consist wholly of appropriate selections from Deuteronomy, showing him to be thoroughly learned in the Scriptures and committed to uphold the laws, and skilled in their application (grasp of and commitment to the laws being the point of connection here with the encomium).

The opening chapters of Matthew, then, affirm the honor of Jesus in categories that would be readily recognized by the inhabitants of the first-century Mediterranean world. He has been given a high honor-rating in terms of ascribed honor and has already used his education to defeat the enemy of the human race in the game of challenge-riposte. He enters the story as God's appointed deliverer of the people, upon whom God's favor rests and through whom God's favor is extended to others, with whom God is "well pleased." This assures that the readers will be aligned with Jesus, will perceive hostility toward Jesus as base and unjust, and will hear Jesus' words as the way to please God and stand in God's favor as well.

2. Deeds of Virtue

Encomia proceeded from the praise of the origins and nurture of their subject to his or her deeds, the acts that showed the realization of his or her noble potential and exemplified recognized and praiseworthy virtues. Part of the encomium would also treat the manner of death and, if possible, the beneficial results of death.[14]

Jesus achieves honor in the first instance through his mighty acts of healing and exorcism (4:23-25; 8:1-4, 5-12, 14-17; 8:28–9:1; 9:18-26, 27-31, 32-33; 15:29-31; 17:14-21), the primary cause of the spreading of his "fame" or reputation in the gospel (cf. 9:8, 26, 31, 33). According to Aristotle wealth "consists rather in use than in possession" (*Rhet.* 1.5.7): it is not the one who hoards wealth, but the one who uses it for the benefit of clients and city who gains honor for his or her wealth.

Jesus is certainly not portrayed as wealthy in the sense of material possessions, but he displays wealth in terms of non-material endowments. He is sought out as a patron (more properly a mediator of God's favors), whose resources include healing the sick and casting out demons. People approach him with reverence, acknowledging the superiority of a patron (note the physical representation of this acknowledgment by both a leper [8:2] and a ruler of the synagogue [9:18]). Jesus responds favorably to these requests, showing his character to be one of mercy, benevolence, and compassion. He acts in the interest of others and not out of self-interest: the interpretive quotation from Isa 53:4 ("he took our infirmities and bore our diseases," 8:17 NRSV) shows, indeed, that he is a benefactor even to his own harm. The crowds give honor to God as a response to witnessing Jesus' deeds, thus acknowledging that God's favor is poured out through Jesus (9:8; 15:31).

These healings serve another function for Matthew, namely to demonstrate Jesus' ascribed honor as God's anointed one, the Messiah. From prison John the Baptist sent messengers to Jesus to ask, "are you the one who is to come, or are we to wait for another?" (11:2-3 NRSV). This was, in effect, a challenge to Jesus calling for a riposte that might demonstrate Jesus' honor as "the one who is to come." It was a challenge to Jesus to clarify for John and the gathered crowd the nature of his position. Jesus answered: "Go and tell John what you hear and see: the blind receive their sight, the lame walk, the lepers are cleansed, the deaf hear, the dead are raised, and the poor have good news brought to them" (11:4-5 NRSV). The works Jesus did—the healings of the blind, the lame, the deaf, and the lepers, the raising of the dead, and the proclamation of God's kingdom and justice to the poor—are offered as the most conclusive demonstration of his identity. Matthew brings together here passages from Isa 29:18-19; 35:5-6; and 61:1. The last two of these passages, in their historical context, look forward to the time of God's deliverance of the people from exile in Babylon; in the first century they become portraits of God's activity in the end time. Among the documents found at Qumran is a text *(4Q521)* that bears independent witness to a messianic reading of these Isaiah passages from the first century B.C.E. Jesus' honor as God's appointed end-time agent, then, is confirmed by these healings (as well as by the proclamation of good news to the poor), which show his divinely-endowed strength.[15]

The manner of Jesus' death posed a greater challenge to the early Church: it was indeed a "scandal," "offense," and "folly" (1 Cor 1:23; Gal

5:11). Nevertheless, the earliest proclamation of Jesus' death as "for our sins" (cf. 1 Cor 15:3) already set the degrading experience of crucifixion within the noble framework of the beneficial death. Paul would place this more clearly in the context of patronage when he declared that "he died for all, so that those who live might live no longer for themselves, but for him who died and was raised for them" (2 Cor 5:15). Jesus' favor and gift should elicit corresponding gratitude from his clients (those whom he has benefited), namely life for life. Matthew, like the other evangelists, is also concerned to present the death of Jesus as a noble death rather than the deserved end of a dishonorable criminal.

The parable of the Wicked Tenants, which is about to be played out in the drama of the gospel, provides one of many interpretive keys offered by Matthew before the actual depiction of Jesus' passion. In 21:42 Jesus cites Ps 118:22-23 as the moral to be drawn from the parable: rejection of Jesus does not signal his dishonor; it is God's election of Jesus as cornerstone that constitutes his true honor and signals the ignorance and baseness of those who rejected him. As Jesus undergoes the status-degradation ritual of trial, mockery, and crucifixion the reader is aware that this experience is but the rejection of the "builders," and that this dishonored one has been chosen by God for the highest honor.

Matthew's presentation of the passion demonstrates first that the trial and crucifixion constituted injustice: punishment was undeserved and the execution was unjust. Having been bested by Jesus in every public debate (challenge-riposte), his enemies turn to a secret plot to eliminate him. Their dishonorable motives and manner appear in 26:3-5, 14-16, and especially 59-61, where the highest ruling body of elders is explicitly charged with promoting deception and the bearing of false witness (and is thus guilty of a serious breach of Torah). Even Pilate can see that "envy" motivates these accusers (27:18). Envy was considered a base passion felt by dishonorable rather than honorable people. Unlike "emulation," in which the success of another spurred one on to seek similar rewards through similar virtuous action, envy provoked no virtue in the envious, but only the desire to deprive the virtuous of the rewards that are their due (Aristotle, *Rhet.* 2.11.1).

Not only are Jesus' opponents dishonorable in the extreme (envious deceivers, lawbreakers), but Jesus' innocence is maintained throughout the trial and execution. The trial is interrupted by Pilate's wife, who protests Jesus' "justice" or "innocence" on the basis of information received in a dream—notably a supernatural source (27:19). Jesus' innocence is also affirmed by the centurion who bears witness to the signs occurring after Jesus' death (27:54). The centurion upholds Jesus' identity as Son of God against the charges of his accusers that he was a criminal, and even against the verdict of Pilate.

If Jesus' death was indeed undeserved, the result of the actions of envious and deceptive people, the dishonor of his death does not attach itself to him but rather to his accusers. That perpetrating injustice was baser than suffering unjustly had been argued by Plato in his *Gorgias*:

> I tell you, Callicles, that to be boxed on the ears wrongfully is not the worst evil to befall a man, nor to have my purse or my body cut open, but that to smite and slay me and mine wrongfully is far more disgraceful *(aischion)* and far more evil; aye, and to despoil and enslave and pillage, or in any way at all to wrong me and mine, is far more disgraceful and evil to the doer of the wrong than to me who am the sufferer (508D).

Seneca (*Const.* 16.3) also claims that insults and injuries are only dishonorable if they are deserved:

> One does not need to be a wise man to despise these, but merely a man of sense—one who can say to himself: "Do I, or do I not, deserve that these things befall me? If I do deserve them, there is no insult—it is justice; if I do not deserve them, he who does the injustice is the one to blush."

By showing Jesus' death to be unjust Matthew both preserves Jesus' honor and charges Jesus' opponents with acting dishonorably, indeed with being shameful people.

The narration of the arrest, trials, and crucifixion is replete with verbal and physical representations of dishonoring and shaming. Recalling that the head and face are the physical "location" of honor, we are not surprised to find considerable attention being given to the dishonoring of this part of Jesus' body. First the Sanhedrin itself slaps, strikes, and spits on Jesus' face (26:65-68), challenging him with taunts that go unanswered. Then the Roman soldiers gather together to dishonor Jesus through a mock "crowning" (accompanied by mock prostration), followed by more affronts to his honor through striking his head (27:27-31). Binding (27:2), the assertion of power over another by restricting his or her ability to act, and flogging (27:26), the mutilation of the physical person, were also part of this "status-degradation ritual," culminating in the crucifixion itself (27:35), the fastening of a now impotent person in a public place for open contempt (cf. the ongoing taunts in 27:39-44).[16] With the preparation Matthew has given the reading of this narrative, however, the reader already knows that none of this degradation touches the honor of Jesus, but only redounds to the dishonor of those who treat the Son of God, the one approved by God, so improperly.

Jesus' death was not, however, merely an unfortunate miscarriage of justice. It was at the same time an intentional death, a noble death. Alongside the base motives of Jesus' opponents, the narrative shows that Jesus has his own motives for submitting to crucifixion. Matthew clearly demonstrates that this death was voluntarily accepted and enacted for the benefit of others, thus qualifying it as a noble death and act of supreme courage.[17] The passion predictions (16:21-23; 17:9-12, 22-23; 20:17-19) function largely to show that Jesus' trial, experience of dishonor, and death were not a surprise, but seen from afar and voluntarily endured since he had ample opportunity to avoid them. Matthew's frequent interjections of remarks concerning Jesus' foreknowledge of the time and manner of his betrayal and arrest (26:18, 21, 31-32, 45) also contribute strongly to the impression that his death was voluntary, as does Jesus' prayer in Gethsemane, in which he expresses his intentional acceptance of suffering and death in obedience to God's plan (26:39, 42).[18] Matthew includes a tradition unique to his gospel concerning Jesus' ability even after his arrest to escape the power of his enemies with the aid of legions of angels (26:52-53), again emphasizing that Jesus is laying down his life voluntarily. Finally, the silence of Jesus before Pilate in the face of his accusers' charges—Jesus' refusal to interrupt with some defense the labeling process that would lead to his execution—confirms that his is a voluntary death.

Matthew makes it clear throughout his narrative that this death was endured to benefit others. As early as 1:21, which announces Jesus' destiny (the destiny etymologically contained in his name) as saving his people from sin, Matthew is preparing for the passion to be interpreted as a death "for others." In 20:28 Jesus claims to have come "to give his life a ransom for many" (NRSV), coupling voluntary action ("give") with beneficial death ("ransom for many"). Jesus' words at the Last Supper, especially the words spoken over the cup, reinforce this interpretation of his death when it occurs: "Drink from it, all of you; for this is my blood of the covenant, which is poured out for many for the forgiveness of sins" (26:27-28 NRSV). While space prevents a thorough discussion of the topic here, Matthew's connection of the progress of the Passion to the Jewish Scriptures (greatly expanding on Mark's efforts in this direction) also contribute to the interpretation of Jesus' death as noble, as it represents an essential part of God's plan to bring the promised eschatological blessings to God's people.

The manner of Jesus' death, while potentially dishonoring, is shown to be actually quite consonant with his honor as God's anointed one: the act of self-giving and beneficence that closes a ministry of self-giving and beneficence. The signs recorded by Matthew that accompanied Jesus' death, like the signs that accompanied his birth, enhance his honor and the significance of his death. Of course it is God who offers the final riposte to the taunt of Jesus' enemies (27:43) through the resurrection, which also constitutes God's appointment of Jesus to the position of highest authority in the cosmos, hence of greatest honor and potential for ascribing honor and dishonor (28:18-20). Thus Matthew is able to include a report of the "time subsequent to our hero's death" (Quintilian, *Inst.* 3.10.17), witnessing to Jesus' honor.

Our brief survey of Matthew's gospel using major headings of the encomium has shown that the gospel is intensely interested in demonstrating the honor of Jesus. Although he writes to believers (i.e., those already convinced of Jesus' honor as Messiah and Son of God), in a situation in which a group's honor is challenged from outside it is often necessary to affirm that honor in part by defending the leader around whom the group formed. Jesus' honor, in particular, was the target of non-Christians. Matthew defends Jesus' honor in order to affirm those who follow in Jesus' way: as long as they are assured of their leader's nobility and the error of the outsiders' opinion, they will be insulated against the attempts to draw them away from commitment to that leader. Moreover, in reminding the audience of Jesus' death on their behalf Matthew also reminds them of their debt of gratitude and loyalty to their Patron: their honor is secure as long as they act honorably toward this exalted Benefactor.

3. Jesus' Honor and Credibility and the Pharisees' Dishonor

We learned from such sources as A.W.H. Adkins and Julian Pitt-Rivers that both Homeric-age Greeks and modern Mediterranean people will engage one another in challenge-riposte exchanges as part of competition for honor. This appears also to be true for first-century inhabitants of Palestine as well, since the challenge-riposte form is so common in the gospel (cf., e.g., 9:1-8, 10-13, 14-17; 11:2-6; 12:1-8, 9-14, 24-42; 15:1-20, 21-28; 16:1-4; 19:3-9; 21:15-17, 23-27, 28-32, 33-46;

22:15-22, 23-33, 34-40, 41-46). A sizable amount of Matthew's gospel portrays Jesus and various representatives of Judaism (especially the Pharisees and scribes) as competing for honor and the results of honor, influence and authority as interpreters of God's Law. Jesus' repeated victory in these contests contributes to establishing his greater authority to teach the ways of God as the superior interpreter of Torah in particular and Scripture more broadly. Jesus' victory (and achieved honor) is confirmed both by the crowd—the honor-granting "public" that witnesses the contests and determines the victor—and by God, whose verdict is uncontestable. Specific censure (shaming) of the Pharisees and scribes also abounds as a special Matthean emphasis. These aspects of the Matthean material will also have an important impact on the audience, leading them to exclude their contemporary representatives of the Pharisees from their court of reputation and to look exclusively to Jesus as the teacher of the divinely-approved way of fulfilling Torah.

Jesus appears at the opening of his public ministry as a teacher, particularly one in competition with other teachers. Matthew 5:17-20 is an important passage in the development of Jesus' teaching ministry, at once deflecting the charge of being a deceiver or false teacher (Jesus claims to teach more accurately the way of keeping Torah so as to stand approved by God) and setting up competition between Jesus' followers and the Pharisees and scribes. The "righteousness" of the Pharisees is insufficient, but Jesus shows the path to the "better righteousness": the disciple, therefore, is assured that he or she stands approved by God and that censure or reproach from non-disciples shows them to be deficient in the knowledge of living righteously. Jesus' invitation in 11:28-30, the call to take up his yoke, is a call to accept Jesus as the teacher of God's way. In the world of the narrative and the world of Jewish Christians it would stand in direct competition with the Pharisaic-Rabbinic yoke. This competition is highlighted by Jesus' warnings against the *halakha* of the Pharisees (16:5-12).

A quick survey of the challenge-ripostes reveals especially an interest in showing Jesus to be the superior interpreter of Torah and Scripture. These challenge-riposte exchanges may indeed be comparable to the challenges hurled especially at Jewish Christians by non-Christian Jews (although Justin Martyr, for example, depicts a Gentile Christian and a Jew in an extended debate—i.e., an extended challenge-riposte scenario—in the mid-second century). Certainly Jesus' victory in these exchanges would encourage the believers that the norms of their group are truly the way to arrive at honor before God, and may even arm them to offer "ripostes" in their own setting. The challenge is most frequently offered by Jesus' opponent (rarely initiated by Jesus himself until the climactic conflicts of Matthew 21–23 when Jesus begins to put the opponents on the defensive).[19] Frequently the challenge consists of an accusation that Jesus or his disciples have acted contrary to the Torah and the norms approved by God. The "riposte" consists of a remark or action of Jesus showing that he (or his disciples) have indeed acted in accordance with God's Law,[20] and that the Pharisees or scribes or Sadducees would have known this if they were just more faithful to Torah or adept in the Scriptures themselves.[21] These exchanges end in the opponents standing "amazed" (22:22; in 22:33 the crowds' amazement bears witness to Jesus' victory) and, at the end, completely silenced and defeated by Jesus. Matthew 22:46 marks Jesus' final and uncontested victory in the long history of challenge-ripostes that fills this gospel. The opponents cannot offer a riposte to his challenge and are so tired of defeat they no longer seek to engage him. This allows Jesus to have the last word, offering his scathing censure of the Pharisees and scribes (Matthew 23).

Confirmation of the honor Jesus acquires in these exchanges and his legitimacy as teacher of God's way comes in the first instance from the "public" who witness the competitions and Jesus' credibility. In 7:28-29 Matthew notes the crowd's comparison of Jesus with the scribes: they are struck by Jesus' authority, and the scribes are found wanting in the comparison. Further, the crowds give honor to God as they witness Jesus at work (9:8; 15:29-31), acknowledging in this manner that ultimately Jesus acts from the power of God (and not the power of demons). The very high public opinion of Jesus (9:33b), which verges on messianic confession ("can this be the Son of David?" 12:23), highlights on the one hand the public honor achieved by Jesus and on the other the envy of the Pharisees who stand to lose their respected position as Jesus' fame and authority grow. Finally the crowd is "astounded" at Jesus' riposte to the Sadducees (22:33), showing their admiration for his victory.

The more important confirmation of Jesus' honor, and of his legitimacy as a teacher and interpreter of the Law, comes from God. The transfiguration scene (17:1-8) is very important in this regard. In it God speaks for the second and last time in Matthew's gospel. The first time, at Jesus' baptism, was to affirm Jesus as God's well-pleasing Son. This second utterance from God (17:5) reminds the audience of Jesus' divinely-ascribed honor as Son and confirms God's approval of his deeds and teaching.

Moreover, it contains God's direct and unambiguous command to "listen to him," to heed Jesus' teaching as the way to live so as to be approved and honored by God. All who oppose Jesus are shown, in this scene, to oppose God and live contrary to the way God approves. It is they, and not the Christians, who ought to be ashamed of their behavior, and so the Christians may again deflect the force of outsiders' censure and not be moved to seek honor in their eyes at the cost of honor in God's eyes.

Finally God affirms Jesus by responding to his execution with resurrection—the sign of God's approval and vindication of the righteous (cf. 2 Maccabees 7). The resurrection demonstrates that Jesus was not in fact a "blasphemer" (26:65) but rather taught "the way of God in accordance with the truth" (22:16). God's affirmation of Jesus' honor and legitimacy as teacher of God's way is heightened by God's appointment of Jesus over all creation (28:18-20), especially as judge (3:11-12; 16:27; 24:30-31; 26:64). This appointment is a weighty ascription of honor. The believers are called to look forward to Jesus' future coming in the full display of God's honor, or in the full display of his own honor and power,[22] seated at the "right hand" of God (note the physical expression of honor, namely being seated at the place of highest honor). This elevation of Jesus leads to the command to teach others to observe Jesus' commandments, as he now stands as judge and as representative of God, ruling on behalf of his Parent.

Matthew's gospel, therefore, affirms the teaching of Jesus as the way to fulfill Torah so as to receive God's approval. The ultimate expression of this conviction is, of course, the installation of Jesus as the eschatological judge who will separate the righteous from the wicked on the basis of the standards he himself taught during his earthly ministry. The ways in which the gospel establishes Jesus' honor, then, constitute an effective and thoroughgoing appeal to *ethos*, affirming the credibility of the leader of the minority group. The future coming of Jesus also establishes Jesus as the one reliable, honorable guide to right knowledge and conduct and the one with ultimate authority to delineate the group's norms and to grant honor or ascribe blame within the group (and beyond).

The audiences are also supported in their commitment to discipleship and assisted in deflecting any pressure put upon them by non-Christian Jews by Jesus' censure of the Pharisees, which is given considerable weight not only by Jesus' victory over them in public challenges (hence his assertion of superior honor and credibility), but also by God's explicit affirmation of Jesus as the spokesperson of God's values. Matthew depicts the Pharisees in dishonorable terms. They experience envy at Jesus' growing honor in the eyes of the people, resulting in slander and deviancy labels (9:34; 12:24). This is recognizable as envious activity, as it attempts to deflect from Jesus the honor that is his due as a virtuous and beneficent person. Their loss of honor in the open contest of challenge-riposte motivates them to seek to defeat Jesus dishonorably through secretive and, ultimately, deceptive means.

The Pharisees are, however, explicitly denounced by honorable characters as unfaithful to Torah and unreliable teachers. John the Baptist begins this attack (3:7-9), which is taken up in earnest by Jesus. In 15:1-20, after the Pharisees offer a challenge concerning the disciples' alleged transgression of ritual washings and purity regulations, Jesus begins his riposte with a counterchallenge concerning the Pharisees' own practices. They break Torah for the sake of their traditions (15:3); they dishonor God through their insincerity and teaching merely human precepts (15:8-9); they are blind guides—teachers without knowledge who also endanger their followers. The effect of such shaming of the Pharisees for Matthew's readers is succinctly surmised by Hagner:

> Pharisees claimed to be interpreters of Torah whereas actually they cancelled it (cf. 15:3, 6, 8-9). This would have had special meaning for Matthew's community given their own situation. . . . [They] saw themselves as faithful followers of Torah, as expounded in the teachings of Jesus, and they justified their position from this clash between Jesus and the Pharisees with the argument that they themselves and not the synagogue were in true succession to Moses.[23]

The audience would be insulated even further by Jesus' warning against the *halakha* of the Pharisees (16:5-12), and especially by his final denunciation of the scribes and Pharisees in 23:1-36. The seven "woes" pronounced by Jesus were likely to have been heard as reproaches for shameful behavior, the opposite of a "makarism" (see below). K. C. Hanson has analyzed the form of the "woe" and concludes from a survey of comparable texts that such reproaches are "imputations of shame on specific groups" that work by "uncovering shameful behaviors."[24] As in 15:3-9 specific behaviors of the Pharisees are censured as dishonorable, and they themselves are labeled "hypocrites" (23:3, 5, 13, 15, 23, 25, 27-29) and "blind guides" (23:16, 17, 19, 24).

While Jesus, the leader of the Christian group, is affirmed as an honorable guide to right conduct who teaches reliably the way to stand in honor before God, the leaders of rival (Jewish) groups are censured as dishonorable teachers whose ignorance of God's Law leads them together with their followers to "fall into a pit" (15:14). Attention to Matthew's development of Jesus' honor and the Pharisees' dishonor has in this way helped open up part of Matthew's rhetorical strategy, particularly as it appears in parts 1c and 1d of our paradigm (given at the end of Chapter One). Matthew censures outsiders—here specifically the representatives of the leadership of non-Christian Judaism—as unreliable guides to conduct, as shameless or dishonorable, as influences that ultimately jeopardize the well-being of individuals (1c). He affirms the character of group leaders, strengthening the group's inner-directed focus on such people—here specifically Jesus—as reliable, honorable guides to right knowledge and conduct, bolstering the leaders' authority to delineate the group's norms and to grant honor or ascribe blame within the group. This reminder of who is the reliable and who the unreliable guide to living so as to please God will also have an important social effect. The believers, though pressured to return to the "ways of their ancestors," will be strengthened to remain committed to the way of discipleship. The social boundaries of the group will be solidified rather than weakened so that the minority group will retain its distinctive identity and constituency vis-à-vis the parent religion.

HONOR, GROUP VALUES, AND SOCIAL ENGINEERING IN MATTHEW

We turn now in the second half of our investigation of Matthew's gospel to the ways in which the material Matthew has preserved and shaped would impact honor-sensitive hearers. In this investigation we follow closely our agenda of discerning the boundaries of the "court of reputation" drawn by the gospel (through the cumulative effect of its sayings and other traditions) as well as the way in which the gospel proposes honor to be gained or lost before that alternate court of reputation. In this way we hope to gain a sharper picture of the relationship of the community addressed by Matthew to other groups in the first-century world, together with an impression of the *ethos* of this community as promoted by the social sanctions of honor and dishonor.

A. Whose Approval Matters?—Delineating the Court of Reputation

Matthew has preserved and shaped many Jesus traditions that would have the effect of bracketing the opinion or evaluation formed by the parent body (the Jewish ethnic subculture) concerning the minority group. Jesus' characterization of the Pharisees and scribes as "an evil and adulterous generation" (12:38; 16:4 NRSV) shows that their character is essentially dishonorable. They do not embody God's values, but rather are aligned with the forces of sin and shamelessness. The opinion formed by dishonorable people is not worthy of consideration. The rhetorical effect of such denunciations is to undermine the *ethos*—the credibility—of the representatives of the non-Christian way of keeping Torah. To follow the opinion of the dishonorable is to risk becoming dishonorable oneself. We have seen above how Matthew's decision to include so many challenge-riposte exchanges between Jesus and Jewish leaders (especially the Pharisees and scribes), as well as Jesus' reproaches directed at these figures (e.g., the scathing denunciation of the Pharisaic-Rabbinic understanding of how to live lives approved by God in ch. 23), would reaffirm for the addressees the essential error of the non-Christian Jewish community and negate the effect of their attempts to shame believers into returning to their way of keeping Torah.

In numerous other passages, however, this effect is reinforced. For example, the readers are told that

> the people of Nineveh will rise up at the judgment with this generation and condemn it, because they repented at the proclamation of Jonah, and see, something greater than Jonah is here. The queen of the South will rise up at the judgment with this generation and condemn it, because she came from the ends of the earth to listen to the wisdom of Solomon, and see, something greater than Solomon is here (12:41-42 NRSV).

Before the judgment seat of God those who opposed Jesus during his ministry, and by extension the disciples of those Pharisees who now oppose the Christian way of doing Torah, will be condemned. Their lack of honor and virtue will be exposed. In light of God's eternal verdict those who reject Jesus and his followers are shown to be a court of reputation that ultimately does not matter. To give in to its pressures to conform now would only lead to the believer's own condemnation before God's judgment seat. A similar effect would be produced by 11:20-24, in which Jesus censures unrepentant Judean cities (i.e., the majority of Jews who did not respond positively to his preaching), and declares that pagan cities like Tyre, Sidon, and even Sodom would fare better before God's court. Disgrace that outstrips Sodom's shame awaits those who reject Jesus.

The parable of the wedding banquet further reinforces this evaluation of those who were invited but refused to respond when called, i.e., refused to respond to Jesus, as "unworthy" (22:8). First, the original invitees are guilty of dishonoring the host by "making light" of his invitation (22:5). These invitees, who clearly represent the detractors of Jesus and his followers, only show their own lack of honor when they refuse the message of the Christian community, and all the more when they move into contempt for or open hostility against Jesus' followers and bring upon their heads God's satisfaction of God's servants' honor (22:6-7). One recognizes in the "anger" of the host the response of one who has received insults from those he desired to benefit (see Aristotle, *Rhet.* 2.2.8). Such passages depict the outsiders (for example, the non-Christian Jews who exert some measure of pressure on their Jewish relatives and neighbors who have joined themselves to the Christian sect) as dishonorable, eliminating the force of their critique.

The lengthy passage about almsgiving, prayer, and fasting (6:1-18) in the first instance warns against engaging in religious activity for the wrong reasons, namely human approval (specifically the approval of the "synagogue," hence those persons who do not conceive of piety in the same manner as the Christian community; 6:2, 5). Piety was a central virtue for both Jews and Gentiles (though defined differently by different groups), and thus an essential component of honor. Jesus' words warn the believers against giving in to the desire to be approved by outsiders (non-Christian Jews and Gentiles) by engaging in acts of religion that might suggest an implicit renunciation of one's exclusive commitment to Jesus. The phrase "your Father who sees in secret" (6:4, 6, 18 NRSV) points to God as the ultimate "court of opinion" to the explicit exclusion of the court of opinion formed, in the first instance, by the Jewish synagogue. The synagogue no longer supplies affirmation, but rather denies the validity of the new community, whose members must be insulated against the pull and pressure of Jewish opinion. Matthew thus directs the Christians' attention to the God who sees in secret, and encourages them to withstand the pressure to perform what non-Christian Jews would approve as pious actions for the sake of their acceptance. This would also not fail to impact Gentile Christians, who would be pressured as well by their neighbors to perform the public acts of piety the Greco-Roman society approves as tokens of loyalty and civic virtue: the prayers of such outsiders are vain babbling, but the One God hears the prayers of Jew and Gentile offered in Jesus' name.

The contrast between the "narrow" and "wide" gates (7:13-14) serves to offset the minority (i.e., deviant) status of the Christian group: they are a minority because only a small number from the mass of humankind finds the divinely-approved way. If the majority, who are entering the broad and easy road to destruction, think that the Christians are fools, dishonorable, or disgracefully lacking in virtue, the Christians will be able to neutralize the force of such pressure to conform by contemplating the end of outsiders as, ultimately, destruction. The way of life promoted within the Church, even if held as dishonorable by the majority of people, is nevertheless the narrow and difficult road to life and eternal honor before the court of God and the Son. Moreover, Jesus' teaching about what constitutes true greatness shows that the world's conception of what is "great" and "honorable" is upside down (20:24-28): those who adhere to such values cannot correctly evaluate the behavior of Christians. This is also important insofar as the Christians themselves were, in most cases, brought up as members of the dominant culture (or the Jewish subculture). They must therefore not evaluate their own honor or lack of honor based on the worldly standards they learned as adolescents and lived as adults, but only according to the new standards as revealed by the teachings of Jesus.

Another passage that is likely to have a strong impact on the believers' formulation of their court of reputation is Matt 10:26: "Have no fear of them; for nothing is covered that will not be uncovered, and nothing secret that will not become known" (NRSV). When all things come out in the open the honor of the minority group will be vindicated and the critics outside shown up for what they are. The counter-definitions of the Christians will be vindicated. There is a greater court to which always to address oneself, whose values one dare not transgress since the penalty is so much greater. Thus the believers are to "fear"—that is, take care not to live so as to provoke—God, and not to be concerned lest this way of life provoke outsiders to acts of hostility (cf. the immediate context of 10:24-25).

Christians are thus directed to look for God's approval, and especially to regard Jesus as the one teacher who is explicitly named by God as the Approved One, the One to hear and obey, who shows the way to live honorably before God. As we have seen above at length, Matthew's narrative effectively establishes Jesus as the credible and authoritative counselor. Just as Matthew sought to undermine the ethos of Jesus' opponents (those who present a rival teaching concerning how to fulfill God's Torah and please God), so he has sought to establish beyond the shadow of a doubt Jesus' honor and credibility as a reliable guide in contrast to the "blind guides" (23:16, 17, 19, 24). God's explicit approval and legitimation of Jesus and his teaching is shown not only at the baptism (3:17) and the transfiguration (17:5), but most powerfully in the resurrection. In the face of the world's contempt and disapproval (shown in the extreme by crucifixion) God vindicates Jesus and the way he taught, raising him to the place of highest honor in the cosmos: "Sit at my right hand, until I make your enemies a footstool for your feet" (22:44). This reminds the believers not only of Jesus' honor and his ability to grant honor to his faithful followers, but also of the outsiders' dishonor: those who oppose Jesus (through attacking and shaming, for example, his family on earth) will be subject to lasting disgrace at Jesus' triumphant return.

Reaffirmations of the basic conviction that Jesus is risen and coming again in the capacity of judge serve to reinforce the believers' willingness to endure the society's disapproval and rejection now in order to gain the greater, eternal honor when his angels "will gather up his elect from the four winds" (24:30-31). This is further fortified by the sayings about judgment (e.g., 10:32-33), which point the believer very firmly toward having regard for what the judge, namely Jesus, will say about one on that day of judgment, encouraging him or her to seek approval before that court no matter how strongly human courts of reputation pressure believers to give up their commitment to the minority group: "do not fear those who kill the body but cannot kill the soul; rather fear him who can destroy both soul and body in hell" (10:28 NRSV).

The believers are also gathered together to form a strong body of support and mutual reinforcement. Indeed, the fellowship of the followers of Jesus is depicted as an honorable body. The conversation about paying the Temple tax reveals that they are the "children" of the King, namely the God on whose behalf the tax is collected, whose children should indeed be held exempt from the tax (17:24-27). As those who do the will of God they are the family of the Son of God, hence part of God's family (12:48-50) and partners in the honor of the head of that family. Such use of kinship language also reinforces a high level of attachment and mutual support within the community, so that the affirmation one receives from fellow-believers offsets the negative pressure one receives from non-Christians.

Matthew's discourse on the life of the community (ch. 18) also provides for strong group reinforcement. Matthew's distinctive placement of the parable of the lost sheep in the context of care for straying group members (18:10-14) sets up a measure of reinforcement for the commitment of those who are wavering within the group: the community is to encourage its wavering members and keep individuals focused on the certainty of the group's values, restoring the fallen (that is, not letting pressure from outside pull them away). We should also note the importance of the command warning the believers not to "despise one of these little ones" (18:10; NRSV). Within the group all the faithful must be honored, must receive approval and affirmation. There is no room for holding the weaker members in contempt, for then how will they remain faithful? What will strengthen them not to give up and give in to the outside pressures? The honor of the "little ones" in the community is upheld by their angels who "continually see the face of my Father in heaven" (18:10; NRSV), who are thus able to obtain the aid of their heavenly Patron if their honor is abused. The community is thus activated to work to restore the fallen, not preen themselves for their commitment while members of weaker constitution are allowed to fall away.

The Christian community as "court of reputation" is given considerable authority in the detailed directions concerning handling a dispute between two believers. After a private confrontation and a meeting with two or three witnesses, the whole Christian community is called upon to enforce discipline, and the verdict of the community is witnessed by Jesus who is present in their midst and binding in both realms of earth and heaven (18:15-18). The Church is in a position to enforce the wayward member's conformity with the ethical ideals of Jesus, for what member would willingly endure excommunication from the Church as long as he or she believed that it truly has the authority to bind and loose, and remains the place where the presence of God as mediated by Jesus can be known? If the narrow road is the way to the eternal inheritance of God's kingdom, the Church is the gateway to that inheritance. Attachment to the community and vital engagement of its values is therefore a strong assurance also of God's approval of one's life and worth, a strong counterbalance to society's claims to the contrary.

B. *Defining Behaviors and Values That Lead to Honor*

How honor and shame uphold group values may be uncovered by investigating what behaviors lead to honor and what behaviors lead to dishonor within the view of reality espoused by the text. The instructions concerning the fuller keeping of Torah that Matthew preserves in

5:21-48 are bracketed by appeals to honor. First, 5:17-20 declares that these behaviors (and, one may assume, an approach to the rest of Torah that follows these models) constitute the "greater righteousness," that is, the "greater virtue" and therefore a "greater claim to honor," than that possessed by the Church's rivals, the scribes in their synagogues. It is, moreover, *this* righteousness that receives God's approval and recognition in the form of admittance to the kingdom of God, the reward prepared for those who embody God's will. Matthew's treatment of the attainment of righteousness and the doing of Torah begins to sound like subcultural rhetoric with regard to the Jewish ethnic subculture (thus supporting again the hypothesis that he writes to reassure Christians that they fulfill the cultural values better than the parent body of Judaism). It is the follower of Jesus who will perform more perfectly what the ethnic subculture claims to prize, namely fulfilling the Torah.

Second, these behaviors are said in Matt 5:45 to make one a "child of the Father who is in heaven," giving the person assurance of the honor of adoption into God's family (hence, ascribed honor) since one has brought one's character and life into line with the character of God. The believer will therefore pursue the virtues that are given as the path to honor, namely the renunciation of anger, grudges, lust, untruthfulness, vengeful aspirations, and hatred, and will instead pursue love for the enemy, prayer for the persecutor, reconciliation with the brother or sister, and so forth. Noteworthy in this passage is the striking way in which Jesus' teachings run counter to the cultural expectations for responding to such a challenge to one's honor as a slap in the face (the face and head, we recall, being special physical symbols of honor). The believer is called to offer as a "riposte" not an act of satisfaction but acts of mercy, forgiveness, and generosity, thus honoring God by imitating God's mercy, forgiveness, and generosity (cf. 18:23-35). Jesus presents this as a better way of preserving and even augmenting honor in the sight of God (if not in the sight of unbelievers).

The Sermon on the Mount closes with another passage that speaks close to home for those who are sensitive to honor: "Not everyone who says to me, 'Lord, Lord,' will enter the kingdom of heaven, but only the one who does the will of my Father in heaven" (7:21-23 NRSV). The hearer is taken to the eternal court of reputation whose verdict results in either lasting disgrace (being labeled an "evildoer" and excluded from Jesus' presence) or lasting approval. This appeal motivates the hearer to seek to "do the will of the Father who is in heaven" as Jesus reveals it.

Matthew 10:24-39 is rich in language resonant with the rhetoric of honor and shame. We have seen that 10:24-26 contributes to believers' freedom from the opinion of non-Christians and to their assurance of vindication when all that is now hidden (e.g., the lordship of Christ) becomes manifest (i.e., at the Last Judgment). Matthew 10:32-33 uses language of honor and disgrace to sustain loyalty to and confession of Jesus in the face of pressure to deny association with the name: "everyone, then, who acknowledges me before human beings I also will acknowledge before my Father who is in heaven; but whoever denies me before human beings I also will deny before my Father." Desire for honor before the eternal court, secured by Jesus' character witness, should lead believers to accept disgrace before the human court on account of their loyalty to Jesus. There is a new point of reference for one's honor: one must prove oneself worthy of Jesus rather than worthy of the affirmation of natural kin or the larger society: "Whoever loves father or mother more than me is not worthy of me; and whoever loves son or daughter more than me is not worthy of me; and whoever does not take up the cross and follow me is not worthy of me" (10:37-38 NRSV). While the way of discipleship may cost a person his or her place in the natural kinship group, and while it may lead to contempt (symbolized by the cross), it is still the way that one is found worthy of Jesus, and therefore worthy of honor before God.

Matthew shares Mark's emphasis on the definition of true greatness in God's sight: it consists in serving (20:24-28); true life is found when one loses one's life for the sake of the gospel (16:24-27); the way of the cross is the way to glory, for the same God who vindicated the honor of Jesus, once despised by his society as deviant and shameful, will also vindicate the followers of Jesus as their walk of discipleship leads them to experience society's contempt. Matthew emphasizes this new definition of greatness with a number of additional sayings: "Those who humble themselves like this child, they are the greatest in the kingdom of heaven" (18:4); "The one who is greatest among you shall be your servant; those who exalt themselves will be humbled, and those who humble themselves will be exalted" (23:11-12). These reinforce for the hearers the essential posture of discipleship, namely serving rather than self-promotion, as the only path to real and lasting honor. This path to honor is explicitly contrasted with the dominant cultural assessment of honor (what the "rulers of the Gentiles" do, 20:25), the definition of honor as "precedence over," sought by James and John "over" their ten comrades (who respond with "anger" at this attempt by these two to gain honor at their expense). Both Matthew and the dominant culture agree that honor is a value worth pursuing, but Matthew preserves sayings of Jesus that invert the dominant culture's definition of honor.

It may be fitting at this point in our survey of Matthew's presentation of acts or attitudes leading to honor to discuss the numerous "makarisms" ("beatitudes") in the gospel (5:3-12; 11:6; 13:16-17; 16:16-19). In a lucid essay K. C. Hanson has distinguished between "blessings" and "makarisms" in the following way: blessings are "formal pronouncements . . . bestowing God's positive empowerment"[25] while makarisms "represent the public validation of an individual's or group's experience, behavior, or attitude as honorable."[26] He thus proposes that the opening of a "beatitude" be translated not "blessed" or "happy" or "enviable," but "how honorable." Makarisms, therefore, articulate "socially ideal behavior and commitments" or those "conditions and behaviors which the community regards as honorable."[27] I would consider this argument basically correct, with a single, minor nuance. Hanson bases his observations concerning the difference between blessings and makarisms on the work of Waldemar Janzen, who rightly depicts a makarism as public affirmation that an individual (or group) has been blessed by God in receiving some "positive empowerment" from God. I would suggest, therefore, that a makarism could also be introduced by the formula "how favored" in many instances. Those who are "favored" are, nevertheless, still quite possibly "honored" by the gift God provides.

Matthew uses a concentration of makarisms to open Jesus' teaching ministry (5:3-12). In them Jesus articulates those attitudes, actions, and states that are regarded as signs of divine favor or individual honor within the new community. Many of these are not altogether surprising, as mercy, gentleness, peacemaking, purity, and passionate concern for justice are values shared by many groups. The final makarisms in the series, however, are somewhat more striking:

> Favored are those who are persecuted for righteousness' sake, for theirs is the kingdom of heaven. Favored are you when people slander you and persecute you and, lying, say every base thing about you on my account. Rejoice and be glad, for your reward in heaven is great, because thus people persecuted the prophets who were before you (5:10-12).

Endurance of the larger society's attempts at shaming what it perceives to be deviants—its attempts at social control through assaulting the honor of those it hopes to "correct"—is transformed into a sign of honor and divine favor, a token of sharing the reward of God's prophets. Where believers accept this interpretation of their experience of dishonor at the hands of outsiders the larger society will be powerless to sway them from loyalty to the Church. Related to these makarisms is 11:6: "favored/honored are those who take no offense at me." Those who cling to Jesus and his teaching rather than reject him as at odds with obedience to Torah and God[28] are affirmed as standing in honor before God.

Two other makarisms appear in Matthew, both directed at the original disciples (one specifically at Peter), but both perhaps speaking also to the congregations reading the gospel. The first declares that those who see Jesus' ministry and hear his words are "favored" above many righteous persons and prophets who did not live to see the advent of the Messiah (13:16-17). In the context of the chapter, moreover, the disciples are "favored" insofar as they actually "hear" in the midst of a generation that may "hear but never understand" (13:14). The second makarism is addressed to Peter upon his confession of Jesus as the "Messiah, the Son of the Living God" (16:16). Jesus pronounces Peter "favored/honored" because this confession comes only through a special revelation from God. In both makarisms it is easy to see how the addressees might have applied them to themselves as well, as pronouncing them favored by the privileges they enjoy (hearing Jesus, acknowledging correctly who he is) but that are not enjoyed by many others. These makarisms thus not only point to markers of honor in the new community (confession of Jesus) but also, like 5:10-12, function to reinforce the difference between believers and outsiders, and the exclusion of the latter group from the court of reputation.

The counterpart to desiring honor is seeking to avoid disgrace. A wedding guest who lacks the appropriate garb is singled out, shamed by the host, and cast out into "outer darkness" in front of all the other guests (21:11-14). The parable contains an unnamed example who is censured for some lack of virtue, making the hearer aware that gross shame awaits those who fail to do the will of God, motivating the hearer to bring forth the appropriate fruits of righteousness as Jesus has defined them. One interpersonal behavior Matthew emphasizes quite heavily is forgiveness. Not only is this underscored in the Lord's Prayer and the verses that follow it (6:9-15), but the lengthy parable that closes the discourse on community life returns to this theme (18:23-35). A slave owing his master an enormous debt is sentenced to be thrown into prison and have his family sold off to recover what portion of the debt the master may. He begs for forgiveness, the master is moved, and the slave is forgiven the debt. He goes out and collars a fellow-slave who owes him a small sum; unmoved by his fellow-slave's pleas for forgiveness, he has him cast into prison. The master castigates the unforgiving slave: "'You wicked slave! I forgave you all that debt because you pleaded with me. Should you not have had mercy on your fellow slave, as I had mercy on you?' And in anger his lord handed him over to be tortured until he would pay his entire debt" (18:32-34 NRSV). The parable closes by warning the addressees: "So my heavenly Father will also do to every one of you, if you do not forgive your brother or sister from your heart" (18:35 NRSV).

The hearers are motivated to practice mutual forgiveness lest they come to dishonor when they stand before their God who forgave them so great a debt. Why should the king have expected the slave to show mercy to his own debtors? The "anger" of the king in the parable (18:34) may offer an important clue. This shows that his honor has been engaged when the slave refused to forgive a debt. The slave's actions make an implicit claim that the slave's honor is of greater value than the king's: the latter was willing to forgive an offense against his honor and forego satisfaction, and that offense was incomparably greater than the offense offered to the slave by his peer. The addressees are thus cautioned, when confronted with an affront from a fellow believer, not to think more highly of their honor and desire for satisfaction than God did when God forgave them their offenses. If they fail to emulate the generous heart of God, if they fail to make God's virtue their own, they, too, shall come to disgrace for showing so little regard for God's honor and patience.

The four eschatological "parables" in Matt 24:45–25:46 reinforce commitment to seek honor and avoid disgrace in the terms defined by the group. In each of these parables (the fourth is really not a parable, but a sort of vision of the Last Judgment), honor awaits those who have lived out their lives faithful to Jesus' word, and dishonor awaits those who fail to take his word to heart and commit their lives to bearing the fruits of righteousness. In the first parable (24:45-51), which may be addressed particularly to local community leaders (those appointed to care for their fellow servants until the master's return), the servants who are continually occupied with the business to which the master has appointed them will receive honor within the household of the master at his return (24:47); those who neglect their service to the master, however, will be shamed and cast out from the household (24:51). In the second parable, the parable of the wise and foolish bridesmaids, admission to the wedding (a symbol of the kingdom for which Jesus' followers are waiting) depends on being prepared to meet the bridegroom at any hour: there will be no opportunity for last-minute preparations (25:1-13), but one must be equipped to meet him whenever he shall come. In the third parable, the parable of the talents (25:14-30), language of approval and honor and language of disapproval and dishonor become much more prominent than in the second parable. Those who use what the master has entrusted to them to increase the kingdom will receive advancement and honor when the master returns: the interim is a time for fruitful labor, for the use of time, resources, and gifts for the building up of what Jesus values. Those who fail to use what the master has entrusted to them to this end will come to shame: they will be branded "worthless," "wicked and lazy," and excluded from the kingdom.

The final parable returns to an explicit delineation of behaviors the Lord looks for in people, and that receive either the reward of honor and approval—"Come, you who are approved by my Father, inherit the kingdom that has been prepared for you from the foundation of the world" (25:34)—or the shame of exclusion and disapproval—"Go away from me, you cursed ones, into the eternal fire that has been prepared for the devil and his angels" (25:41). These strong sanctions are used to support works of love, deeds of charity and mercy toward the hungry, weak, sick, poor, and imprisoned. This concluding vision helps the hearers understand that ultimately their honor depends not on networking with the rich and powerful but with responding in mercy and generosity toward the needy and nobodies.[29]

C. Dealing with Dishonor from Outside

Matthew seeks to insulate his readers further from the pressure of the disapproval of the outside world by providing them with a means of withstanding society's (and particularly non-Christian Jews') attempts at shaming them back into conformity. He begins to do this by pointing out the outsiders' lack of knowledge concerning what truly pleases God. Their attempts at shaming are to be understood as the hostility of the ignorant.[30] Moreover, Matthew presents disgrace and opposition from the dominant culture and the parent religion as experiences to be expected; they should not therefore catch the believers unaware so as to disconfirm their convictions about their place in God's favor and truth. The first disciples were told to expect such attempts at social control (10:17-18), and the generations of believers that would follow are warned that hostility from outside is inevitable (24:9-10).

Matthew closely links believers' experience of persecution first with Jesus' own experience at the hands of the ungodly (10:24-25). Just as the attempts to shame Jesus reflected rather the dishonor of his opponents, and just as God was the ultimate guarantor of Jesus' honor, raising him from the dead and exalting him to the highest position (honor) in the cosmos, so the believers would be insulated from society's attempts at social control by the assurance that these measures again reflect the dishonor and error of the non-Christians. Matthew also links the believers' experience of dishonor at the hands of outsiders with the return of the Son of Man, so that believers are given hope for certain and imminent vindication (13:41-43; 24:30-31).

Finally, we recall the sayings included (and extended) by Matthew that pronounce these believers honored, favored, and approved when they are subjected to disgrace and persecution for the sake of the name: "You are honored when people slander you and persecute you and lie about your character on my account. Rejoice and be glad, for your reward in heaven is great, because thus they persecuted the prophets who were before you" (5:11-12). Just as the prophets of old stand in honor before God, so the believers are assured that they, too, stand in honor with them. Given the community's definitions of reality, according to which Jesus himself will come to judge the nations and reward his own, it becomes actually "honorable" to suffer contempt, reproach, insult, and hostility now on his account.

CONCLUSION

The foregoing investigations are certainly not intended to be an exhaustive treatment of honor discourse in Matthew's gospel, but merely an example of how to discern the presence of honor discourse and how to interpret its rhetorical and social effect upon the audience. Many exchanges between characters in the story could be profitably investigated in depth as challenge-riposte scenarios (e.g., the exchange between Jesus and the father of the epileptic or the Syro-Phoenician woman). While the opportunities are fewer in Matthew than in Luke or John, still there are numerous places where the activities of women could be investigated against the background of female honor (conceived as chastity and as location in private spaces). Many individual details of the replication of honor in physical postures have been bypassed.

Nevertheless, this cursory look at how Matthew uses honor discourse may begin to highlight the benefits of this line of inquiry. As we attend to a text's use of honor discourse we see what behaviors the hearers are being led to emulate or avoid, as well as how the document works to reinforce group boundaries and values by answering for the hearers the question "whose approval should I seek?" and by motivating the sorts of behavior within the group that aid group solidarity and commitment. We also see how such investigation provides insights that might nurture theories concerning the situation of the churches Matthew envisioned as his audience (and this need not be limited to reconstructions of a particular "Matthean community"). Here the fact that Matthew preserves so much material challenging the Pharisees' ability to recognize what God values and demonstrating Jesus' superiority as reader of Scripture and teacher of Torah supports theories that place the Church in tension with the local Jewish communities, emphasizing the need for the Christians to be especially well-insulated in that direction. Matthew promotes among the churches that read his work (however broad that audience becomes) a subcultural relationship to emerging Pharisaic/Rabbinic Judaism, claiming to fulfill a commonly-held set of values (Torah) better than the Jewish ethnic subculture.

Matthew's gospel also establishes a relationship with Greco-Roman culture. Both cultures agree that piety is a central value, but Matthew rejects the dominant culture's expression of piety as worthless; both agree that honor and preeminence are highly desirable goods, but Matthew inverts the dominant culture's definition of how honor is displayed and attained. The majority culture, whether Jewish or Gentile, suggests that affronts (challenges to honor) demand satisfaction; Matthew preserves Jesus' sayings that point to forgiveness and even benevolence as the only appropriate responses to injury and affront (having revealed these to be the essential characteristics of God). This points to a more countercultural relationship with the Greco-Roman world and with Mediterranean majority culture more broadly.

While Matthew establishes God and the Christian group as the primary court of reputation it is also clear that he does not entirely withdraw from an interest in the impression made on outsiders. On the one hand believers are to have no regard for the outside world's criticisms, reproaches, or other attempts at shaming them. On the other hand believers are urged to conduct themselves virtuously in the eyes of outsiders so that their "good works" will result in the outsiders' coming to revere the One God (5:16). The parting commission of Jesus, moreover, explicitly envisions the conversion of outsiders to the group's way of life (28:18-20). Matthew erects strong boundaries for the preservation of the group and its culture, but the boundaries are to be fluid as outsiders are converted.

Careful investigation of occurrences of honor discourse can thus help uncover the rhetorical effect of a gospel on its first hearers as well as provide valuable insights into the setting of the evangelist and audience and the social formation the evangelist seeks to achieve. In cooperation with other exegetical disciplines it can give our work an added and useful dimension that leads us closer to an appreciation of the very real, three-dimensional issues faced by the first-century churches.

NOTES: CHAPTER 2

[1] For some intriguing forays into the rhetorical analysis of gospels see the studies of selected passages in light of the rhetorical elaboration of the *chreia*, which opened the door to the rhetorical investigation of the gospels, in Burton L. Mack and Vernon K. Robbins, *Patterns of Persuasion in the Gospels* (Sonoma, Cal.: Polebridge, 1989); Burton L. Mack, *Rhetoric and the New Testament* (Minneapolis: Fortress, 1990).

[2] Bruce J. Malina and Jerome H. Neyrey, "Honor and Shame in Luke-Acts: Pivotal Values of the Mediterranean World," in Jerome H. Neyrey, ed., *The Social World of Luke-Acts: Models for Interpretation* (Peabody, Mass.: Hendrickson, 1991) 25–66; Bruce J. Malina and Richard Rohrbaugh, *Social-Science Commentary on the Synoptic Gospels* (Minneapolis: Fortress, 1992).

[3] The appeal to *ethos* is "indirect" insofar as Matthew is not interested in building up his *own* credibility as a speaker, but rather in underscoring *Jesus'* authority to prescribe the courses of action believers are to follow.

[4] Nowhere has this been more forcefully displayed than in Wayne A. Meeks, "The Son of Man in Johannine Sectarianism," in John Ashton, ed., *The Interpretation of John* (Philadelphia: Fortress, 1986) 141–173.

[5] See the collections of essays in Richard J. Bauckham, ed., *The Gospels for all Christians* (Grand Rapids: Eerdmans, 1998). Such questioning is not without important precedents. See, for example, Luke T. Johnson, "On Finding the Lukan Community: A Cautious, Cautionary Essay," *SBLSP* 1 (1979) 87–100.

[6] Bauckham, *Gospels* 27–30.

[7] Bauckham, *Gospels* 30–44. This is a particularly compelling and well-documented section of Bauckham's essay.

[8] Bauckham, *Gospels* 12–13.

[9] Bauckham, *Gospels* 15.

[10] Bauckham (*Gospels* 47) is, of course, acutely aware of this himself.

[11] Donald A. Hagner, "The *Sitz im Leben* of the Gospel of Matthew," in David R. Bauer and Mark Alan Powell, eds., *Treasures New and Old: Recent Contributions to Matthean Studies* (Atlanta: Scholars, 1996) 27–62, at 29–32. Graham N. Stanton places great importance on Matthew's heightening and extending the polemic in the traditional material, focusing it even more sharply against the Pharisees and scribes in particular (*A Gospel for a New People* [Louisville: Westminster/John Knox, 1993] 146–168).

[12] "To their Jewish kinsfolk, Jewish Christians have always had to answer such charges as disloyalty to the religion of Israel, disloyalty to the Mosaic Law (or at least charges of association with others who fail to observe it), and of joining an alien, indeed pagan, religion, the large majority of whose adherents are Gentile" (Hagner, "*Sitz im Leben*," 46).

[13] On labeling and deviancy—topics closely associated with the social control function of dishonor—see Bruce J. Malina and Jerome H. Neyrey, "Conflict in Luke-Acts: Labelling and Deviance Theory," in Neyrey, ed., *Social World* 97–122.

[14] Cf. *Rhet. ad Her.* 3.7.14, which includes as an element of the encomium the answer to the question, "If he is dead, what sort of death did he die, and what sort of consequences followed upon it?" Giving one's life to secure benefits for others especially led to a most honored remembrance, as for the soldiers praised in Pericles' Funeral Oration (Thucydides, *Hist.* 2.35-46).

[15] Two passages in which Jesus demonstrates power over nature (8:23-27; 14:28-33) also enhance his honor in the sight of witnesses, for example in the confession of Jesus by disciples as "Son of God" (14:33).

[16] For more detailed discussion of the dishonor of crucifixion see David A. deSilva, *Despising Shame: Honor Discourse and Community Maintenance in the Epistle to the Hebrews* (Atlanta: Scholars, 1995) 166–168; Martin Hengel, *Crucifixion in the Ancient World* (Philadelphia: Fortress, 1977); Jerome H. Neyrey, "Despising the Shame of the Cross: Honor and Shame in the Johannine Passion Narrative," *Semeia* 68 (1996) 113–137.

[17] On the pattern of the noble death see David Seeley, *The Noble Death. Graeco-Roman Martyrology and Paul's Concept of Salvation* (Sheffield: Sheffield Academic Press, 1990). Aristotle, among others, links the virtue of courage with the noble death: "The courageous man . . . will be he who fearlessly confronts a noble death" (*Nic. Eth.* 3.6.10).

[18] The notion of an obedient death leads to the possibility of its being an expiatory death, as in 4 Macc 6:28-30; 17:20-22.

[19] Jesus initiates a challenge-riposte-counterchallenge exchange in 21:28-32, 33-36; 22:41-46.

20 This is clear in the challenges to Jesus over Sabbath *halakha* (12:1-8, 9-14), purity *halakha* (9:10-13; 15:1-20); and divorce (19:3-9). In the challenge to his authority to forgive sins, it is his function as mediator of God's favors (such as healing) that proves his function as mediator of God's forgiveness as well.

21 Jesus scores several times by offering as a riposte a lesson in closer reading of Scripture (21:15-17; 21:33-46; 22:23-33; 22:41-46). The implication of three of these four ripostes is that if the opponents were better versed in Scripture they would have recognized Jesus' messiahship and understood what the Christian Jews have come to understand. This is also in view in the challenge calling for a "sign" from Jesus (16:1-4). The fourth shows the Sadducees' denial of the resurrection to stem from their failure to think through adequately the implications of something as central as God's revelation of God's own self as the "God of Abraham, the God of Isaac, and the God of Jacob."

22 The expression "in glory" refers to the visible display of honor and status. "Glory" *(doxa)* was a word tightly wed to conceptions of honor: its meaning ranged from "opinion" and "reputation" to "honor" itself (a synonym for *timē*) to the visible manifestation of honor, e.g., in splendid apparel or other trappings which visually represented the honor or status of the one wearing such symbols (cf. LXX Esther 14:1; 15:6, 13). For a fuller discussion of "glory" see deSilva, *Despising Shame* 212–215.

23 Hagner, "Sitz im Leben," 56.

24 K. C. Hanson, "How Honorable! How Shameful! A Cultural Analysis of Matthew's Makarisms and Reproaches," *Semeia* 68 (1996) 81–111, at 102.

25 Hanson, "How Honorable," 85.

26 Ibid., 90.

27 Ibid., 93, 100–101.

28 Comparison with 13:54-58, where the inhabitants of his home village "took offense at him" (13:57), also suggests that the "favored" ones are those who understand, as does Matthew's audience (cf. Matthew 1–4), that Jesus' honor rating derives from a greater ancestry than most people suspect. He is thus not to be seen as "the carpenter's son" but the "Son of David" and "Beloved Son" of God.

29 While G. N. Stanton has provided an admirable argument that this passage declared that judgment of all the nations would proceed on the basis of how they received the Christian missionaries (*A Gospel for a New People* 207–231), it does not seem to me to be the only likely reading of this vision by first-century Christians. Indeed, the discussion of the "little ones" elsewhere may point to the weak members of the community, such that the vision adds to the directions in ch. 18 to care for the needy, powerless, and marginalized members of the Christian community. See David A. deSilva, "Renewing the Ethic of the Eschatological Community: The Vision of Judgement in Matthew 25," *Koinonia* 3 (1991) 168–194.

³⁰ This is a familiar technique found also in both Jewish and Greco-Roman circles. The censure of Gentiles as "alienated from the truth" (3 Macc 4:16), for example, helps to support commitment to the rejection of Gentile values (such as idolatrous worship) and to the maintenance of Jewish values ridiculed by Gentiles; similarly, holding the non-philosopher to be ignorant of what truly matters frequently enables the philosopher to hold onto his or her ideals in the face of ridicule or insult (cf. Epictetus, *Diss.* 1.29.50-54; 4.5.22; Seneca, *Const.* 13.2, 5).

3

Honor Discourse in the Fourth Gospel

The Fourth Gospel stands apart from the synoptic gospels in so many ways that a survey of its use of honor discourse alongside our investigation of Matthew may be helpful. As with so many other points of comparison between John and the synoptics, its use of honor discourse on the one hand bears marked similarities to what one finds in the other three gospels but, on the other hand, there are also a number of points of intensification. Like Matthew, John presents Jesus as an honorable person whose death on the cross in no way detracts from his honor, but rather augments it. John deals much more directly, however, with Jesus' honor rating and intensifies the honor that attaches to the endurance of the cross itself; it becomes nothing less than the hour of glorification. John pursues many of the same strategies as Matthew for excluding non-Christians from the court of reputation and for insulating believers from the power of shaming (whether from the dominant culture or the ethnic subculture of Judaism), but again he goes even farther in drawing the lines around the body of significant others for whose approval one is to have concern. John also provides the reader with an understanding of the believer's honor and the way for him or her to preserve or enhance that honor, but while Matthew uses the sanctions of honor and dishonor to support a wide variety of behaviors, John uses these in a much more focused way.

For the sake of a clearer comparison, then, we will approach John in much the same way as we did Matthew. We will begin with the evangelist's presentation of Jesus as an honorable and reliable figure worthy of trust and allegiance, and with the way in which the shameful execution of Jesus is interpreted as a noble death. In the second part of the chapter we will turn to analyze the rhetorical and social effects of honor discourse in John on its readership: How does it delineate and maintain an alternate court of reputation? How does it negate social pressure exerted on group members from outside the group? How does it help the readers to locate their claim to honor in specifically Christian identity and behaviors? Once more there is no claim here to present an exhaustive discussion of honor discourse in John, but rather a preliminary sketch of its most central features as a starting point for future studies. Our leading question will remain: How would the use of honor discourse in this text affect the first-century reader?

THE SETTING AND PURPOSE OF JOHN'S GOSPEL

This is not the place to solve the much-debated question of the setting and purpose of the Fourth Gospel.[1] Our investigation of honor discourse, however, can connect with and possibly even refine the larger scholarly conversation at a number of points. As one discovers how the gospel orients the believer toward the outside world, or the groups and criticisms against which the evangelist seeks to insulate the believers especially well, one gains additional internal evidence for determining setting and purpose and discovers conections that have not yet entered into the larger scholarly conversation. We begin here to catch a glimpse of how investigation of honor discourse can assist the larger task of the reconstruction of the historical and social setting of an ancient text.

One purpose that receives frequent mention concerns the disciples who continued to follow John the Baptist long after the early Christian movement had emerged. Raymond E. Brown and G. R. Beasley-Murray,[2] for example, affirm the likelihood of the evangelist's interest in replying to followers of John the Baptist by promoting the superiority of Jesus. Beasley-Murray even suggests the possibility that John addresses Jews who were not followers of the Baptist *per se,* but who might have found it useful to portray Jesus as a disloyal disciple of John who broke away from the latter's healthier teachings. Attention to honor discourse supports such a theory, since John the Baptist himself is made repeatedly to bear witness to Jesus' precedence over him in God's court and to accept the diminution of his own honor and following in favor of Jesus' honor and following (1:8-9, 20, 30; 3:28, 30; 10:41).

Brown and Beasley-Murray, joined by C. K. Barrett, agree that John's gospel reflects controversy with Judaism, or the synagogue.[3] This appears, in part, to involve defending the ascription of the title "Messiah" to Jesus.[4] The controversy appears to be social as well as theoretical, however. Brown posits that John uses the term "Jews" frequently "almost as a technical title for *the religious authorities, particularly those in Jerusalem, who are hostile to Jesus.*" These were the spiritual ancestors of the "Jews of his own time" who were pressuring Christian Jews either to hide or renounce their convictions about Jesus as the Messiah or risk excommunication from the synagogue.[5] Donald Hagner has exposed the fallacies of putting too much weight on the "benediction against heretics" or the date of 85 C.E. for the implementation of a universal expulsion of heretics from the synagogue. Aside from the questions surrounding the contents, date, and implementation of this "benediction"[6] it is rightly noted that hostility between non-Christian Jews and Christian Jews began much earlier and was not necessarily settled quickly throughout the Mediterranean by a universal policy issued in 85 C.E.[7] Moreover, Bauckham has rightly pointed out that were such a benediction in fact included in the synagogue liturgy it would have been used in a large number of cities. John would not be addressing the needs only of a "Johannine community," but of Jewish Christians throughout the Mediterranean (in whatever places the *birkat ha-minim* was employed).[8]

Analysis of honor discourse suggests that John was in fact quite concerned about the effect of the synagogue's negative evaluation of Jesus and those who followed him. Expulsion from the synagogue is a recurrent concern in John (9:22, 12:42, and 16:2), and twice this eventuality is linked with the open confession of Jesus. While we may agree with Witherington and Hagner that the eighties C.E. brought no new "social crisis between the synagogue and the Johannine community,"[9] we are pushed to consider that John understood non-Christian Jews as at least a potentially significant voice for his audiences—a voice the effects of which he would need to negate. Perhaps the local synagogues were growing more rigorous in their attempts to bring the deviant members of their race back to the right way of keeping Torah and abandoning aberrant messianic convictions. In any event the gospel preserves much material that suggests that the believers needed special insulation with regard to the evaluation of non-Christian Jews, and even more specifically this issue of having to choose between honoring Jesus and being honored or affirmed by the synagogue.

It is increasingly less certain that John's gospel is concerned with the refutation of heretic Christians:[10] the polemic in 1 John is clearly pointed in this direction, insulating the believers who remained within the congregations addressed by that letter against the pull of their own former sisters and brothers, but the gospel is much more concerned with insulating the believing community from the social pressures of shaming from the synagogue.

There is much debate concerning whether or not John is written with an evangelistic aim in mind, or rather for the encouragement of those who have already become Christians. Barrett and Beasley-Murray regard both aims as of equal importance to the evangelist,[11] while Brown denies the work any missionary thrust and Witherington promotes evangelism of outsiders as the gospel's primary objective.[12] The debate formerly hinged on the finer (and impossible) textual and grammatical arguments surrounding John 20:31 ("these things are written so that you may come to believe/keep on believing that Jesus is the Messiah, the Son of God"), but has moved to consider more broadly the attitude of the evangelist toward nonbelievers throughout the gospel. Witherington is correct to point out that disciples within the Johannine community have a responsibility to bear witness to the world (cf. John 15:27; 17:18), but it is difficult to concur with his claim that the primary audience addressed by the gospel is a non-believing one rather than those who are already disciples.[13] He states his position better earlier in the same book when he claims that the Fourth Gospel was meant to assist believers in evangelism, not to be handed out as a "missionary tract."[14]

Witherington's statement of the purpose of John comes as a response to a number of studies that read the Fourth Gospel as a primarily sectarian work that encourages little positive interaction with the outside world: "it seems to me a significant mistake to simply read this gospel as a manifestation of dualistic sectarianism bent on nurturing an 'us versus them' mentality."[15] This remains a useful caveat, since the gospel certainly does indicate ongoing witness to the world. Our analysis of honor discourse in the Fourth Gospel suggests, however, that it does indeed reinforce strong boundaries between the believing community and the world "outside"—in fact, it appears better suited to explaining the failure of mission rather than motivating new missions. Witherington, too, recognizes that the gospel prepares the disciples for rejection and persecution as a result of their "aggressive witness" since "the world is indeed a dark place."[16] On the one hand, then, the disciples are "sent" into the world to witness as Jesus did; on the other hand an expectation of widespread success is not engendered by the gospel (which sets it apart from Matthew and Luke, where hostility and persecution do not mute the enthusiasm for universal mission).

The gospel surely addresses those who are already followers of Jesus, both Jews and Gentiles. In Beasley-Murray's words, the Fourth Gospel is written in order "to elucidate the revelation brought by Jesus and how it answers the Jewish objections, to encourage Christians to maintain their Christian confession despite the sufferings they endure from Jewish opponents."[17] The words and stories about Jesus are as much concerned with keeping the disciples "from stumbling" (16:1) as with inculcating faith (20:31, unless the disputed clause *hina pisteu[s]ēte* is taken to mean "in order that you may keep on believing"). Analysis of honor discourse can greatly enhance the discussion of the ways in which John encourages believers and insulates them from the pull of nonbelievers (protecting them from stumbling), and help elucidate the behaviors and attitudes he inculcates for the sake of the ongoing life of the community.

JESUS' HONOR

A. The Honor of Jesus Revealed in His Ministry

Like Matthew, John anchors Jesus' honor in disclosures of Jesus' origins, but unlike Matthew he does not base this in claims about Jesus' human lineage or city of origin. Jesus' honor is not secured by tracing his descent from the noble house of David. While John records the low esteem in which Nazareth, the city with which Jesus was associated, was held (1:46), he does not defend Jesus' honor by claiming that he was really born in Bethlehem as does Matthew. Rather, John concentrates fully on the exposition of the honor ascribed to Jesus by his special embeddedness in God and his heavenly origin.

First, honor is ascribed to Jesus not as "Son of David" but as "Son of God." As early as the Prologue itself Jesus' "glory"—his "honor" or "status" as revealed in the signs and to the resurrection witnesses—is said to be that of the unique Son of the Father:

> The Word became flesh and lived among us, and we have seen his glory, the glory as of the Father's only Son, full of grace and truth. . . . From his fullness we have all received, grace upon grace. The law indeed was given through Moses; grace and truth came through Jesus Christ. No one has ever seen God. It is God the only Son, who is close to the Father's heart, who has made him known (1:14, 16-18 NRSV).

Part of the ascribed honor of Jesus involves his role as mediator of the Father's favor. As Son, Jesus has special access to his Father, and his proximity to his Father guarantees the success of his brokerage for those who seek favor from God through the Son.[18] Jesus is, moreover, the only means of access to God's favor (cf. 14:6-7: "no one comes to the Father except through me," NRSV). This gives Jesus special honor as the unique source of access to the highest Patron, underscored by the comparison with Moses in 1:17. Not only is Jesus "full of grace (favor)," but he is also full of "truth," that is, reliable knowledge upon which true evaluations of honor and dishonor can be made. Considerable emphasis is placed throughout this gospel on the superior knowledge Jesus brings and on the ignorance and error of those who do not receive his revelation of "truth" (see pp. 81–82).

John repeatedly shows the embeddedness of Jesus' honor in the honor of God. Disrespect shown the Son becomes dishonor shown the Father: "whoever does not honor the Son does not honor the Father who sent him" (5:23; cf. 3:36). God, however, desires that the Son be honored by all, and guarantees the honor of Jesus: "I honor my Father, and you dishonor me. And I do not strive for glory—he is the one who strives for it and evaluates it" (8:49-50). Jesus has acted in the world as an obedient Son: he acts to defend the honor of God's house, endangered by profiteers (2:16); he seeks to honor God in his testimony, not himself, proving his reliability (7:18); he even endures death in obedience to the Father's will (18:11). He is thus certain that the Father will uphold his honor against the affronts of his enemies. The source of Jesus' honor is not other human beings (5:41), but God in heaven: "it is my Father who manifests my honor, of whom you say 'he is our God'" (8:54). God has further ascribed honor to Jesus by appointing him as "judge," the one who will determine the eternal destiny of all people. John connects Jesus' appointment to this position—a position of matchless authority (5:27)—specifically with God's plan to bring honor to the Son: "The Father judges no one, but has given all judgment to the Son, that all may honor the Son, just as they honor the Father" (5:22-23 NRSV).

With regard to Jesus' place of origin John claims for Jesus an honor surpassing any that could be granted by association with even the most noble earthly city. Jesus is the one "from above": "the one who comes from above is above all; the one who is of the earth belongs to the earth, and speaks about earthly things. The one who comes from heaven is above all" (3:31 NRSV; cf. 8:23). Place of origin still helps determine one's honor rating and establishes precedence in terms of honor (who is more honorable than another), but John makes the superlative claim that Jesus is "above all" in terms of honor. He is unique among people because he has entered the world from heaven, which places him in an entirely different and superior league: "No one has ascended into heaven except the one who descended from heaven, the Son of man" (3:13 NRSV; 6:33-35, 38). The honor John claims for Jesus on the basis of parentage and place of origin is bitterly contested by the "Jews," who think they know enough about Jesus' parentage and origin to deny him the honor he claims: "Is not this Jesus, the son of Joseph, whose father and mother we know? How can he now say, 'I have come down from heaven'?" (6:42 NRSV).

How do those individuals who become disciples come to recognize the truth of Jesus' claims? In John the miracles of Jesus are manifestations of Jesus' honor and divine endowments: they are not merely marvels, but "signs" that point away from themselves to something else, namely Jesus' "glory": "Jesus did this, the first of his signs, in Cana of Galilee, and revealed his glory; and his disciples believed in him" (2:11 NRSV). The sign is the medium by which Jesus revealed his true status, honor, and authority to his disciples. As certain figures encounter Jesus' signs they make claims about his honor on his behalf. Nicodemus affirms that Jesus is a "teacher who has come from God" since "no one can do these signs that you do apart from the presence of God" (3:2 NRSV); the crowd fed by the loaves affirms Jesus' honor as "the prophet who is coming into the world" (6:14); an unnamed "royal official" comes to "believe" on account of a sign (4:54); the collective impact of the signs leads many to suggest that Jesus deserves to be recognized as the Messiah (7:31); the blind man healed by Jesus claims before the Pharisees that these signs—unparalleled from the beginning of the world—should lead all to recognize that Jesus is from God and that God hears Jesus, thus that Jesus is honorable and no sinner (9:30-33); finally, Jesus himself declares that Lazarus' illness will bring honor to God and the Son (11:4, 40).

Jesus' deeds substantiate his claims to be "Son" of God and to speak the truth on behalf of God. While Jesus does indeed claim to be the Son, more often claims are made about Jesus by others rather than by himself. The titles of honor ascribed to Jesus in response to the signs, together with other claims made about Jesus (John the Baptist's testimony that Jesus is the "Son of God," 1:32-34; the Samaritan disciples' claim that Jesus is the "savior of the world," 4:42; the Judean disciples' claims that Jesus is Messiah, Son of God, King of Israel, the "one coming into the world," 1:41, 49; 11:27), all show Jesus' honor being recognized by others, not claimed for himself (as Jesus himself argues in 5:31-47; 7:16-18; 8:54-55). Jerome H. Neyrey points out that in this way Jesus behaves honorably: "he does not seek honor by making vain claims to such-and-such status, but he is regularly ascribed great honor by others."[19]

The Fourth Gospel, then, develops Jesus' honor as the unique Son of God, the one invested by God with authority to judge the inhabitants of the world. Though his status is contested by nonbelievers, Jesus' works testify to his honor and the legitimacy of the claims made about him by his followers. Those who refuse to acknowledge his honor—who presume to judge him—will encounter him as their judge and God as the guarantor of Jesus' honor.

B. The Honor of Jesus Revealed in His Death: The Hour of Glorification

Like Matthew, John is especially concerned to interpret Jesus' death favorably. It is not the shameful execution of a criminal, and in no way does it diminish the honor that is claimed for him throughout the gospel. Like Matthew, John uses topics that transform the crucifixion into a noble death: it is voluntary, courageous, and of benefit to others. John will augment both the voluntary and courageous aspects of this act, and goes farther to present the whole episode as the "glorification" of Jesus as well as of God.

We have already discussed briefly the effect of crucifixion on one's honor rating in the eyes of the dominant and majority culture.[20] Throughout the passion narrative itself John records numerous attempts by enemies to degrade Jesus: he is bound (18:12, 24); his face is struck (18:22; 19:1-3); he is flogged and then taunted by the soldiers by means of the crown of thorns and the mocking tokens of honor (19:1-3); he is made to carry the crossbeam (19:17) and finally affixed to the cross, naked, powerless to stop the soldiers from casting lots for his clothing (19:18, 23-24). As Neyrey rightly observes, however, "despite all the shameful treatment of Jesus, he is portrayed, not only as maintaining his honor, but even gaining glory and prestige. Far from being a status degradation ritual, his passion is seen as a status elevation ritual."[21]

Jesus' death is shown, however, not to be an act inflicted upon him from without but as voluntarily chosen by himself for the sake of accomplishing a noble and beneficent goal. In the words of Aristotle, "sometimes indeed men are actually praised for deeds of this 'mixed' class, namely when they submit to some disgrace or pain as the price of some great and noble object" (*Nic. Eth.* 3.1.7). This transforms the endurance of degradation and suffering into a mark of courage, an honorable virtue.

Jesus' death is shown to be voluntary first in Jesus' claim to have authority over his own life: "For this reason the Father loves me, because I lay down my life in order to take it up again. No one takes it from me, but I lay it down of my own accord. I have power to lay it down, and I have power to take it up again. I have received this command from my Father" (10:17-18 NRSV). John preserves a saying that explicitly stresses that Jesus' death is an act accomplished by Jesus, not inflicted upon Jesus. He is shown to be in control of the situation from beginning to end, even to the point of taking up his life again. The expression in 19:30 that Jesus "gives up" his spirit recalls this earlier claim concerning the voluntary character of the death. As in Matthew, the voluntary nature of the death is also demonstrated by Jesus' foreknowledge of the passion. John provides several passion predictions, although in a more cryptic idiom than one finds in the synoptic gospels (7:33-36; 8:21-29; cf. also 3:14; 12:32). Their function, however, is the same: "I have told you this before it occurs, so that when it does occur, you may believe" (14:29 NRSV). The reader is reminded when Pilate sentences Jesus to die by crucifixion that this sentence fulfills Jesus' predictions concerning the manner of his death (3:14; 12:32).

John introduces the notion of the "hour" of Jesus' passion, which Jesus knows in advance and which must arrive before his enemies are permitted to move against him. This is introduced as early as the wedding at Cana (2:4; cf. 7:6, 8: "my time"). There is a time appointed by God that Jesus foreknows (12:23; 13:1) and accepts. None can harm him before that hour, and even then he lays down his life. None has power over his life. It is important to John to demonstrate that the crucifixion does not occur because of Jesus' weakness or because his enemies prevail. Indeed, they are continually foiled in their attempts to arrest Jesus until "his hour" arrives (7:30; 8:20; 12:23). John also underscores Jesus' knowledge of the identity of the betrayer and the time of betrayal (6:71; 13:11), going so far as to portray Jesus as ordering Judas to perform the deed at a specific time, orchestrating his own sacrifice (13:18-19, 21-30). This heightens the perception of Jesus not as victim but as a willing benefactor who is proactive even in his death.

As the passion proceeds Jesus remains a powerful figure, acting in ways hardly appropriate for a weak victim. When the soldiers approach Jesus to arrest him, for example, they fall down when Jesus declares who he is (using words suggestive of the divine name, "I am," 18:6, 8). At his arrest, Jesus commands the soldiers to let his disciples go.[22] At his trials Jesus speaks with the "boldness" *(parrhēsia)* of the free citizen,[23] displaying courage and even gaining the upper hand in both his exchanges with Annas and with Pilate. John is thus careful to show that Jesus never loses his power or authority. Everything he suffers he endures voluntarily because he has undertaken to achieve a noble goal.

That nobility derives in part from the fact that Jesus dies on account of his obedience to God, his Father. When the "hour" arrives Jesus declares that he will not pray to be saved from it, since it was for this very purpose that he came into the world (again quite different from Matthew's Gethsemane scene). The cross is the accomplishment of the Father's work as well as an opportunity for the Son to bring honor to the Father: "Father, glorify your name" is the prayer Jesus offers in lieu of a plea for avoiding the cross (12:28). By allowing himself to be "lifted up" Jesus will draw all people to himself, realizing God's plan to "gather together the scattered children of God" (11:52). The cross, in short, is the cup God has given him to drink (18:11), and he takes it courageously and obediently, demonstrating the honorable "virtue of *andreia* or courage."[24]

Again as in Matthew, John stresses the benefit Jesus brings to others by means of his death in order to portray that death as noble. John the Baptist presents Jesus as the "Lamb of God who takes away the sin of the world" (1:29 NRSV), which already places his death within the framework of the sin offering that restores the relationship between God and the sinner. His death is a saving death (Jesus entered the world "that the world through him might be saved," 3:17) bringing the benefaction of eternal life to those who believe (3:14, 16). This is echoed in the Samaritan believers' confession of Jesus as the "savior of the world" (4:42): the crucifixion is the means by which others receive this deliverance. Again the "Honorable Shepherd" discourse contains information relevant for understanding the passion: Jesus lays down his life "on behalf of [his] sheep" (10:11, 15) in order to bring them the gift of more abundant "life" (10:10). Even the high priest, Caiaphas, is made an unwitting witness to Jesus' death on behalf of others: "He did not say this of his own accord, but being high priest that year he prophesied that Jesus should die for the nation, and not for the nation only, but to gather into one the children of God who are scattered abroad" (11:51-52 RSV).

Finally, the hour of Jesus' passion is also the hour of glorification (12:23; 17:1). It marks the manifestation of Jesus' honor to the world as its benefactor, but it also marks the beginning of Jesus' return to the

Father, and to the "glory [the honor, position, and power] I had in your presence before the world existed" (17:5). As Neyrey observes, "Jesus belongs to a kingdom where he is honored as he should be (5:23; 17:5, 24)"[25]—this is his return to that greater realm where his glory is not concealed and his claims to honor meet with affirmation and respect. Because Jesus honors the Father in this death Jesus also anticipates that God will honor him through it (13:31-32; 17:4-5).

Jesus preserves his honor, and indeed augments it, through his endurance of dishonor and pain in the trial and crucifixion. It is a noble act by which Jesus brings eternal benefits to his followers, that is, to those who recognize his claim to honor. It is an act of obedience to God by which the honor both of Father and Son is displayed and enhanced before the world. John's depiction of Jesus' death as an act that honors God and brings honor to Jesus has special meaning when one considers that Peter's martyrdom is also referred to as an act that will bring honor to God (21:19). Jesus provides an example for the believers to follow, namely seeking honor from God and seeking to honor God in obedient service, even if this means being shamed and afflicted by nonbelievers. Just as Jesus' honor remained intact through his passion, so the honor of believers will remain untarnished by the assaults of non-Christians as long as they remain loyal and obedient to the God who drew them to himself in Jesus.

HONOR DISCOURSE AND THE AUDIENCE'S RESPONSE

We have already seen how John maintains Jesus' honor and thereby his reliability as the ultimate leader of the group and the one who is vested with the authority to ascribe honor or dishonor (especially in his role as judge, 5:22-23, 27). As in Matthew, we can also observe how John's presentation of the discourses and controversies of Jesus would serve to promote adherence to the values of the minority culture as the path to honor, carefully excluding nonbelievers from the court of reputation and disarming their attempts to shame believers or to label them as deviants. Once again, as long as believers tend to seek the affirmation of their honor among non-Christians their commitment to the values and worldview espoused within the Christian culture remains in jeopardy. John will certainly urge the believers to seek to advance their own honor, but only in the sight of God and one's fellow-believers, so that desire for honor is channeled into activities that sustain the distinctive *ethos* of the Christian culture.

A. Drawing the Boundaries of the Court of Reputation

John draws a sharp contrast between seeking honor from people and seeking honor from God—much sharper than one finds in Matthew. Seeking honor from people repeatedly hinders trusting in Jesus: "How can you believe, who receive honor from one another and do not seek the honor that comes from the only God?" (5:44 RSV). Notably, honor before the human court of reputation and honor before God's court are posited as mutually exclusive options between which one must choose. The eternal, hence superior, value of the latter should make the choice clear for the believing audience at least. "Fear of the Jews," specifically fear of being labeled a dishonorable deviant through expulsion from the synagogue, also repeatedly surfaces as a hindrance to open confession of one's attachment to Jesus or acknowledgment of Jesus' claim to honor (9:22; 19:38). Especially salient is 12:42-43: "many even of the authorities believed in him, but for fear of the Pharisees they did not confess it, lest they should be put out of the synagogue: for they loved the praise of men more than the praise of God" (RSV).

The readers are thus confronted with a choice: have concern for their reputation in the eyes of human beings, especially the synagogue, or have concern for their honor before God's court. John seeks to reinforce their commitment to the latter, of course. He does this in part by presenting Jesus as an example, seeking to honor God rather than to advance his own honor in the eyes of the world (7:18). He also includes much material that calls into question the reliability of the opinion of people, particularly those people who have not received the testimony Jesus brought from God.

First, John suggests that nonbelievers are of a vicious and dishonorable character, hence their opinion concerning what is honorable or shameful carries no weight:

> This is the judgment, that the light has come into the world, and people loved darkness rather than light because their deeds were evil. For all who do evil hate the light and do not come to the light, so that their deeds may not be exposed. But those who do what is true come to the light, so that it may be clearly seen that their deeds have been done in God (3:19-21 NRSV).

One's response to Jesus thus reveals one's moral character: a positive response shows that a person is virtuous (doing works "in God"); a negative response shows that the person is a worker of vice and evil who is afraid of conviction. These verses are not merely about believing or not believing, but also attach value judgments to the character of groups of people such that believers are enabled to exclude unbelievers from their court of reputation as unreliable and immoral people. This is further reinforced in 5:41-42 where Jesus refuses to accept honor from people because he knows that their hearts are base and therefore their opinion is not valuable or acceptable: the "love of God" is not within them. This recalls what we find in Stoic literature concerning the disregard of the wise person for the opinion of the non-philosopher, save for the different criterion for what makes a heart "virtuous" (having the "love of God").

Not only do unbelievers show themselves to be unethical, they are also shown to be ignorant of essential knowledge, possessing an inferior knowledge base. They are ignorant of Jesus' identity (1:10, 26) and so cannot receive adoption as God's children (highlighting a qualitative difference between the believers and outsiders). The nonbelievers do not accept Jesus' testimony even though he is "above all things" and able to impart revelations of what he sees and hears "above" (3:31-32). Those who refuse to receive his testimony thus do not have all the facts about reality and are unable to make reliable judgments. They remain "in darkness" (8:12; 12:46), a symbol of their ignorance and error. Jesus is thus able to censure their power of evaluation as faulty: "do not judge by appearances, but judge with right judgment" (7:24 RSV); "you judge according to human standards" (8:15 NRSV). Whether such people ascribe honor or dishonor to the believer, the believer is to consider that their opinion stems from their vice and ignorance and thus to place no weight on it.

Reliable opinions and evaluations are only possible among believers: "whoever follows me will never walk in darkness but will have the light of life" (8:12 NRSV); "I have come as light into the world, so that everyone who believes in me should not remain in the darkness" (12:46 NRSV). The believers are "enlightened," having received Jesus' testimony and accepted the fullness of "truth" he embodied (1:14, 17). Among human beings only one's fellow believers are equipped with the proper knowledge base to offer reliable evaluations of the honorable and shameful. Moreover, they are of such a moral character as to render them reliable (they have come toward the light, showing their commitment to do the works of God, 3:18-19). Having drawn the lines around the "alternate court of reputation" as consisting of God, from whom one seeks honor, Jesus, the judge who will ascribe honor or censure on the last day, and the believing community, John further strengthens the bonds within the community. The single commandment Jesus gives is that disciples "love one another" (13:34), even to the point of laying down their lives for one another (15:12-13). This is calculated to intensify the affection and mutual support within the community, so that the encouragement and affirmation from within outweigh any censure and discouragement from without.

If John has provided ample material to motivate the believers to lay aside concern for gaining honor in the eyes of the outside world he has also given them many considerations that will disarm the sting of the outsiders' negative opinion. Casting unbelievers as fundamentally ignorant of "truth" (1:10-11, etc.) and as morally deficient (3:17-19) will already go far toward negating their attempts to shame the believers. John presses even further, however, identifying unbelief itself as a mark of non-privilege, and hence dishonor. Unlike those who do respond positively to Jesus, the unbelievers were not chosen by God, not drawn by God to the elect community (6:65). They are not part of the special flock of the Son of God (10:25-27) and so do not respond to his voice. Their non-election is expressed even more strongly as Jesus labels those who are hostile to him "children of the devil," the liar in whom no truth dwells. They are simply "not from God." Their spiritual descent from the archenemy is revealed in their refusal to listen to the truth from Jesus (8:45; 18:37). It is they, and not the Christians, who are the deviants in the big picture.

In two rather extended passages John deals directly with the believers' experience of dishonor and persecution at the hands of the outside world. The first of these brings together a number of elements that should strengthen believers in the face of pressure from outside:

> If the world hates you, know that it has hated me before it hated you. . . . Because you are not of the world, but I chose you out of the world, therefore the world hates you. Remember the word that I said to you, 'A servant is not greater than his master.' If they persecuted me, they will persecute you; if they kept my word, they will keep yours also. But all this they will do to you on my account, because they do not know him who sent me (15:18-21 RSV).

The disciples receive no more than the master endured, and the believers should not expect to be treated with greater justice than their Lord. Matthew makes similar use of the same saying—one of very few sayings shared by John with the synoptic tradition (Matt 10:24). Moreover, hostility from nonbelievers is to be understood as a product of their ignorance of God (hence their dishonor), and as a mark of the honor that befell the believers in their election by Jesus and by God out from the world. Such considerations will certainly help insulate the believers from the society's social sanction of shaming and make it less likely that believers will seek to relieve that shame by conforming again to the values and convictions of the outside world.

Jesus' warnings about the world's social control techniques are given specifically in order to keep the disciples from "stumbling" (16:1, 4). John understands that "forewarned is forearmed," that what is anticipated by the gospel cannot disconfirm the correctness of the gospel. This foreknowledge is to prepare believers to meet the assault head-on and negate its power by the repeated assurance that it stems from the outside world's shameful ignorance about God and the Son (16:3). Even though outsiders believe that their persecution of Christians is an act of piety the believers are not to accept the world's attempts to label them as deviants and deal with them as ungodly persons. Jesus' final word in his farewell discourse, before his prayer, also speaks to this subject: "in the world you face persecution. But take courage; I have conquered the world" (16:33 NRSV). Ultimately the world's assaults are those of a defeated enemy, and no lasting advantage would accrue to the one who exchanges loyalty to the conqueror for peace with the vanquished. Even if the world's hostility should reach the pitch of martyrdom, here too death is an honorable means of "glorifying God" (cf. 21:19). The believer, therefore, is not to fear dishonor and marginalization in the eyes of the world: he or she is rather to remain constant in the quest for honor before the court of God.

B. Gaining Lasting Honor

Before the court of God, what gives the believer honor? How does John use the promise of honor to motivate specific behaviors? Believing in Jesus itself brings an extraordinary grant of honor as the believer joins the family of God: "to all who received him, who believed in his name, he gave power to become children of God; who were born, not of blood nor of the will of the flesh nor of the will of man, but of God" (1:12-13 RSV).[26] Their honor rating is no longer determined by their natural birth but has become incomparably higher through birth into God's family and thus a share in the honor of the Almighty. This new birth also highlights the "set-apartness" of those who do receive the Son, who are given incomparably higher honor than those who do not accept him (1:10-11). This topic is developed further in 3:5-6 where it becomes clear that since flesh and spirit are qualitatively different, the former counting "for nothing" (6:63), one's ascribed honor from human birth, race, and city also counts "for nothing" when compared to birth into God's family. John has already demonstrated this conviction in his presentation of Jesus' ascribed honor—not in terms of human lineage or cities of origin as in Matthew, but wholly on the basis of his origin in God.

This devaluation of criteria used among people to weigh relative honor appears again in 8:34-36: "everyone who commits sin is a slave to sin. The slave does not continue in the house forever; the son continues for ever. So if the Son makes you free, you will be free indeed" (RSV). What is decisive for one's status is not a matter of wealth, noble birth, or fame, but whether or not one has committed sin. Servile status is shameful, and only the Son can bestow honor on the individual, granting freedom to the slave (the one who is a slave to sin). True honor, then, is a gift from the Son, and the believer derives honor from his or her embeddedness in the honor of Jesus, which is itself embedded in the honor of God. Indeed, Jesus has ascribed to the believers the same "glory" God has given Jesus (17:22). Jesus, introduced as the sole mediator of God's favor, has also extended to the disciples the honor of being mediators of Jesus' favor (13:20), and has even named them "friends" (a term of social equality and reciprocity) rather than "servants" (a term of social inequality).

If this is the starting point for the believer's honor John also makes him or her aware of how to preserve that honor through noble behavior. The honorable path consists first in serving Jesus: "Whoever serves me must follow me . . . whoever serves me, the Father will honor" (12:26 NRSV). Such commitment to service results in being honored by God's own self: no more secure and no greater hope for preserving and gaining honor could be given. What does this service look like? It involves, in part, hating one's life in this world in order to gain eternal life (12:25). Moreover, it involves serving the other members of the believing community. Jesus himself shows the servants how to serve one another (13:14-16), to take up postures of service within the group rather than making claims to precedence (they are not, after all, greater than the master who served them!). This is very strikingly reminiscent of the synoptics' portrayal of the way to honor as the way of mutual service within the community (cf. Matt 20:25-28). The grant of honor Jesus has given to all believers, namely the ascription of the same honor

Jesus received from God, is meant to lead to unity among the believers (17:22). John's emphasis on honor coming from God rather than from other people may help curtail attempts to gain precedence over others within the group, which would endanger unity by reviving competition for honor within the group.

One's personal honor or dishonor is, for John, ultimately a matter of how one has honored or dishonored God. These are strong sanctions, since honoring God is the heart of the virtues of piety and justice and dishonoring God brings the grave danger of God's seeking satisfaction for the affront by punishing the offender (which God is certainly able to enforce). This is developed forcefully in John 3:33-36:

> Whoever has accepted his testimony has certified this, that God is true. He whom God has sent speaks the words of God. . . . The Father loves the Son and has placed all things in his hands. Whoever believes in the Son has eternal life; whoever disobeys the Son will not see life, but must endure God's wrath (NRSV).

Receiving Jesus' testimony (accepting Jesus) is sanctioned as honoring God by affirming God's truthfulness, reliability, trustworthiness, since God sent Jesus. The converse, not receiving Jesus' testimony, would mean insulting God, calling God a liar, dishonoring God (3:33). Further, disobeying Jesus (thus showing him contempt) means dishonoring the Father, provoking the Father. The threat of "wrath" or "anger" signals God's perception that God's honor has been violated and God's desire for satisfaction against the affronts of those God desired to benefit (recall Aristotle, *Rhet.* 2.2.8). This is, notably, the opposite of experiencing God's favor (cf. 1:14, 16-18). This connection between the failure to honor Jesus and the failure to honor God recurs at 5:22-23. God is honored not only when God's Son is accepted and served but also when one remains a disciple and bears fruit (15:8). This "fruit" is left undefined, but it may be most naturally linked with acts of love and service within the community (suggested by the context of 15:1-17), and possibly witness to and conversion of outsiders. Finally, God is honored by the faithfulness of God's witnesses even unto death (21:19).

Rather than use honor discourse to promote a wide variety of behaviors and curtail a wide variety of other behaviors John simply focuses the believers on the honor they enjoy as members of the family of God and urges them to preserve that honor through continued loyalty to Jesus, acceptance of his message, and faithful service to him in the person of the sister or brother. Service within the community replaces status-seeking in the eyes of humans, as the believers are assured the honor God ascribes to them.

CONCLUSION

Our investigation has shown that the Fourth Gospel, for all its differences from the synoptic gospels, still shares many of the same concerns with the other evangelists. Like Matthew, this evangelist seeks to present Jesus as an honorable figure who inspires trust and loyalty. John accomplishes this, however, not by arguing for Jesus' honor in terms of noble descent from the house of David or birth in a city with a noble heritage, but by relativizing all worldly claims to honor in an appeal to Jesus' divine lineage and heavenly origin. This marks a strategy that spills over into other uses of honor discourse in the Fourth Gospel, such as the complete negation of the value of honor in the eyes of human beings in favor of seeking honor in the eyes of God. John also uses many of the same topics to transform the crucifixion into a noble death (voluntary, courageous, beneficial to others), but in underscoring it as the hour of glorification also highlights the radical opposition between this world's values and what is honorable before God.

John collects and preserves material that will also serve to shape the readers' awareness of whose opinion—whose evaluation of their honor—should count in their eyes. As we have seen, this is an essential consideration for the maintenance of a minority culture with marked differences from the majority culture. Again, John uses many of the same techniques for bracketing the opinion outsiders may form of the group: unbelievers lack the necessary knowledge to form reliable judgments; they are themselves morally deficient and hence dishonorable. John heightens the group boundaries with imagery suggestive of election and strong dualistic elements; moreover, outsiders dishonor God by rejecting the Son, and so stand under God's negative evaluation (judgment). John is also more directly aware than Matthew, for example, of the need to insulate the audience against the experiences of dishonor and disapproval from outsiders. God's evaluation of the believer is the sole criterion for his or her honor, and God has ascribed incomparable honor to the Christian through adopting him or her into God's family. The believers' commitment to Jesus, to bearing witness to the world, and to acts of love and service within the community are the ways in which they bring honor to God, and thus preserve the honor they have received from God.

Investigation of honor discourse in John opens up new dimensions in John's social and rhetorical strategy for the modern reader. It contributes much to our understanding of the ways in which the Fourth Gospel encourages believers to remain faithful in the face of pressure and censure from outside the group. It may provide additional data for the reconstruction of the setting and purpose of the gospel—certainly helping us understand how the evangelist wishes to orient the believer toward the outside world (and possibly different groups within the outside world) and toward other believers. Witherington reminds us that the gospel, as ancient biography, is also intensely concerned with the subject of the biography, namely the person of Jesus.[27] Attention to honor discourse also helps us to uncover the evangelist's understanding of this figure and the ongoing interpretation of his death in the early Church. Interestingly, it has also shown that while John's idiom is quite distinctive many of his interests are not so very different from other voices in the early Church, including the synoptic evangelists.

NOTES: CHAPTER 3

[1] All the more as this question has been complicated recently by the important critique in Richard J. Bauckham, ed., *The Gospel for All Christians: Rethinking the Gospel Audience* (Grand Rapids: Eerdmans, 1998). See the discussion of this book in the previous chapter.

[2] Raymond E. Brown, *The Gospel According to John*. 2 vols. AB 29, 29A (Garden City, N.Y.: Doubleday, 1966) 67–70; G. R. Beasley-Murray, *John*. WBC 36 (Dallas, Tex.: Word Books, 1987) lxxxix.

[3] C. K. Barrett, *The Gospel According to St John* (London: SPCK, 1960) 53; Brown, *John* 1:71–75; Beasley-Murray, *John* lxxxix.

[4] Brown, *John* 1:70; Beasley-Murray, *John* lxxxix.

[5] Brown, *John* 1:71, 74–75.

[6] Gale A. Yee (*Jewish Feasts and the Gospel of John* [Wilmington, Del.: Michael Glazier, 1989] 23–24) strikes a sensible balance in her demonstration that, on the one hand, the "benediction" was not aimed specifically at Jewish Christians but that, on the other hand, the Jewish Christians who were themselves struggling for self-definition were likely to have regarded it as a direct assault.

[7] Donald A. Hagner, "The *Sitz im Leben* of the Gospel of Matthew," in David R. Bauer and Mark Alan Powell, eds., *Treasures New and Old: Recent Contributions to Matthean Studies* (Atlanta: Scholars, 1996) 27–62. Ben Witherington (*John's Wisdom: A Commentary on the Fourth Gospel* [Louisville:

Westminster/John Knox, 1996] 29) points to evidence in Acts that expulsions from Diaspora synagogues may have happened much earlier than any such official ban in the eighties.

[8] Bauckham, *Gospels* 22–23.

[9] Witherington, *John's Wisdom* 39.

[10] Barrett (*John* 21) viewed this as the driving purpose of the gospel, but Brown (*John* 1:76) explicitly rejects the hypothesis on the basis of too little internal evidence. Beasley-Murray (*John*) and Witherington (*John's Wisdom*) do not even mention it as a possibility.

[11] Barrett, *John* 21; Beasley-Murray, *John* lxxxix.

[12] Brown (*John* 1:73) holds that the gospel is not meant to convert Jews to Christianity: "the violence of the language in ch. viii, comparing the Jews to the devil's brood, is scarcely designed to convert the Synagogue." He further doubts that it was written to convert Gentiles, but thinks it was intended rather to encourage Jews and Gentiles who were already believers (*John* 1:77–78).

[13] Witherington, *John's Wisdom* 32.

[14] Witherington, *John's Wisdom* 4. Assisting evangelism efforts, of course, can hardly express the sole purpose of the gospel.

[15] Witherington, *John's Wisdom* 39.

[16] Witherington, *John's Wisdom* 40.

[17] Beasley-Murray, *John* lxxxix.

[18] See the discussion of the importance of Jesus' "Sonship" for his role as mediator in the chapter on Hebrews in this volume.

[19] Jerome H. Neyrey, "Despising the Shame of the Cross," *Semeia* 68 (1996) 113–137, at 126–127. We might point out that historical-Jesus research has frequently sought Jesus' self-understanding in the limited claims he makes on his own behalf, regarding claims made about him as of secondary importance. Neyrey's insight helps to show why this approach is fundamentally flawed.

[20] See Martin Hengel, *Crucifixion* (Philadelphia: Fortress, 1977) 22–32; summarized in Neyrey, "Despising the Shame of the Cross," 113–114.

[21] Neyrey, "Despising the Shame of the Cross," 114.

[22] Neyrey comments helpfully ("Despising the Shame of the Cross," 120): "Weak people do not tell a cohort of Roman soldiers what to do. This proves, moreover, that his word of honor is true and trustworthy: 'This was to fulfill the word which he had spoken, "I did not lose a single one of those you gave me"' (18:9)."

[23] Neyrey ("Despising the Shame of the Cross," 121) rightly contrasts this *parrhēsia*, or boldness of speech, which "denotes courageous and honorable

behavior," with those "shameful people who are afraid to speak openly about the Christ."

[24] Neyrey, "Despising the Shame of the Cross," 120. *Andreia* is often translated as "manliness," showing the way in which this particular virtue is rooted in ancient conceptions of what behavior is "appropriate" to the male gender. For a male to fail to display courage (e.g., to endure pain for the sake of a noble goal) is to fail to embody his own masculinity, in effect. This is not to say that "courage" is peculiar to males, as the author of 4 Maccabees, for example, lauds the mother as "more courageous [i.e., manly] than men in endurance" (15:30).

[25] Neyrey, "Despising the Shame of the Cross," 124.

[26] John uses the language of ascribed honor here, but there is also an element of achieved honor in the sense that the status of being a child of God comes through a commitment made by the believer. This already begins to elevate believing, or continuing to believe, as a desirable value to maintain since one's place in God's family and the honor that results from occupying that place depend on faith.

[27] Witherington, *John's Wisdom* 4.

4

Honor Discourse in 1 and 2 Thessalonians

*M*oving into epistolary texts brings with it the possibility of a more precise understanding of the challenges being faced by a believing community, and therefore a better comprehension of how honor discourse is being employed to help believers meet those challenges. In Thessalonica believers had to deal with the hostility, reproaches, and challenges they received from their neighbors because of their withdrawal from the behaviors valued by citizens of a Roman colony, especially participation in ruler cult and in traditional Greco-Roman religion, which showed one's reliability and one's commitment to the welfare of family, city, province, and empire.

As we analyze the Thessalonian letters for honor vocabulary, limitations on the court of reputation, and promotion of certain behaviors as honorable before that court of reputation we find that these epistles do not merely seek to answer questions about Paul's credibility (1 Thessalonians 2), the resurrection (1 Thessalonians 4–5) or the end-time (2 Thessalonians 2), or to admonish the "idle" (2 Thessalonians 3),[1] but are chiefly concerned to establish the new believers' commitment to the alternative culture of Christianity to which they had joined themselves through responding to Paul's preaching.[2] Once again attention to honor discourse opens up new avenues for the investigation of the rhetorical strategy and effect of the New Testament texts.

THE COMMUNITY'S SITUATION: SUBJECTED TO SOCIETY'S SHAMING

Paul expressly refers to the Thessalonian believers' situation as *thlipsis* (1 Thess 1:6; 3:3-4; 2 Thess 1:4, 6) and speaks of the believers as "suffering" (*paschein*: 1 Thess 2:14; 2 Thess 1:5). While social scientists have shown that "suffering" may be real or perceived, objective or subjective, we should not too hastily disregard these references to the negative, disconfirming, discouraging experiences of the believers in Thessalonica,[3] particularly when they are a prominent rather than a casual feature of the author's depiction of the situation. Moreover, such pressure is readily understandable as a society's attempts to shame what it considers to be deviant members into returning to what the dominant culture regards as a suitable way of life.

Thessalonica was the capital of the Roman province of Macedonia, with a long history of devotion to the emperor. This concern to show loyalty to Rome began in earnest after Antony's defeat at Actium in 31 B.C.E., since the city had previously sided with Antony and needed to express quickly and enthusiastically its loyalty to Augustus. The emperor cult and a cult "of Rome and Roman benefactors" were both prominent in the city, such that civic events were even dated by the terms of the priests of these cults. The cults of the traditional Greco-Roman gods are also well attested in this city.[4]

Recent decades of scholarship have helped us appreciate the meaning of these cults for the participants, and the importance of participation.[5] The spectres of enforcement of emperor worship from above or of the "sham religion" of the idolatrous cult have given way to a new understanding of the local and grassroots motivation for such cultic activity. Participation in the cults of Rome, the emperor, and the traditional pantheon showed one's *pietas* or *eusebeia*, one's reliability, in effect, to fulfill one's obligations to family, patron, city, province, and empire. Participation showed one's support of the social body, one's desire to do what was necessary to secure the welfare of the city, and one's commitment to the stability and ongoing life of the city. Moreover, participation was an important expression of gratitude toward those who were perceived to be the city's benefactors. Imperial cult in all parts of the empire focused attention on the emperor as the patron of the world. Since his gifts matched those of the deities (peace, protection from enemies, and the like), it was deemed only fitting that expressions of gratitude and loyalty should take on the forms used to communicate with the patron deities themselves. As long as the emperor was strong and his clients faithful, peace and prosperity would remain and the horrors of civil war and foreign invasion would be prevented.

Joining oneself to the Christian movement meant sharing in the same avoidance of all forms of idolatry that marked the practice of the parent religion, Judaism. Jews, though admired by some more philosophically-minded Greeks and Romans, were never free from suspicion and slander. Their devotion to One God to the exclusion of all others—the gods honored by Gentile peoples as true gods—made them appear little better than "atheists" in the eyes of many. Moreover, this religious exclusivism was seen to be replicated in social exclusivism, as Jews were censured for alleged lack of concern for the public welfare (cf. 3 Macc 3:3-7; LXX Esther 13:4-5) and for "hatred of outsiders."[6] People who *withdrew* from participation were subject to even greater suspicion, for it is always more threatening to find one's own withdrawing their support from one's worldview and *ethos* than to deal with a group that has never supported these.[7] It should not be surprising, therefore, that there should be a fair amount of local resentment, suspicion, and even hostility directed at the potentially anti-Roman, anti-establishment proclamation of Jesus, the Messiah crucified by the Romans, as the coming Ruler and Judge. This was a proclamation that threatened Roman order and the security posited in the ideology of "Eternal Rome," the city that insured the Thessalonians' enjoyment of peace. It was, moreover, a proclamation which moved formerly reliable citizens of Thessalonica to withdraw from cultic displays of gratitude toward the city's most important benefactors and from religious displays of loyalty and dedication to the welfare of the city.[8] The group gave all the warning signs of becoming a source of disunity, a cancer in the social body requiring treatment. It is thus quite significant that Paul will locate the believers' honor before God as originating with their turning "toward God away from idols, to serve a living and true God" (1 Thess 1:9): the very act that was also the beginning of their loss of honor and approval in the eyes of their fellow citizens.

While officially sanctioned persecution of the Church was extremely rare in the first century this did not mean that deviant groups like Jews or Christians would not be subject to unofficial acts of hostility and abuse. A believer suffered affliction even if the persecution only took the form of frequent cold shoulders, of hearing some term of abuse while passing a former colleague, or conspicuous exclusion from circles of former friends. We know from Josephus and Philo, however, that such unorganized persecution could take more violent forms. The racial violence in the American Southeast during the Civil Rights Movement, for example, shows how formidable unofficially sanctioned social control techniques could be. There is, however, no mention of martyrdom in the letter (which would have led to a different sort of assurance about the dead believers' destiny), but only reference to the natural deaths of believers. Therefore we may surmise that the persecution was the sort that was normally leveled at people whose lifestyles were now considered deviant and a threat to the city's way of life.[9]

Persecution was, therefore, society's way of expressing disapproval for the believers' new loyalties, of reaffirming its own commitment to the traditional religious expressions of duty toward family, city, province, and empire. It was an attempt to draw the deviants back from the error of their ways by the power of shaming.[10] It is of central importance to Paul as he sends Timothy to visit the congregation (a visit recounted in 1 Thessalonians), and follows up the visit with the letter itself, to counteract the power of these attempts by the dominant culture to reclaim its deviant members. First Thessalonians coheres mainly not as a response to questions about Paul's character or the resurrection of the dead, but as an attempt to negate the effects of being shamed by outsiders, to fix the believers' eyes on those whose opinion of one's honor truly and lastingly matters, and to spur them on to the behaviors and acts that lead to honor before that alternate court of reputation. Second Thessalonians (whether authored by Paul or by another member of his circle) will be seen to continue the social-engineering work accomplished by 1 Thessalonians.

TIMOTHY'S VISIT: COUNTERACTING SOCIETY'S DEVIANCY-CONTROL TECHNIQUES

Paul was concerned lest this device of shaming should work in society's favor, drawing the believers away from their new-found, costly faith. This is particularly evident in 2:13-16 and 3:1-5, which introduce and explain Paul's motivation for sending Timothy back to visit the new community. Paul appears by both the accounts in 1 Thessalonians and in Acts to have left before he would have wished: 1 Thess 2:17 uses the image of being "bereft," a metaphor of mourning over a separation that is not willed by the parties involved. Concerned because of the troubled circumstances of that church, and frustrated with not being able to return himself to see them (2:17-18), he sends Timothy to encourage them in the midst of their afflictions, to do whatever he could to offset the influence of the dominant culture on the new community:

> We sent Timothy, our brother and God's servant in the gospel of Christ, to establish you in your faith and to exhort you, that no one be moved [i.e., shaken, disturbed] by these afflictions. You yourselves know that this is to be our lot. For when we were with you, we told you beforehand that we were to suffer affliction; just as it has come to pass, and as you know. . . . When I could bear it no longer, I sent that I might know your faith, for fear that somehow the tempter had tempted you and that our labor would be in vain (3:2-5 RSV).

Paul did not want the believers to be "shaken" (3:3) by their loss of honor, that is, to doubt their choices because of society's disapproval as manifested in the "affliction" they were experiencing. The outside world is even censured as the agent of the "tempter," Satan, the enemy of the divine order. Society's attempts at reintegrating the deviant are labeled as a demonic "temptation" (3:5) that could lure them away from the path that leads to safety "from the wrath that is coming" (1:10). In this way Paul is helping to insulate the believers against yielding to those social pressures: they are not benign, but malevolent.

Paul apparently received a positive report from Timothy about the state of the congregation. Nevertheless he prays "earnestly night and day that we may see you face to face and supply what is lacking in your faith" (3:10 RSV). That is, Paul understands that Timothy's work in reaffirming the group's values and encouraging renewed commitment in the face of society's negative sanctions was only the first step in the ongoing work of maintaining the group's integrity. What Paul desires to do "face to face" is here as elsewhere accomplished through the letter itself, the epistolary replacement for the apostle's presence. From Timothy, moreover, he has learned of any concerns the believers had—concerns that left chinks, as it were, in the armor of the world-construction Paul calls his "gospel." First Thessalonians responds to both needs and serves as a whole to further cement the community's commitment in the face of society's hostility.

1 THESSALONIANS AND PAUL'S SOCIAL-ENGINEERING PROGRAM

Paul is addressing people whose honor, whose basic measure of worth, has been challenged by society—indeed, has been questioned and negated by society. This is the effect of the "affliction" they have endured. These are people who realize that attachment to Jesus and this new community has cost them the respect they formerly enjoyed from their neighbors, and to that extent has made them question their own self-worth. How does Paul build on the work already done by Timothy to address this problem? When we apply the paradigm developed in the first chapter for uncovering the use and effect of honor discourse Paul's strategy in 1 Thessalonians, in all its intricacy and complexity, becomes transparent.

A. Reinforcing the Court of Reputation

First we may look at Paul's negation of the validity of the opinion of outsiders regarding the believers' commitment to Jesus and the new social entity, the *ekklēsia tou theou*. We have already noted how society's pressures, effected through the "affliction" suffered by believers, have been set by Paul within the framework of the activity of the Tempter, the primeval enemy of God and God's cosmos (3:5). Paul also suggests that the outsiders stand under God's disapproval on account of their harassment of the Christians. The Thessalonian believers' neighbors are repeating the same sort of hostility against God displayed by the Jewish believers' neighbors in Judea:

> For you, brothers and sisters, became imitators of the churches of God in Christ Jesus that are in Judea; for you suffered the same things from your own compatriots as they did from the Jews, who killed both the Lord Jesus and the prophets, and drove us out; they displease God and oppose everyone by hindering us from speaking to the Gentiles so that they may be saved (2:14-16 NRSV).

Outsiders—specifically those who persecute the believers, attempting to pull them away from their new-found commitments—stand under God's displeasure. Paul emphasizes group boundaries, drawing a clear distinction between the outsiders who displease God (2:15) and are therefore acting dishonorably—both Jews (2:15-16) and Gentiles (2:14b; 4:3-6; 5:3-8)—and the insiders who do seek to please God (4:1). The believers are thus not to have regard for the persecutors' evaluation of their behavior, for the persecutors are shown themselves to be working against God's purpose.[11]

The unbelieving Gentiles are censured as given over to shameful lust and ignorance of God—a familiar pair in Hellenistic Jewish anti-

Gentile polemic (cf. Wis 13:1-9; 14:22-27; Rom 1:18-32; Eph 4:18-19): the believers are to act "not in the passion of desire like the Gentiles who do not know God" (4:5). This contrast of lifestyle between the (Gentile!) believers and the (unbelieving) Gentiles was a common feature of early Christian rhetoric, serving to mark the different values served by the two groups and the incompatibility and inferiority of the unbelievers' values with the enlightened *ethos* of the Christian group (cf. 1 Pet 4:1-4; Eph 4:17-20). Here, too, such a contrast serves to censure the unbelievers as base and therefore also to denigrate their ability to form a reliable judgment about what is honorable or not (since they themselves live dishonorably). The focus in this context on "sanctification" (*hagiasmos*, 4:3)—being "set apart" for God from profane use—further emphasizes the boundary between the Christian community and the unbelieving world. This is a boundary anchored in the very will of God ("for this is God's will: your sanctification," 4:3), assuring the believers of the ultimate legitimacy of their new group loyalties and the illegitimacy of society's resistance to this group formation.

1 Thessalonians 5:3-8 constructs an even more elaborate contrast between the believers and the outsiders:

> When people say, "There is peace and security," then sudden destruction will come upon them. . . . But you are not in darkness, brethren [and sisters], for that day to surprise you like a thief. For you are all children of light and children of the day; we are not of the night or of darkness. So then let us not sleep, as others do, but let us keep awake and be sober. For those who sleep sleep at night, and those who get drunk are drunk at night. But, since we belong to the day, let us be sober (RSV).

The outsiders are the deluded proclaimers of peace (an ironic reference to the *pax Romana?*) but they shall be utterly surprised and overturned on the "day of wrath," which is in many ways a cornerstone of the Christian minority culture's world-construction. The believers are as different from outsiders as day is from night, light from darkness, wakefulness from sleeping, sobriety from drunkenness. Outsiders, moreover, fare badly in each contrastive pair: this is not a matter of apples and oranges, of differences without value-laden appraisals. Paul also creates a sort of genealogical distinction between the group members and outsiders: they are two different families or races now, the offspring of light and the offspring of darkness.

A final blow is dealt to the opinion of outsiders in Paul's contrast between how the believer is to face death (i.e., the death of significant others) and how the unbeliever faces death. The unbelievers grieve as those without hope (4:13): their perception of reality crumbles in the face of death and cannot adequately answer this threatening phenomenon. Indeed, Paul's discussion in 4:13-18 is meant to strengthen the believers' world-construction at precisely this point, so that the death of members of their court of reputation, their significant others, will not be taken as disconfirmation of the group's distinctive counter-definitions of reality.[12] Paul therefore provides them with the necessary information to integrate even this most marginalizing of experiences. This distinction reinforces the difference between insider and outsider, stressing the inferior access to information, and hence inferior ability to discern between the honorable and dishonorable, of the latter.

While Paul through a number of deliberate contrasts with outsiders reinforces the group's boundaries and gives believers ample cause to disregard the opinion of unbelievers as unreliable and erring, he also devotes considerable attention to reminding the addressees of who does constitute their court of reputation, and to whom they should look for their honor and confirmation of their self-worth. The primary significant Other in this letter is, of course, God. The thanksgiving section of the Pauline letter consistently functions as an admirable reminder of this basic fact: it is before God that the authors and addressees are conducting their lives and ministries, so that both giving thanks to God and remembering the addressees before God serve to raise again to consciousness this One in whose sight one lives and before whom one seeks remembrance, recognition, and reward: "We give thanks to God always for you all, constantly mentioning you in our prayers, remembering in the presence of our God and Father your work of faithfulness and labor of love and constancy of hope in our Lord Jesus Christ" (1:2-3). In God's presence the believers are praised by Paul for their Christian commitment and perseverance in their new relationships.

The authors further highlight this point by recalling for the Thessalonian believers their personal example: the very example the believers have imitated (1:6) and are called to imitate further in order also "to please God" (4:1): "just as we have been approved by God to be entrusted with the gospel, so we speak, not to please mortals, but to please God who tests our hearts" (2:4 NRSV). Pleasing people, that is, living for approval and honor from the non-Christian court of opinion, is not the way of the apostles, and it is not the way to please God. Ultimately it is God's evaluation that counts far more than society's, for on the Day of the Lord God's evaluation and its eternal effects will be made manifest: it is always with a view to that "court" that one seeks to live in the present, preferring temporary danger and loss from human courts of opinion to the eternal danger and loss from God's court (1 Thess 1:5; 2:19-20; 3:13; 5:9).

Believers are called to seek to please God, not people: seeking human approval leaves one susceptible to the seduction of society's call to the deviant to return; seeking God's approval, however, leads to the approval of one's fellow believers who are also seeking to please God. Paul and his co-authors are concerned that there be strong social reinforcement of God's approval or disapproval, and so they continually call each hearer's attention to the company of the "brothers and sisters" who now form their primary reference group. This is a limited group defined by God's choice, which is reflected in their positive response to the gospel: "we know, brothers and sisters beloved by God, that he has chosen you; for our gospel came to you not only in word, but also in power and in the Holy Spirit and with full conviction" (1:4-5 NRSV). It is these "brothers and sisters" who become the group of significant others for each individual member as they enact Paul's injunctions to "exhort one another" (5:11; cf. 5:14), "build one another up" (5:10), "love one another" more and more (4:9-10),[13] and "comfort one another" (4:18).

The strong, meaningful bonds between group members forged through this level of interaction will strengthen individual believers' commitment to the group and insulate them from the negative opinion and treatment of outsiders. Feelings of attachment and experiences of encouragement within the group outweigh feelings of disconnectedness from society and experiences of discouragement at the hands of outsiders. Care for and being cared for by the brothers and sisters leads to an increased desire to conform to the values of the group so as to be held in esteem by those who are important for one's daily life.[14] Even though Paul will also exhort the believers to "abound in love for one another and for all" and to "do good to one another and to all" (3:12; 5:13), thus admirably moving the group to reach out beyond group lines as benefactors of the community, the very form of this exhortation reinforces (with the mention first of "one another") the meaningfulness of those group boundaries. The local court of reputation formed by the church in Thessalonica is consciously extended by Paul to include the churches of God in all of Macedonia, Achaia, and Judea, thus connecting the member of the local "chapter" of this minority culture to a larger network of believers throughout the world.

Finally, Paul's directions to honor local church leadership and to follow their instructions, as well as his affirmations of his team's honor and exemplary conduct, also help provide a focus for the believers as they seek affirmation and reliable guides to honor before God's court. This provides a positive counterpart to his denigration of outsiders, his censure of their conduct and ignorance, and therefore the unreliability of their evaluation of Christians and their new commitments. It is in this light that we may make sense out of Paul's so-called "defense" of his apostleship in 1 Thess 1:5; 2:1-12. It is not that the integrity of Paul and his team was openly called into question or challenged (as in Galatia or Corinth). It is rather part of a larger strategy of equipping beleaguered and possibly wavering converts to continue trusting the figures who have called them out from the society into this minority group (and looking to such figures as reliable guides to what behaviors are honorable and what dishonorable) and to continue resisting the chastisement of their former compatriots.

Ethos was an essential component of the art of persuasion, and Paul must here reaffirm the reliability of his character not against the slander of opponents but in a vital contrast with the character and reliability of the other voice that threatens to seduce the believers away from the truth, namely the voice of the outside world (3:3-5). This contrast is made clearer by the juxtaposition of the honorable example of Paul's team in 4:1 with the dishonorable pattern of conduct of the (unbelieving) Gentiles in 4:4. Moreover, Paul claims that his message "does not spring from error or uncleanness" (2:3), the very stains upon the (unbelieving) Gentile's honor ("the passion of lust" characterizes the "Gentiles who do not know God," 4:5). As a corollary to reaffirming his own reliability as a guide to honorable conduct Paul exhorts the believers also to respect the local Christian leadership that was left in charge of the new congregation by Paul and his team: "respect those who labor among you and are over you in the Lord and admonish you, and . . . esteem them very highly in love because of their work" (5:12-13 RSV). The believers' regard for these figures will give weight to the leaders' approval or admonition of the group members, for they play an essential role in maintaining the group's values and conduct.

Throughout 1 Thessalonians, therefore, we find Paul concerned with delimiting and reinforcing the "court of reputation" before which the believers are to live, and whose opinion they are to regard. The unbelieving society acts out the role of Satan, the Tempter; it lives shamelessly without regard for God or God's standards; it belongs to the darkness, and its members even constitute a different order of being. The opinion of unbelievers, therefore, is not to be regarded as meaningful, and hence should be in no way determinative of the believer's choices and values. The believer is called to live so as to please God, to gain God's approval: this is mirrored in the interaction of the believing community, as its reliable and ethical leaders offer admonition and praise and as the group members reflect back to one another the group's values and ideals. In this way the minority culture is freed from the dominant culture's social-control techniques to pursue the goals deemed honorable within the group.

B. Affirming and Augmenting the Honor of the Group Members

As Paul reinforces the boundaries of the believer's "court of reputation" he also labors to assure the believers of their honor before that court in a variety of ways. The loss of esteem they have suffered in society's eyes receives ample compensation in the honor they now enjoy within the group of those who are better equipped to evaluate what is truly honorable.

First Paul gives clear indications of the believers' worth in the eyes of the group. They receive praise from Paul for their "work of faithfulness and labor of love and constancy of hope" (1:3), for their reception of the gospel in the face of society's opposition (1:6; 2:13-14). Paul's giving thanks to God for these aspects of the community's life shows his team's approval of the believers' progress, and also assumes God's approval—indeed, God's agency in effecting this progress. "Election" itself serves the goal of strengthening commitment to the community. The very fact that an individual is now a part of the Church becomes a mark of God's favor and approval, and remaining a part of the Church becomes a mark of obedience to God, hence of piety and proper gratitude (1:4; 2:12; cf. 2 Thess 1:11-12; 2:14). Paul also affirms them in their mindfulness of seeking so to live as to please God (presumably here with regard to Paul's ethical instructions, 4:1), their expressions of love toward their fellow believers (4:9-10), and their preservation of the Christian view of reality through mutual encouragement in pursuing group ideals (5:11).

Paul also greets them with a declaration of their growing reputation among the churches throughout the regions of Macedonia (of which Thessalonica was the capital) and Achaia.[15] They enjoy a supra-local honor because of their eager reception of the gospel, their welcome of

God's emissaries, and their endurance of affliction. Within the larger network of Christian communities they enjoy fame, a good report:

> You became imitators of us and of the Lord, for you received the word in much affliction, with joy inspired by the Holy Spirit; so that *you became an example to all the believers in Macedonia and in Achaia.* For not only has the word of the Lord sounded forth from you in Macedonia and Achaia, but *your faith in God has gone forth everywhere, so that we need not say anything.* For they themselves report concerning us what a welcome we had among you, and how you turned to God from idols, to serve a living and true God, and to wait for his Son from heaven, whom he raised from the dead, Jesus who delivers us from the wrath to come (1:6-10 RSV; emphasis mine).

This is comparable to a city's delight in achieving preeminence among the other cities of a given province, or fame among those cities and beyond for some peculiar civic virtue or achievement.[16] Even though they are dishonored by their fellow-citizens for their adherence to the gospel they have gained a good name in places far beyond their local community.

Paul here begins to reinterpret society's attempts to disgrace Christians as actually leading toward honor within the alternate court of reputation. Indeed, the society's main complaint against the Christians is their neglect of the traditional Greco-Roman gods and benefactors and therefore their political and civic unreliability. Significantly, the very posture that caused them to lose approval and esteem from their non-Christian neighbors becomes the believers' claim to fame among all the churches in Greece (1:9-10).

Moreover, Paul assures them that such hostility was "normal," only to be expected from the unbelieving world: "You yourselves know that this is to be our lot. For when we were with you, we told you beforehand that we were to suffer affliction; just as it has come to pass, and as you know" (3:3-4 RSV). Paul develops a mimetic pattern that demonstrates the normality or predictable nature of this resistance: Paul and his team carry out their response of faithfulness to the word in the face of "great opposition" (2:1-2); the churches in Judea, where the Christian movement had its beginnings, experienced hostility and rejection from their non-Christian neighbors and fellow Jews; now the Thessalonians endure hostility and bear the brunt of the social control techniques of the dominant culture, imitating the pattern of Paul and the churches in Judea (1:6; 2:14). Paul's claim regarding the normality of opposition has a firm basis in the experience of believers worldwide. This emphasis on normality is important since the society is trying to get the believers to see themselves as deviant and in need of change. As Paul inverts this, society's rejection actually assures the believers that they are right where they should be, and not "out of line." Encountering resistance from the outside world is part of the normal course of making progress toward the honor God has in store for the faithful. Indeed, Paul also transforms his team's own experience of dishonor at society's hands as an occasion to display courage, to act nobly in the face of great opposition (2:2): they hold onto their *parrhēsia*, their freedom of speech, in the face of danger, and so prove faithful to the trust with which God entrusted them.

Finally, we see Paul throughout the letter urging the believers to shape their behavior ever with an eye toward attaining the honor and security Jesus will provide to his faithful clients on the Day of the Lord. The opinion of outsiders during these days of struggle is inconsequential compared to the opinion God forms of the believers on that day of visitation. Indeed, the gospel has given the Thessalonian believers an incomparable advantage: "But you, brothers and sisters, are not in darkness so that the day will come upon you like a thief" (5:4). Unlike the unbeliever, the Christian has received advance warning and is in a privileged position to prepare for that day by seeking to please God in the present.

The certainty of that day and its promise of wrath and disgrace for all who have not sought to please God through responding to God's favor in the gospel message provide a powerful motivation to the believers to endure the temporary dishonor and danger of marginalization in order to attain the greater honor and security of being approved on that day. Paul therefore appreciates the strategic value of elevating the Day of the Lord throughout the letter:

> You turned to God from idols, to serve a living and true God, and to wait for his Son from heaven, whom he raised from the dead, Jesus who delivers us from the wrath to come (1:9b-10 RSV).

> We exhorted each one of you and encouraged you and charged you to lead a life worthy of God, who calls you into his own kingdom and glory (2:11-12 RSV).

> May the Lord . . . establish your hearts unblamable in holiness before our God and Father, at the coming of our Lord Jesus with all his saints ["holy ones"] (3:12-13 RSV).

> God has destined us not for wrath but for obtaining salvation through our Lord Jesus Christ (5:9 NRSV).
>
> May the God of peace himself sanctify you entirely; and may your spirit and soul and body be kept sound and blameless at the coming of our Lord Jesus Christ (5:23 NRSV).

The ethics of the Christian community—the new kinship relations and the associated obligations, the admonitions toward continence, the response to death—are focused toward this future event, this day of reversal on which their faith will be vindicated and their honor as children of God manifested. Paul applies this focus even to his own missionary work: "For what is our hope or joy or crown of boasting before our Lord Jesus at his coming? Is it not you? Yes, you are our glory and joy" (2:19-20 NRSV). On that day Paul's only claim to honor will be his faithfulness in carrying out his commission to call together for God a sanctified people: knowing this, he seeks no other claim to honor before the unbelieving world. His self-respect comes from his preparedness for that day. As for the believers, honor will be granted to them on the basis of their leading "a life worthy of God": it is their faithfulness to God's selection of them to be "set apart" for God that secures their future honor and provides the new standard by which they are to evaluate their worthiness, or their honor, in the present.

It should be noted, however, that Paul does not give in to the impulse to withdraw and shut out unbelievers completely, nor does he allow his converts to do so. This response was far from unknown in the ancient world, as the literature of Qumran, for example, attests. Rather believers are urged to reach out not only to fellow believers (though, of course, this must be the primary arena of support) but also to all people: "May the Lord make you increase and abound in love for one another and for all" (3:12); "See that none of you repays evil for evil, but always seek to do good to one another and to all" (5:15 NRSV). The exhortation to "seek to do good to all" orients believers toward the society as potential benefactors of their local community: by acting as benefactors they will be able to dispel, to some extent, society's suspicion of them, and perhaps even begin to regain respect (although, of course, their behavior must remain detached from the opinion of outsiders). Their lifestyle is not to confirm society's opinion of them as disruptive, dissentious, non-contributing parts of the social body. While freed from concern for society's opinion, they are still called to "behave becomingly toward outsiders" (4:12), in order to make known the noble character they have received from God.

CONCLUSION

Attention to honor and shame discourse, guided by observations of how this language is used in the ancient world to reinforce cultural identity and boundaries, has opened up a new dimension of the rhetorical strategy of 1 Thessalonians. Because there is stronger opposition to this fledgling community in Thessalonica than in other cities Paul devotes much of 1 Thessalonians to the problem of social engineering: strengthening the boundaries of the group, delegitimating the opinion (and thus the social pressure to conform) of outsiders however this is actualized (the shape of "affliction"), and promoting the course of action that leads to the survival and growth of the group. Society's vigorous application of social control techniques such as shaming through insult, exclusion, and abuse calls forth a more vigorous counter-program from Paul's team (both Timothy's visit and 1 Thessalonians). Honor discourse, as an essential component of social control in the ancient Mediterranean, is thus a prominent feature of this correspondence.

Much of 1 Thessalonians reflects Paul's attempt to do precisely what he could not do through a personal visit, namely to "supply what is lacking in your faith" (3:10). "Faith" in that context clearly refers to the believers' "firmness" in their commitment to the new social reality called the *ekklēsia tou theou* in the face of the dominant culture's resistance and disapproval. Paul responds by reinforcing the court of reputation, which involves (1) invalidating society's attempts at making the believers ashamed of their new commitments (2:4; 3:5; 4:1-4, 13; 5:3-8), (2) redirecting the believers' attention to pleasing God, whose approval alone has eternal significance (1:2-3, 5, 6; 2:4, 19-20; 3:13; 4:1; 5:9), (3) encouraging believers to reinforce one another's sense of worth as members of Jesus' household and commitment to those pursuits that result in honor before God (1:4-5; 3:12; 4:9-10, 18; 5:10-14), and (4) affirming the importance of local church leaders, to whom members should look for approval insofar as the leaders reflect the values of the group (5:12-13).

Paul is also engaged in affirming the believers' sense of worth as rooted in distinctively Christian values and identity, and in urging believers to advance in honor by pursuing behaviors characteristic of the Christian ethos. Paul thus uses the promise of honor to promote acts of love, steadfastness in faith, preparing for Christ's return (the Day of the Lord), avoidance of idolatry, sexual purity, holiness, and hospitality toward Christian missionaries (1:3-10; 2:1-2, 11-14; 3:12-13; 4:1-4, 9-10;

5:4, 11). One especially important contribution of this letter is its emphasis on the encounter of the Christian with the unbelieving society. Christians are urged not only to offer deeds of love and generosity toward one another, but also to unbelievers (3:12; 4:12; 5:13). Christians are not allowed to cocoon up in their "alternative court of reputation," but must continually seek to have a positive impact on the world around them. Paul's group-maintaining techniques, while highly critical of outsiders, do not result in a countercultural movement—a group that seeks deliberately to violate the dominant culture's values. While there are certain non-negotiable areas, such as all forms of idolatry as opposed to the single-hearted devotion to the One God, Paul's advice in the letter moves the group also toward the possibility of future *rapprochement* with the dominant culture.

2 THESSALONIANS AND THE PAULINE CIRCLE'S CONTINUING INTEREST IN GROUP MAINTENANCE

Second Thessalonians bears many similarities to 1 Thessalonians: both deal heavily in eschatology, both have similar opening thanksgivings, both have a second "thanksgiving." This similarity, however, is not merely formal.[17] There appears to be a similarity of purpose such that 2 Thessalonians extends Paul's work in 1 Thessalonians to create a strong and vital sense of community, to prevent the Christians from nurturing any regard for messages and suggestions from outsiders leading believers away from loyalty to the group, and focusing the believers on those aspects of the Christian worldview (e.g., eschatology) that will reinforce those boundaries and commitments. The importance of convictions about the end (a primary support for the group *ethos* concerning life in the present) is reflected in the author's[18] desire to preserve the original contours of Jewish-Christian eschatology from any innovation or revision.

A. Reinforcing the Court of Reputation

God is again the primary significant Other who, together with Jesus, presides over the ultimate court of reputation, the court that ascribes lasting honor or disgrace according to the individual's response to truth (i.e., the saving gospel, 2:11-12) and to the call to holy living (1:11; 2:12). As in 1 Thessalonians, the initial thanksgiving immediately calls to mind this Other whose approval, mirrored in Paul's giving thanks to God for the progress of the believers, matters above all else (1:3). This opening thanksgiving also calls to mind the larger network of churches, whom Paul calls as witnesses to the Thessalonian believers' supra-local honor (1:4).

Paul also uses the court of reputation formed by the local congregation to support his admonitions concerning certain deviants—the *ataktoi* (the "idle" or "unruly") and any who will not follow Paul's team's instructions (3:14). Paul calls the group to exercise pressure on the *ataktoi* to return to an orderly life, to a productive occupation, rather than a disorderly life led as if all norms were called off due to the advent of the end. Idlers, as potential sources of social disturbance within the group, would not help the group in its coexistence with the outside world.[19] The group is now strong enough to exercise internally the same sort of social control the society had been attempting, however unsuccessfully, to use on believers to call them back to conformity with the dominant culture's norms.[20] The social-engineering device of shaming becomes a tool for promoting adherence to the values of the group, and to Paul's directions in particular:

> Now we command you . . . in the name of our Lord Jesus Christ, that you keep away from any brother who is living in idleness and not in accord with the tradition that you received from us. . . . If any one refuses to obey what we say in this letter, note that man, and have nothing to do with him, that he may be ashamed. Do not look on him as an enemy, but warn him as a brother (3:6, 14-15 RSV).

The goal of such shaming is the eventual inclusion of the wayward back into the fold of the group, which was, no doubt, also the goal of society's shaming of the believers.

Paul also continues his work in delegitimating the opinion and "public knowledge"[21] of outsiders, that is, of the unbelieving Greco-Roman world. This occurs largely through the discussion of the "man of lawlessness" in 2:1-12. Scholars believe that the addressees knew exactly what Paul was referring to in this cryptic passage, but it is equally possible that it was as opaque to them as to us: after all, Paul was not seeking to encourage speculation about the time of the end, but rather to affirm its certainty and, more to the point, its futurity. First, Paul posits the possibility of deception lurking in those voices that do not agree with his teaching (2:3). There is an intangible yet active enemy "out there": "the mystery of lawlessness is already at work" (2:7) and will culminate in the end-time deception. Who will be deceived?

"Those who are perishing," who "did not welcome the love of the truth in order that they might be saved" (2:10), who "did not believe the truth but approved unrighteousness" (2:12). Those who do not receive the message of salvation (i.e., the gospel of Jesus Christ)—indeed, the same people who had sought to shame the Christians away from their faith—are thus censured as liable to Satan's power of deception (2:9-10), participants in the rebellion against God (2:3), shameless in their conduct (2:12), erring in their knowledge of reality ("not believing the truth," 2:12; "believing a lie," 2:11), and therefore unreliable in their opinion.

The outsiders are susceptible to deception in a way in which the believers are not. Their positive response to the gospel has given them the advantage of "true" knowledge, even if that knowledge is "deviant" in the eyes of the society. The second "thanksgiving" section brings home this point, emphasizing further the boundary between the nonbeliever and the Christian:

> But we must always give thanks to God for you, brothers and sisters beloved by the Lord, because God chose you as the firstfruits for salvation through sanctification by the Spirit and belief in the truth. For this purpose he called you through our proclamation of the good news, so that you may obtain the glory of our Lord Jesus Christ. So then, brothers and sisters, stand firm and hold fast to the traditions that you were taught by us, either by word of mouth or by our letter (2:13-15 NRSV).

The thanksgiving, far from beginning a new section or functioning as the exordium of a letter or oration, actually completes the contrast between those who are alienated from the truth, hence liable to Satan's deception and God's judgment, and those who have received the truth and follow the implications of that truth unto honor and security on the Day of the Lord. This division is further echoed in Paul's own prayer for deliverance from hostile non-Christians (3:1-2): "pray for us . . . that we may be delivered from unnatural and evil people; for faith does not characterize everyone." Those who have not aligned themselves with the new community (who have not come to "faith") are censured as "deviant and dishonorable people" (*atopoi kai ponēroi anthrōpoi*, 3:2): their character deficiencies explain their hostility to the gospel and its followers. The choice of *atopos* to describe those who do not "have faith" is particularly interesting: it turns society's claim that the Christians are "deviant" or "out of place" back upon its own head.

B. Affirming and Augmenting the Honor of Group Members

Paul also gives considerable attention in 2 Thessalonians to affirming the believers' honor in God's sight and in the sight of the "assemblies of God," pointing the believers ever forward to the day of reversal as the guide to their conduct in the present. In the thanksgiving section Paul and his co-authors again dwell on God's approval of the community (the fact that they can "give thanks" to God reflects God's accomplishment of God's good purpose among the believers, and hence God's approval, 1:3) based on their continued dedication to the minority culture's counter-definitions, their deepening loyalty (*pistis*, 1:3) to God and the group, and their continued efforts at meaningful, group-sustaining interaction ("the love of each one of you all for one another increases," 1:3). Rejection by the host society again becomes a source of honor within the group: "therefore we ourselves boast of you in the churches of God for your steadfastness and faith in all your persecutions and in the afflictions which you are enduring" (1:3-4 RSV). The believers' perseverance in the face of society's hostility and attempts to shame them into conformity leads to the Thessalonian Christians' having a real claim to honor: the "boast" that Paul makes on their behalf to other churches, that larger network of the believer's significant others and source of supra-local honor and fame.

Society's hostility, insults, and rejection are reinterpreted not only as a source of honor before the supra-local Christian community but also as a sign of God's approval and acceptance. The affliction does not reflect their deviance or lack of honor (as society would have it understood), but rather qualifies them for eternal honor before God. It is the noble contest that leads to lasting honor in God's sight. Enduring affliction is actually transformed into the path to the fulfillment of the believer's ambition, as it makes him or her "worthy" of the desired end: "This is evidence of the righteous judgment of God, and is intended to make you worthy of the kingdom of God, for which you are also suffering" (1:5 NRSV). Here Paul builds on a strategy employed in Hellenistic Jewish literature, turning the negative experiences of members of the minority culture at the hands of "unbelievers" into a positive experience that, however painful, qualifies them for God's reward by exercising their fidelity to God.[22] Wisdom of Solomon, for example, turns the shameful treatment of the loyal Jew at the hands of apostate Jews into a form of educative suffering that exercises the person in those traits (such as loyalty/faith) that are necessary to please God: "having been disciplined a little, they will receive great good, because God tested them and found them worthy of himself" (3:5 NRSV). Hebrews 12:4-12 also uses an extended version of this metaphor to render the believers' afflictions by outsiders meaningful and salutary within the group's world-construction.

The Pauline team then focus on the "big picture" that provides the basis for disregarding society's opinion and clinging only to God's evaluation of the group, and thus of continuing steadfastly in loyalty to the group and its divine Benefactor. On the day of judgment a great reversal will take place, and the believers' honor and security will be manifest and actualized while the unrepentant members of the host society will suffer punishment (God's censure and disapproval of their lives), exclusion from the promised rest (a non-privilege, hence dishonor). Indeed, the lasting disgrace will cling to the unbeliever, not the believer:

> Since indeed God deems it just to repay with affliction those who afflict you, and to grant rest with us to you who are afflicted, when the Lord Jesus is revealed from heaven with his mighty angels in flaming fire, inflicting vengeance upon those who do not know God and upon those who do not obey the gospel of our Lord Jesus. They shall suffer the punishment of eternal destruction and exclusion from the presence of the Lord and from the glory of his might, when he comes on that day to be glorified in his saints, and to be marveled at in all who have believed, because our testimony to you was believed (1:6-10 RSV).

The Christian's affliction is made endurable because it leads to honor and inclusion (again, cf. Heb 12:5-12); the affliction posited for the host society in the future will not lead to a noble end, but rather actualizes God's evaluation of the unbelievers' lives by this dishonorable end. Paul repeats his claim that such perseverance fulfills the Christian's ambition to be "made worthy" of God's call. Dropping down, or even off, the social ladder is thus transformed into a move up on a different, and eternally more important, ladder.

The final result will be Christ's manifestation of his honor through his clients, and the manifestation of the believers' honor in Christ. The "many sons and daughters" will share in the honor of the Son (cf. Heb 2:10), an inducement repeated in 2:14:

> To this end we always pray for you, that our God may make you worthy of his call, and may fulfill every good resolve and work of faith by his power, so that the name of our Lord Jesus may be glorified in you, and

> you in him, according to the grace of our God and the Lord Jesus Christ (1:11-12 RSV).
>
> To this [God] called you through our gospel, so that you may obtain the glory of our Lord Jesus Christ (2:14 RSV).

The believers may look forward to honor and safety on the day of judgment since God chose them for salvation and set them apart by the Spirit and "belief in the truth" (2:13). They will therefore have a very different end than the unbelievers who now afflict them (1:6), but will only attain that end if they maintain firm their commitment to the group, its ideals, and its values: "So then, brothers and sisters, stand firm and hold to the traditions which you were taught by us, either by word of mouth or by our letter" (2:15 NRSV). Only by thus "standing firm and holding on" (2:15) can they escape the delusion that ensnares the unbelieving world and brings God's judgment upon it (2:9-12). The Christians must therefore seek in their own lives the fulfillment of Paul's prayer for them, "that our God will make you worthy of his call, and will fulfill by his power every good resolve and work of faith" (1:11 NRSV) in order that the believers may attain the promised honor at Christ's coming (1:12).

Excursus: The Authenticity of 2 Thessalonians

While again it would be beyond the scope of this chapter to enter into a full discussion of the issues surrounding the question of authorship,[23] the above observations may offer some helpful considerations. First, 1 Thessalonians and its sequel appear to address several of the same issues at different stages of development. On the one hand the "idle" or "disorderly" *(ataktoi)* of 1 Thess 5:14 (cf. 4:11) have become a more evident problem (2 Thess 3:6-15); on the other hand, the believers have also made some positive progress in the direction in which 1 Thessalonians has urged them (cf. 1 Thess 4:9-10 with 2 Thess 1:3b; 1 Thess 3:10 with 2 Thess 1:3a). More strikingly, however, 2 Thessalonians clearly builds on the social engineering of the previous letter, using many of the same techniques: the alternate court of reputation remains the same (God; the supra-local network of churches; the local believing community); eschatology functions in the same way in both to motivate group-sustaining activity (1 Thess 2:12; 3:13; 5:8-9; 2 Thess 1:11-12; 2:13-15) and to undermine the opinion of outsiders (1 Thess 5:3-8; 2 Thess 2:9-12).[24] The success of Timothy's visit and 1 Thessalonians with regard to strengthening the minority culture's solidarity and commitment in the face of the dominant culture's hostility is apparent in Paul's ability now, in 2 Thessalonians, to use shaming as a social-control technique within the group to reclaim deviants. This clearly attests a strong group identity and a high level of meaningfulness in group relationships, or else such shaming would not work at all (the deviant would be just as happy to rejoin the dominant culture and reenter his or her former network of significant others).

We may briefly address two other objections to authenticity here. First, the differences in lexical usage, style, and the different use of the same terms may be resolved if we take seriously the co-authorship of the letters, which are, after all, written by Paul, Silvanus, and Timothy, and not Paul alone. If we postulate a collegial model of writing, the team discussing the situation and how it might be addressed, then the person holding the stylus would be the one to give the final form its distinctive style and lexical imprint. Thus we find Paul doing the actual writing of 1 Thessalonians: he does not add his "signature" at the end of this letter, so it would follow that the whole is in his own hand. Silvanus or Timothy (perhaps more likely the former, given the latter's junior status) holds the pen as the team forms 2 Thessalonians, to which Paul does add his authenticating signature (3:17).

Second, the alleged difference in eschatology—that 1 Thessalonians presupposes an imminent expectation of the *parousia* while 2 Thessalonians "adopts an anti-apocalyptic strategy"[25]—is overdrawn. Second Thessalonians is by no means "anti-apocalyptic," since the exhortations to the community, and indeed the boundaries of the group, are anchored in the expectation of the end-time reversal. This letter, however, demonstrates Paul's concern to maintain the *futurity* as well as the certainty of the *parousia*, for the *ethos* of the group and the group's boundaries are legitimated in these terms. The collapse of the future judgment of God at the *parousia* into the present ("the day of the Lord has come," 2:2) threatens to shake this pillar of the Christian world-construction, and Paul reasserts the futurity of the Day of the Lord through the use of this "man of lawlessness" tradition. The imminence is not diminished by Paul's discussion of the "man of lawlessness,"[26] whose coming may itself be imminent since the warning signs are already present in the deception that has overtaken unbelievers.[27]

CONCLUSION

Our analysis of honor discourse within the Thessalonian correspondence has led to the discovery of an agenda that runs throughout the various parts of each letter. It has provided, in effect, a more unified conception of the purpose of the correspondence (regardless of one's final conclusions concerning the authorship of 2 Thessalonians)—a purpose frequently overlooked before in the history of interpretation. It provides an additional angle from which to grapple with such questions as the literary integrity of the letters (e.g., 1 Thess 2:14-16) or the order of the letters' composition. Finally, attention to honor discourse has allowed us a more three-dimensional sense of the social dynamics of being a member of the believing community in Thessalonica. We understand the social pressure exerted upon the believer by the dominant culture, and to what end. We grasp the ways in which the believers are urged to interact with one another, how they are taught to view outsiders, and how boundaries are erected between the group and the outside world for the preservation of the distinctive *ethos* of the former. Analysis of honor discourse, enriching in these ways the reading and investigation of a New Testament text, may thus claim a place alongside other disciplines within the exegetical enterprise.

NOTES: CHAPTER 4

[1] Cf. the discussions of the purpose of the letters in Leon Morris, *The First and Second Epistles to the Thessalonians*. NICNT (Grand Rapids: Eerdmans, 1991) 6–11; Earl J. Richard, *First and Second Thessalonians*. SP 11 (Collegeville: The Liturgical Press, 1995) 31. Charles A. Wanamaker (*The Epistles to the Thessalonians: A Commentary on the Greek Text*. NIGTC [Grand Rapids: Eerdmans, 1990] 60–63) does recognize, however, that the "theme of praise" introduced in 1 Thess 1:2-3, 6-9 has "a parenetic goal throughout the letter" (p. 49), which sought to "maintain the boundaries and distinctive features of the Christian world that the Thessalonians had come to inhabit through their conversion" (p. 47, citing Stanley K. Stowers, *Letter Writing in Greco-Roman Antiquity*. LEC 5 [Philadelphia: Westminster, 1986] 77–81). Richard (*Thessalonians* 31) understands the "paraenetic task" as beginning only "after a thanksgiving," but our investigations will show that the paraenetic task begins very much within the thanksgiving.

[2] William Neil (*The Epistle of Paul to the Thessalonians* [Naperville, Ill.: Alec R. Allenson, 1957] 64) and Robert Jewett (*The Thessalonian Correspondence:*

Pauline Rhetoric and Millenarian Piety [Philadelphia: Fortress, 1986] 93–94) have both noted that society's opposition weighed heavily on the minds of the new converts, causing them to question the correctness and validity of their new commitments. These scholars recognize that part of Paul's strategy must include the negation of the negative opinion of outsiders.

³ As does Abraham Malherbe (*Paul and the Thessalonians: The Philosophic Tradition of Pastoral Care* [Philadelphia: Fortress, 1987] 44–48), rightly challenged on this point by Morris (*Thessalonians* 48) and Wanamaker (*Epistles* 81).

⁴ See the impressive body of evidence gathered in Holland Hendrix, *Thessalonicans Honor Romans* (Th.D. thesis, Harvard University, 1984); Charles F. Edson, "Macedonia, II. State Cults in Thessalonica," *Harvard Studies in Classical Philology* 51 (1940) 127–136; idem, "Macedonia, III. Cults of Thessalonica," *HThR* 41 (1948) 105–204.

⁵ Cf. S.R.F. Price, *Rituals and Power: The Roman Imperial Cult in Asia Minor* (Cambridge: Cambridge University Press, 1984); G. W. Bowersock, "The Imperial Cult: Perceptions and Persistence," in Ben F. Meyer and E. P. Sanders, eds., *Jewish and Christian Self-Definition* (Philadelphia: Fortress, 1982) 3.170–182; Leonard L. Thompson, *The Book of Revelation: Apocalypse and Empire* (Oxford: Oxford University Press, 1990) 95–170. These developments are summarized in David A. deSilva, "The 'Image of the Beast' and the Christians in Asia Minor: Escalation of Sectarian Tension in Revelation 13," *Trinity Journal* n.s. 12 (1991) 185–208.

⁶ This complaint reverberates throughout the Greek and Latin literature (cf. Diodorus of Sicily 34.1-4; 40.3.4; Tacitus, *Hist.* 5.5; Juvenal, *Sat.* 14.100-104; Josephus, *Ap.* 2.121).

⁷ The author of 1 Peter, for example, speaks of the origin of the society's hostility in the unbelievers' surprise that their former colleagues no longer join them in their accustomed rituals and practices (4:3-5). While 1 Peter censures these activities as "excesses of dissipation," they included the "lawless idolatry" (4:3) that was the foundation of civic loyalty and solidarity. A view from the "other side" comes from Pliny the Younger (*Ep.* X.96), who sees renewed interest in traditional religious activity as the healthy result of his investigation of the deviant Christians, many of whom are now returning to fulfill their social and civic obligations.

⁸ Cf. discussions of suspicion toward such self-separating groups in R. A. Markus, *Christianity in the Roman World* (London: Thames and Hudson, 1974) 24–47.

⁹ If the deaths that troubled believers were actually martyrdoms (Juan Chapa, "Is First Thessalonians a Letter of Consolation?" *NTS* 40 [1994] 150–160, at 156; Raymond F. Collins, *The Birth of the New Testament* [New York: Crossroad, 1993] 112) one would expect some clearer connection to be made by Paul between the affliction and the removal of beloved sisters and

brothers from the congregation, as well as the use of such traditions as the eschatological *vindication* of the martyr who has died for the sake of his or her loyalty to God (cf. 2 Maccabees 7 and Wisdom 2–5). Such images would have provided more vigorous encouragement about the fate of the dead members, not to mention encouragement to face death through martyrdom oneself.

[10] This technique of social control accounts for much of the persecution of believers one finds in the New Testament, as in, for example, Heb 10:32-34 and 1 Pet 4:1-4 (where the Gentiles' own cognitive dissonance is posited as the cause of the believers' suffering).

[11] Against the view that 2:14-16 is a later anti-Jewish interpolation we should note that the subject matter is not truly out of place in this setting, particularly as an introduction to Paul's attempts at explaining the afflictions the Thessalonian believers suffered at the hands of their Gentile fellow citizens (2:14) in 3:3-5. Bruce C. Johanson (*To All the Brethren. A Text-Linguistic and Rhetorical Approach to 1 Thessalonians* [Uppsala: Almqvist & Wiksell, 1987] 97) labels 2:15-16 a *vituperatio*, an invective that serves a specific rhetorical goal in a specific rhetorical setting. 1 Thessalonians 2:15-16, then, is a fitting parallel to 4:4-5, a vituperation against Gentile outsiders that persists in 2 Thess 1:8-9; 2:10-12; 3:2. God's wrath comes down upon all who hinder or reject the gospel of Jesus, who show themselves to be displeasing to God by that very rejection and hostility, irrespective of ethnic origin (1 Thess 1:10; 2:15-16; 4:1-5; 2 Thess 1:8; 2:11-12), while God's favor rests on all who respond positively to the gospel, irrespective of ethnic origin (cf. Gal 3:26-28; Rom 3:21-31; 1 Cor 1:22-24; Col 3:11).

[12] Cf. Peter Berger, *The Sacred Canopy: Elements of a Sociology of Religion* (Garden City, N.Y.: Doubleday, 1967) 43–44, 80: "Death radically puts in question the taken-for-grantedness, 'business as usual' attitude in which one exists in everyday life. . . . Insofar as the knowledge of death cannot be avoided in any society, legitimations of the reality of the social world *in the face of death* are decisive requirements in any society. . . . Unless anomy, chaos, and death can be integrated within the nomos of human life, the nomos will be incapable of prevailing through the exigencies of both collective history and individual biography."

[13] Paul uses the more limited term *philadelphia*, a word reserved for speaking of love within the kinship group, rather than *philanthrōpia*, "love for humanity" and beneficence in general. This is not because Paul is uninterested in acts of love and benevolence that reach beyond the group (cf. 3:12; 5:13), but because he needs to promote, in the first place, the mutual affection and concern that will lead to the solidarity of the group and to the recognition by the individual member that these relationships are the most significant (hence the construction of a fictive kinship within the group).

[14] This is also a probable effect of Paul's own use of affective language in 2:7b-12a; 2:17–3:1, 6-10.

¹⁵ Scholars have noted that Paul is discussing here the believers' honor (e.g., Richard, *Thessalonians* 50–51), but this has not been linked with the letter's sociological effect or larger rhetorical strategy. Wanamaker (*Epistles* 80) takes a step forward when he recognizes that 1:6 is at least "a subtle piece of parenesis inculcating perseverance in all circumstances through imitation of Paul and the Lord Jesus."

¹⁶ Cf. Dio's attempts to persuade Rhodes to take a certain course of action in order to preserve their civic reputation among other cities and provinces (*Oration* 31), as well as competition between cities for the provincial honor of being named *neokoros* ("temple warden") of the imperial cult (see Price, *Rituals* 126–132).

¹⁷ And therefore indicative of non-Pauline imitation, as Richard (*Thessalonians* 20–22) argues.

¹⁸ For the purposes of this discussion I will refer to the author as "Paul" or the "Pauline team," who are at the very least the implied authors. For a brief attempt to address the question of authenticity see the excursus below.

¹⁹ So, rightly, Wanamaker (*Epistles* 282, 286), following Ronald Hock, *The Social Context of Paul's Ministry: Tentmaking and Apostleship* (Philadelphia: Fortress, 1980) 42–47.

²⁰ This is one reason why I would not favor Wanamaker's hypothesis that 2 Thessalonians preceded 1 Thessalonians (*Epistles* 37–45). If one is going to argue for the authenticity of both letters, as he does, then it seems more likely that the groundwork laid by Timothy's visit and Paul's social engineering in 1 Thessalonians is a necessary foundation for such internal social-control measures. It also seems more likely that the problem of the "idlers" would go from moderate to worse rather than toward improvement. Paul's milder directions to "admonish the idlers" (1 Thess 5:14) being insufficient to correct the problem, he then returns to this item more forcefully in 2 Thess 3:6 from the stronger social base he has been forming. If the order of letters were reversed, and there were still "idlers" idling about, how could Paul have contented himself with the mere passing reference in 1 Thess 5:14?

²¹ To borrow a phrase from Peter Berger, *A Rumor of Angels* (Garden City, N.Y.: Doubleday, 1970) 6.

²² This background to 2 Thessalonians has been admirably demonstrated by Jouette M. Bassler, "The Enigmatic Sign: 2 Thessalonians 1:5," *CBQ* 46 (1984) 496–510.

²³ For a fuller discussion see especially I. Howard Marshall, *1 and 2 Thessalonians*. NCBC (Grand Rapids: Eerdmans, 1983) 28–45, an exposition difficult to match for breadth and depth of interaction in this issue. See also Wanamaker, *Epistles* 17–28.

[24] Cf. Wayne A. Meeks, "The Social Function of Apocalyptic Language in Pauline Christianity," in David Hellholm, ed., *Apocalypticism in the Mediterranean World and the Near East* (Tübingen: J.C.B. Mohr, 1983) 687–705, at 689.

[25] Richard, *Thessalonians* 28.

[26] This figure does not depend on the *Nero redivivus* myth: the activity of Antiochus IV and, more recently, Caligula, have provided Jewish Christians with all the material they need to construct this end time image.

[27] For a contemporary example one need only note how Hal Lindsey's endless talk about the antichrist has heightened rather than diminished apocalyptic anticipation.

5

Honor Discourse in the Corinthian Correspondence

Study of the Corinthian correspondence is often made more challenging because of the serious questions revolving around the literary integrity of the second letter especially, the reconstruction of the sequence of events, and the identification of the sources of opposition to Paul. Space prevents us from offering as a prelude to our investigation any detailed discussion of the first two issues. The literary integrity of 2 Corinthians will not much affect our study: whether 2 Corinthians was originally one or five letters (all written after 1 Corinthians, of course), Paul's use of honor discourse will remain unchanged.[1] More important are the theories about the issues giving rise to the letters. For our investigation, we will posit the following as the driving factors in the history of Paul's dealings with the churches in Corinth.

Social-scientific analysis of the Corinthian letters has underscored the presence of elites, semi-elites, and peasant/artisans among the house churches in Corinth.[2] A great many of Paul's difficulties, however, appear to come from the elites and semi-elites. Part of this stems from the peculiar character of Corinth as a city of the *nouveau riches*. The elites and semi-elites there were not all "old money," but rather third-generation veterans and freed slaves turned entrepreneurs, social climbers, and people of local political prominence. It was a highly competitive environment, with these elites vying in business, in politics, and in claims to status. A host of inscriptions testify to the self-promoting mentality of this echelon of the population, who had many opportunities to rise along various social and political ladders. In a new city there was always the opportunity for would-be benefactors to construct a public building or pave a courtyard and to publicize his or her munificence with an inscription. For example, we know of the famous "Erastus inscription": "Erastus laid this pavement at his own expense in exchange for the aedileship." This especially prominent thirst for honor, and the desire for public recognition attested by these inscriptions, provide the background for many of the problems Paul encountered in Corinth throughout his relationship with the churches there.

First, factions appear to have developed within the Corinthian congregation based on selecting and promoting a favorite orator among what are perceived to be rival orators.[3] Dio Chrysostom remembers rivalries between traveling orators in Corinth as being rather fierce; he paints a picture of the intense divisions that could arise among followers of different orators concerning whose was the best. Dio describes the season of the Isthmian games, which were under Corinth's jurisdiction, as "the time when one could hear crowds of wretched sophists around Poseidon's temple shouting and reviling one another, and their disciples, as they were called, fighting with one another" (*Or.* 8.9). Seneca the Elder's *Controversies* also provide eyewitness testimony to the sophists' activities and rivalries. Orators would ridicule one another and compete for prestige before the crowds, who cheered their favorites as modern Americans cheer their favorite football teams. Stephen Pogoloff provides a helpful summary of the situation:

> Such competition in *sophoi logoi* sometimes became quite divisive. . . . One philosopher and another or one rhetor and another were often strenuous competitors. The group following a particular teacher could be so strong that they could be described as a *secta,* a "sect" or "party." This is the word Seneca the Elder uses to describe the followers of Apollodorus versus Theodorus, rival rhetoricians in Rome in the first century B.C.E.[4]

When different preachers came to Corinth the Corinthians treated them as they would have any other orators: they chose their favorites, argued over who was better, and created "parties" or "divisions" based on their choice. This was fueled further by the patronage system as the few patrons of the new Christian community sought to enhance their own prestige through claiming to have as a client the most illustrious Christian orator. The Christian "declaimers" found these new elites quite willing to enhance their own reputation by collecting client-dependents.

For these elites it became a source of pride and prestige to have the more able and gifted clients. The partisanship in 1 Corinthians 1–4, therefore, belongs to this cultural competition for honor based on collecting illustrious clients, comparing one's own sophist with the sophists of rival households or groups of followers in an effort to claim honor for oneself through one's own sophist. This competitive environment leads to the problem of comparing Paul with other similar preachers, with whom he cannot (or will not) compete in terms of flashy style, speech, and boasting about spiritual revelations—a problem certain itinerant preachers will exploit to the full.

Second, this sort of competition for honor carried on within the community was not limited to the patrons' boasts in their client apostles,[5] but manifested itself in numerous other aspects of the life of the church. The attitude of the "strong" toward the "weak" in the matter of eating food sacrificed to idols (1 Corinthians 8)—labels surely not deriving from the "weak"—reveals a claim to greater spiritual knowledge and power, and hence to honor (in Paul's words, being "puffed up," 1 Cor 8:1) on the part of the "strong." It implies an achieved status possessed by some, but not by others. Moreover, Paul's complaints concerning the celebration of the Lord's Supper reflect the ongoing replication of social status (honor, precedence) at the communal meals of the Christian group.[6] These meals become the occasion to remind many believers of their low status on the social ladder of precedence on which they occupy merely the bottom rungs (1 Cor 11:22).[7] Paul's discussion of spiritual gifts also suggests that competition for honor has led members to prefer the more exotic signs of divine giftedness—speaking in tongues, for example. Here we come close to a central difficulty in Corinth: the believers have not been "giving the greater honor" to the "less noble members" (12:23-26) so as to promote unity, but have been acting in accordance with the cultural norms of competition for honor, promoting division through establishing precedence.

Third, between the writing of 1 and 2 Corinthians a rival Hellenistic Jewish-Christian mission[8] had made its way to Corinth, exploiting the Corinthians' enslavement to society's norms in order to demonstrate its superiority over Paul. These rivals play into the image of the orator who has "honor, power, spiritual gifts, rhetorical skills, and good references and who would accept patronage."[9] The believers' susceptibility to such teachers reveals the degree of their embeddedness in the norms of the majority culture. Paul regards the possibility that some at least will decide to follow these rivals as a genuine threat to their formation in Christ. The very salvation of these believers may be halted and aborted as they return to imitating those who refuse to imitate Christ because they still desire to appear "honorable" and "powerful" according to worldly standards.

Paul's overarching goal is to teach the Corinthians about the true basis for honor. This is reflected in the frequent use of the words for "boast" or "boasting."[10] Most of the problems in Corinth appear to be related to improper boasting, to the believers' failure to comprehend that the gospel of the crucified Messiah also entails a transvaluation of dominant cultural norms of evaluating honor and understanding divine giftedness. Moreover, many of these problems stem from the failure of some of the Corinthians to understand that they are rather to acknowledge and reinforce one another's honor in the body of Christ rather than continue their competition with one another for honor in this new court of reputation. Finally, Paul's own honor comes under heavy attack when he is evaluated on the basis of what he considers worldly standards. This is especially the case in 2 Corinthians, where he expends much effort to defend his honor while at the same time maintaining the new definitions of what constitute honor in the eyes of God. It is especially in connection with the Corinthians' assessment of Paul and his team that their failure to grasp the essential significance of the gospel revealed itself to Paul.

Paul's responses show that many of the Corinthian believers have not been adequately socialized into the ethos of the new group. They have, rather, imported their primary socialization, which included an emphasis on competition for honor and on displays of beauty, power, and charisma as marks of one's honor and giftedness, into the new social body.[11] They have, moreover, imported other markers of precedence, such as wealth or social status, into the life of this new body, so as further to reconstruct the outside world's ladder of honor within the community. Paul seeks to complete their socialization into the culture of the new body.[12]

As Paul addresses these concerns he uses honor discourse in several ways already observed in Matthew, John, and the Thessalonian letters. Part of his socialization of the believers involves drawing a sharp contrast between the "wisdom of the world" and the "wisdom of God," thus also contributing to the exclusion of the one who has not come to embrace God's wisdom in the crucified Messiah from the court of reputation. He also seeks to motivate the believing community to function as a court of reputation, to impose sanctions of shaming as well as conferring upon one another the honor with which God has gifted them (cf. 1 Cor 5:1-11; 2 Cor 2:3-11). His defense of his own ministry and honor as God's legitimate apostle, and his exclusion of those who continue to base their *ethos* on the "wisdom of the world," contribute to this formation of the alternate court of opinion by reaffirming his own authority as a leader to ascribe honor and shame within the group. Within this alternate court of reputation, at which God and the crucified Messiah have the final verdict, Paul outlines the basis of the believers' only claims to lasting honor, teaching them that many of their boasts are ultimately hollow. He spurs them on to honor before the court that matters. We will look at each of these elements of the Corinthian letters in detail, together with an analysis of why Paul believes so strenuously that dominant cultural norms of evaluation must be excluded from the new community, indeed why evaluating honor in a worldly way ultimately signals one's failure to have grasped the gospel itself.

THE ERROR OF WORLDLY WISDOM

The fact of the crucified Messiah, the central feature of Paul's gospel, reveals the upside-down nature of the world's way of thinking and evaluating. Failure to grasp the devaluation of the world's standards as "folly" in God's sight equals, for Paul, failure to grasp the gospel itself:

> The message about the cross is foolishness to those who are perishing, but to us who are being saved it is the power of God. . . . Has not God made foolish the wisdom of the world? For since, in the wisdom of God, the world did not know God through wisdom, God decided, through the foolishness of our proclamation, to save those who believe. . . . We proclaim Christ crucified, a stumbling block to Jews and foolishness to Gentiles, but to those who are called, both Jews and Greeks, Christ the power of God and the wisdom of God. For God's foolishness is wiser than human wisdom, and God's weakness is stronger than human strength. . . . God chose what is foolish in the world to shame the wise; God chose what is weak in the world to shame the strong; God chose what is low and despised in the world, things that are not, to reduce to nothing things that are, so that no one might boast in the presence of God (1 Cor 1:18-29 NRSV).

Such words are calculated to exclude the opinion of "worldly" thinkers from the community's court of reputation, since God's verdict on their ignorance is made manifest: God has specifically targeted those considered "wise" and "powerful" by the world for shaming. Paul needs, however, to convince the Corinthian believers that a particular way of thinking is incompatible with the message of salvation before he can move them to regard those who still think that way as ignorant and dishonorable.

"Christ crucified," the basis of Paul's preaching (1 Cor 2:2), is the point at which God reveals the world's standards of evaluating advantage and disadvantage (its "wisdom") as folly. The one whom God appointed "Lord of glory" (1 Cor 2:8) was not recognized as such by the world, but rather was dishonored by the world through the crucifixion. In showing contempt toward Jesus the world reveals its own ignorance concerning what is honorable and approved in God's sight. "Those who are perishing" (1:18) consider the notion of a crucified Messiah to be foolishness. Their destiny, which is to perish along with the present age that is passing away, shows the folly of their own way of thinking. If they recognized God's wisdom they should enjoy the advantage of surviving the end of this age through the resurrection to life; since they will not survive the end of the age, but will come to nothing, their opinion and evaluation are shown to be ignorance and folly.[13] They have fallen prey to Satan's deceptions, having their eyes blinded to the truth of God (2 Cor 4:1-6). Those who "are being saved," however, recognize in Christ the wisdom and power of God, and based on this recognition should surmise that appearances as judged by worldly standards do not reveal the honor of a person in God's sight. The way to be regarded as wise, and hence honorable, in God's sight is thus to be willing to become a fool in the sight of non-Christians (1 Cor 3:18-20).

Such argumentation seeks to establish that if the Corinthians fancy themselves believers in Christ at all they must recognize that they have become such not on the basis of evaluating as the world does. Moreover, they must recognize the implications of the crucified Messiah for worldly (dominant cultural) standards of assessing honor *tout entier*. They must distance themselves from their own primary socialization and regard those who still operate under that socialization in the majority culture's values as unreliable guides to what is honorable and what is dishonorable. Paul further reinforces these points throughout the letters. The person endowed with God's Spirit is free from the court of reputation formed by those who do not possess that Spirit: "those who are unspiritual do not receive the gifts of God's Spirit, for they are foolishness to them, and they are unable to understand them because they are spiritually discerned. Those who are spiritual discern [i.e., judge] all things, and they are themselves subject to no one else's scrutiny" (2:14-15 NRSV).

One finds similar reflections in Seneca, who claimed that the wise person is the only one able to form reliable evaluations: the opinion of fools, whether they despise or honor the wise person, means nothing.[14] Because of this the believers should be ashamed to present their disputes before the courts of nonbelievers (1 Cor 6:1-7), "those who are least esteemed by the church" (6:4 RSV), who are groping in the ignorance the world calls wisdom, who have not received adoption by God. The nonbelieving Gentiles, moreover, are censured for acting dishonorably, as Paul calls to the believers' minds what they once were in order to emphasize the qualitative difference between the community and those outside (1 Cor 6:9-11). One finds in 1 and 2 Corinthians, therefore, many of the same techniques used elsewhere in the New Testament and other subcultural or countercultural literature to negate the opinion of outsiders, distance group members from their primary socialization, and prepare for an inversion of cultural values within the group.

THE TRUE BASIS OF THE BELIEVERS' HONOR AND ITS HONORABLE EXPRESSION

Paul addresses the issue of how the believers are to redefine their own honor on a basis other than competition in endowments recognized by the majority or dominant culture. To begin this process Paul contrasts the natural endowments of the majority of believers with the honor they have received from God, arguing that indeed in the world's estimation the Christians have little or no honor:

> Consider your own call, brothers and sisters: not many of you were wise by human standards, not many were powerful, not many were of noble birth. . . . God chose what is low and despised in the world . . . so that no one might boast in the presence of God. He is the source of your life in Christ Jesus, who became for us wisdom from God, and righteousness and sanctification and redemption, in order that, as it is written, "Let the one who boasts, boast in the Lord" (1 Cor 1:26-31 NRSV).

Even those who had gained considerable wealth and prestige in the new Corinth might be stung by this remark, recalling the laments attached to the resettling of Corinth with veterans and freed slaves *(libertini)* from Rome and elsewhere in the empire (Syrians, Egyptians, Jews), which elicited disparaging remarks from orators. Crinagoras, for example, can exclaim: "Alas for the great calamity to Greece! Would, Corinth, that you did lie lower than the ground and more desert than the Libyan sands, rather than be wholly abandoned to such a crowd of scoundrelly slaves!" (*Greek Anthology* 9.284).

Paul claims that it is only God's choice of and work in the believer that give him or her a true claim to honor (a "boast"). Just as this is Paul's own source of honor and authority (2 Cor 3:1-6), so also it is each individual believer's source of honor. There can be no vying for status in the Lord's community, no competition for prestige, since God alone supplies this to all (1 Cor 4:7).[15] It is not possible to claim honor within this new community on the basis of credentials recognized by the worldly mind, which has already been censured as foolish by God: "it is not those who commend themselves that are approved, but those whom the Lord commends" (2 Cor 10:17-18 NRSV). The believers have been called out of a dishonorable way of life in their response to Christ, having been washed from every base vice (1 Cor 6:9-11). Moreover, they have been given the privilege of becoming temples of God's Holy Spirit (1 Cor 6:19-20), set apart for the honor or carrying within themselves this divine gift. Indeed, they must continue to remain separate from the vices of their former way of life if they are to preserve this greater honor that God has given them (1 Cor 6:12-20).

This deposit of the Spirit (2 Cor 1:22; 5:5) transforms the believer into the image of Christ, and it is only as he or she comes to reflect this image that he or she moves toward the final honor which God has prepared. We come here to 2 Cor 3:7-18, a passage many have read as a sign that Paul is combating Judaizers in Corinth, but that appears rather to serve a different purpose. Because his opponents commend themselves as credible and honorable teachers on the basis of "letters of recommendation" Paul appeals in 3:1-6 to the Corinthians themselves as his "letters of recommendation" written in their own hearts (since they have received the knowledge of God and the gift of the Spirit through Paul's ministry). The contrast between letters written down and the proof of the Spirit leads Paul to a discussion of the two covenants as an exemplification of the point he is trying to impress upon the Corinthians. He seizes on Moses' veiling of his face, which shone with "glory,"[16] the reflection of God's own honor, after receiving the Torah. The crucial element for Paul is that this glory was "fading" *(katargoumenēn)*, that is, transient, and indeed must be evaluated as possessing no value in the presence of the "surpassing glory" *(hyperballousē doxa,* 3:10) of the "covenant of the Spirit."

Paul's point is made clearly in 3:10-11: "what once had glory has come to have no glory at all, because of the glory that surpasses it. For if what faded away came with glory, what is permanent must have much more glory." The crucial distinction between these two "glories" is that one is fading while the other remains or endures. Paul speaks of more here than two covenants, as the covenant of Sinai did not fade away but rather came to its fulfillment and end "in the fullness of time." Rather what is fading is this present age, the realm of all that is seen (*ta blepomena*). Only what will remain after the consummation is of any value, or gives any claim to honor, in the reign of God. The standards by which the believers had assessed their own and others' honor all belonged to this fading realm. Honor in such terms could not be held as honor at all in light of the revelation of the one claim to honor that lasts beyond death and beyond the end of this age.

Paul's rivals, like Moses, seek to veil this fact, hiding from the converts' eyes the transitory quality of strengths and claims that belonged to the world that was passing away. Paul, however, urges the believer to seek his or her honor only through "gazing with unveiled face at the glory of the Lord, being transformed into the same image from glory to glory" (3:18). What counts, Paul argues, is not the appearance as it exists in this age, but as it is transformed into the image of Christ—an image of suffering and weakness through which the power of God becomes present. This brings the believer eternal honor, next to which any temporary honor that will fade away with the present age must be counted as of no value at all. Indeed, this is the test Paul poses at the close of the correspondence—whether or not Christ is in fact in them (13:5-6)—for ultimately that is the only mark of honor and worth.

One's appearance "in the flesh" therefore cannot contain any clues to one's honor before God's court (2 Cor 5:11-13), where only the transformation of the inner person into the likeness of Jesus brings "glory" or "honor." The reason for this is developed more thoroughly in 2 Cor 4:16–5:8. Paul distinguishes between the condition of the "outer person" and the "inner person" at 4:16, characterizing the former as decaying but the latter as being made new or renewed day by day. By this he intends to link the external person to the realm of what is fading or what is perishing, but the inner person to what endures or is saved. Appearances of physical existence such as Paul's weaknesses or charismatic deficiency belong to the realm of what is passing away and therefore are not reliable criteria for judging the ultimate realities of the new life in Christ, which achieves fullness only after this age has completely faded. The troubles that afflict the apostle afflict only the "outer person." Paul's acceptance of this experience bears witness to the conviction that all such externals belong to the present age and have no normative value to qualify one for or disqualify one from participation in the age that is coming.

Contrasted to the outer person is the inner person that, despite or perhaps by means of the contrary experiences of this present affliction, is being renewed day by day. Thus in the life led by the apostle there is testimony both to the penultimate nature of appearances and to the ultimate or eternal nature of the life lived by hope in God. As the former is indeed passing away visibly in the form of the afflictions the apostle endures (4:17; cf. 4:8-9), the new life is growing within. These afflictions of the present accrue an eternal weight of glory (4:17), replicating the pattern of Christ himself (cf. 2 Cor 4:10-14). The perspective of faith is to regard the unseen (4:18) and not to build on norms that govern and assign value according to what is seen, "for what is seen is temporary, but what is unseen is eternal" (4:18b). The terms "temporary" and "eternal" become important labels for bracketing dominant cultural values and promoting group values.

Paul also attempts to teach the believers about the impropriety of "boasting," that is, laying claims to honor or precedence within the community based on God's gifts. While being favored by God is indeed a basis for honor, Paul does not allow God's gifts to become the grounds for competitive boasting, the basis for competitions for honor.[17] "What do you have that you did not receive? And if indeed you received it, why do you boast as if you were not given it?" (1 Cor 4:7). Paul suggests, indeed, that "boasting" is an affront to the Giver, representing as one's own achievement something that was rather the result of God's generosity. Apostles were not to be the cause for boasting or factions (1 Cor 3:21-23; 4:6-7), for they were—God's gift to the whole community—a sign of God's patronage of the new community and not a ground for the human patrons to promote their own honor. Spiritual endowments—those gifts that demonstrated the Spirit's presence within and guidance of the community—were also not grounds for competitive boasting. The Spirit was indeed a great gift, giving the believer access to "what no eye has seen" (1 Cor 2:9-10). The believers must, however, "understand the gifts given to us by God," namely that they point to God's generosity (1 Cor 12:4-11) and should lead the Corinthian believer to serve the body through the gifts rather than to seek to establish a reputation for being a superior "charismatic" through the display of gifts (1 Corinthians

12–14). Similarly, "knowledge" is not given to create status markers within the community between "strong" and "weak" (1 Cor 8:1-13). Knowledge so used is not knowledge at all, but mere arrogance (1 Cor 8:1-2). True honor, not mere puffery, comes from the display of love that "builds up" the other members, that seeks to secure and augment the honor of one's brothers and sisters. This is the point of Paul's presentation of his own example in 1 Corinthians 9: his "boast," or "claim to honor" consists precisely in not exercising privileges but in taking on servile roles (especially by working with his hands) for the benefit of the Church God is building (9:15-23). For this reason Paul presents love as the highest sign of divine giftedness (1 Cor 12:31b): contrary to the values held by the majority, however, love does not seek precedence over others (1 Cor 13:4-5).

The believer's honor, then, derives solely from God's choice of the believer and the transforming work of the Spirit within the believer, which guarantees the enjoyment of future honor and vindication when Christ is fully formed in them. They are challenged to seek to establish their honor neither on their social status in the world nor on the gifts God has given them. Their lives in this world are to be marked not by competition with one another for honor and recognition, but by mutual upbuilding and service, following the example of Paul and of Christ himself (1 Cor 11:1).

ASSESSING THE MESSENGER, ACCEPTING THE MESSAGE

Paul claims to have distanced his proclamation of the gospel of the crucified Messiah deliberately from the manner of worldly orators (1 Cor 1:17; 2:1-5). Victor Furnish, approving the work of Peter Marshall, comments: "Paul deliberately rejected the Hellenistic cultural conventions his critics valued and with which he himself felt most comfortable. This . . . helps to explain the concern—throughout 2 Cor—to show how suffering and weakness bear witness to the gospel and are the true signs of apostleship."[18] Rather than play into the cultural norms of popular Hellenistic society Paul refused to use impressiveness of voice, gesture, and vocabulary to win over his audience. He realized that to use the world's means of gaining conviction would undermine the transformation the gospel sought to achieve in people's lives. As Paul declares, "Christ sent me not to baptize but to proclaim the gospel, and not with cleverness in the use of words, lest the cross of Christ be emptied of its power" (1 Cor 1:17). It was imperative to him that the hearers be won over "not in plausible words of wisdom, but with a demonstration of the Spirit and of power," and that the faith of his converts rest "not on human wisdom but on the power of God" (2:4-5 NRSV).[19] Paul declares that the proclamation must serve the message, not the tastes of the people and the reputation of the orator. The proclamation itself was about the transcendent power of God—the God who is self-revealed in the crucified Messiah.

If Paul were to win his converts by manifestations of human skill or fleshly excellence he would betray the message itself and deny the hearers an encounter with God's transforming power. Only if the Corinthians could perceive the God at work in weakness, the God who rejected those who relied on human wisdom but moved powerfully through those who allowed God to shine through their cracks, their flaws, their points of weakness, would they understand how radically different salvation was from what their culture led them to believe. Rising up the ladder, gaining clients, increasing one's reputation, gaining wealth to use for beneficence, making a name for oneself: these were the things Corinthian society pursued as if salvation depended on it. The gospel proclaims advancement as serving others and preferring others over oneself, investing oneself not in one's reputation or standing in the community but rather in advancing the well-being of the community, caring for the weak members of the community.

The apostle's presentation of himself, then, was to reflect the content of the gospel: God's power breaking into this age precisely at a place of weakness and contempt, namely the cross of Jesus. It is no wonder, then, that Paul can effectively equate one's response to him with one's response to Christ: those who reject Paul show themselves to be among "those who are perishing" just as surely as they demonstrate their failure to see in Christ the wisdom of God (2 Cor 2:15-16; 1 Cor 1:18). His endurance of shameful treatment and the unimpressiveness of his appearance are not grounds for the believers to think of him as base or dishonorable. Rather, Paul contends, it is precisely in this way that he allows the power of God to break in upon the Corinthians and free them from the error of the worldly mind that regards the standards of this age as of ultimate value.

In 2 Cor 4:7, after describing the climactic grandeur of the "light of the knowledge of the glory of God in the face of Christ," Paul juxtaposes the unattractiveness of the vessels in which this treasure is stored. The apostles who may not appear to be worthy of the treasure they bear, and who therefore come under criticism from "those who boast in appearances" (2 Cor 5:12), in fact conform to the purpose of God. Their appearance is unimpressive precisely "in order that the surpassing greatness of the power might be from God and not from ourselves" (4:7). The apostles' own experience of suffering or affliction keeps them mindful of this all-important fact of the gospel, namely that hope or confidence may only be placed in God who raises the dead (2 Cor 1:8-9). Not measuring up to worldly expectations in appearance and performance cannot justifiably discredit them. On the contrary, this establishes them as emissaries of God since in their weakness God's strength is known and made present for the churches (1:3-7; 4:10-12). Paul relates his sufferings to those of Christ, which gives him the hope of Christ's life manifesting itself in him now and the hope of resurrection from the "One who raised Jesus from the dead" (4:14).

Paul's refusal to display honor in terms comprehensible to the worldly mind allows him to make the claim that he puts no "stumbling block" in anyone's way (2 Cor 6:3). In one sense, of course, Paul's apparent lack of credentials (such as oratorical or charismatic virtuosity) that could be appreciated by "fleshly wisdom" (1:12) is in fact quite a "stumbling block" for the Corinthian congregation, as 2 Corinthians 10–13 especially attests. Nevertheless, by allowing his humanness, his vulnerability, his seeming inadequacies to remain visible he makes it possible for others to see in him God's favor and power glowing through the translucent walls of his clay vessel. Paul claims that his decision not to adorn the earthen vessel of his physical bearing prevents the gospel from being obscured or distorted. He does not allow human strengths to distract from the one sure ground for hope and confidence: God's presence. In this way Paul truly presents no stumbling block to the gospel. The rival teachers, however, do put the stumbling block of their own strengths, boasts, and prowess in the way of the believers, who can see only human strength rather than the power of God reflected in these teachers. An ancient orator and instructor of orators once wrote: "the greatest defect in a person is to show his or her humanness, for then a person ceases to be held divine." Paul's opponents follow such advice. In building themselves up on the strength of their appearance and credentials, however, and asking that their followers evaluate them on this basis they do not allow God's presence to shine through. Rather they remain opaque to God's power, revealing no new basis for trust and confidence but affirming the values of the world and the ultimacy of the strengths of this present age. For such teachers the cultural standards by which honor is displayed, recognized, and measured in competitions for honor remain valid.

Paul goes on, however, to defend his endurance of suffering as a mark not of dishonor but rather of honor in the sight of the One whose opinion alone ultimately matters. First it makes Paul the acceptable and pleasing "aroma of Christ to God" (2:15), by which he "replicates the sacrificial death of Christ"[20] and extends God's benefits to the Corinthians. The apostle's participation in the sufferings of Christ leads to the congregation's own experience of God's encouragement (1:5): "whether we are afflicted, it is on behalf of your comfort and salvation; or whether we receive comfort, it is on behalf of your comfort working through the endurance of the same sufferings which we suffer" (1:6). The apostle's experience of suffering, far from being a disqualifying thing, works toward the comfort and salvation of the Corinthian believers as long as they remain partners with the apostle: "As you are sharers of our sufferings, so also of comfort" (1:7). Paul makes an important claim on the Corinthians here: as the broker of God's "comfort" or "encouragement" (2 Cor 1:3-9) Paul merits the believers' gratitude, which entails respect, loyalty, and obedience (all three of which were at stake in Corinth). Indeed, his endurance of hardship must be rendered noble by the awareness that it is borne "for the sake of others," that is, to bring benefit to the Corinthian Christians: "all things are on your behalf, in order that the gift which spreads through the many may make gratitude increase to God's honor" (2 Cor 4:15).

Paul returns in 2 Cor 4:8-9 to dwell on the conditions of the life of the apostle as a life marked by affliction and suffering at the very limits of human endurance. Its extremity poses something of a mystery, for the trials to which the apostle is exposed, it appears, should be sufficient to crush or destroy the apostle, but instead he endures. Here is, in part, the manifestation of the power of God (4:7). More than that, however, Paul sees the bearing of "the death of Jesus in our bodies" as a means of witnessing to "the life of Jesus in our body" (4:10) and the hope for the resurrection from the dead (4:14) as a result of sharing the sufferings of Christ (1:5). Paul, indeed, is a witness to the worthlessness of the world's standards as he flouts the attempts of the world to shame him into conformity with those values. Moreover, while "death is at work" in the apostle "life is at work" in the Corinthians (4:12), recalling the claim of Paul in 1:6-7 that the apostle endures suffering in order to bring the Corinthians comfort and salvation.

In addition to ennobling these hardships by claiming that they mediate divine gifts to the believers, Paul also claims that they constitute the path to lasting honor and to the experience of God's power, particularly

God's power over death. Noteworthy here is 2 Cor 4:17-18: "this slight momentary affliction is preparing for us an eternal weight of glory beyond all comparison, because we look not to the things that are seen but to the things that are unseen; for the things that are seen are transient, but the things that are unseen are eternal" (RSV). Honor as the world conceives of it is merely temporary, and so pales in comparison with the honor God grants. In light of this it is highly advantageous temporarily to endure dishonor in the world's eyes. Moreover, Paul claims that his union with the sufferings of Jesus also grants him the experience of God's power, both in this life (2 Cor 1:8-9; 12:7b-10; 13:4) and in the next through resurrection (2 Cor 4:14).

Finally, the apostle's endurance of hardships in God's service proves his fidelity to his trust and his courage in the pious execution of his charge:

> As servants of God we commend ourselves in every way: through great endurance, in afflictions, hardships, calamities, beatings, imprisonments, tumults, labors, watching, hunger; by purity, knowledge, forbearance, kindness, the Holy Spirit, genuine love, truthful speech, and the power of God; with the weapons of righteousness for the right hand and for the left; in honor and dishonor, in ill repute and good repute. We are treated as impostors, and yet are true; as unknown, and yet well known; as dying, and behold we live; as punished, and yet not killed; as sorrowful, yet always rejoicing; as poor, yet making many rich; as having nothing, and yet possessing everything (2 Cor 6:4-10 RSV).

Paul's endurance of hardships (expanded upon dramatically in 2 Cor 11:22-28)[21] is the first proof of his loyalty to his divine commission, the task God entrusted to him. He follows this up with a list of virtues that he claims he and his team manifest (6:6-7) together with a reminder of their access to divine power (6:7b). The claims to possess virtue and power are readily recognizable claims to honor, supporting his first claim (6:4-5). The last few verses are quite salient for the Corinthian believers. Paul emphasizes the unreliability of the opinion of outsiders, who treat or regard the apostles in ways inappropriate to their true status (6:8-10) and rather according to the criterion of external appearances. Paul's treatment at the hands of such people cannot in any way be read as a true reflection of his honor, which is established by his courageous fidelity,[22] his virtuous conduct, and his proximity to God's power. The Corinthians will need to learn this lesson for themselves if they are ever to grasp the wisdom of God in the cross and be freed to serve as God requires. The mystery of the apostle's sufferings is that while he appears to be the most marginal of people he has the commendation of God; while he appears to have the least in this world he possesses the assurance of resurrection from the dead and an indestructible life. In this way he is a "better servant" of Christ (2 Cor 11:23) since he more nearly replicates in his own life the pattern of Jesus' own crucifixion in weakness and reception of divine power.

In his "fool's speech," his ironic answer to the boasts of his rivals in 2 Cor 11:21b–12:10,[23] Paul claims to be a "better" servant of Christ than his rivals precisely on account of his endurance of greater and more numerous hardships in Christ's service:[24]

> Are they servants of Christ? I am a better one—I am talking like a madman—with far greater labors, far more imprisonments, with countless beatings, and often near death. Five times I have received at the hands of the Jews the forty lashes less one. Three times I have been beaten with rods; once I was stoned. Three times I have been shipwrecked; a night and a day I have been adrift at sea; on frequent journeys, in danger from rivers, danger from robbers, danger from my own people, danger from Gentiles, danger in the city, danger in the wilderness, danger at sea, danger from false brethren; in toil and hardship, through many a sleepless night, in hunger and thirst, often without food, in cold and exposure (2 Cor 11:23-27 RSV).

Many of these experiences are explicitly linked with the dominant culture's low estimation of Paul and its attempts to shame him into renouncing a base and disapproved way of life. The others reflect his transient, rootless lifestyle, which was itself less honorable than the lifestyle of one who is firmly rooted in a single location enjoying the respect of his or her neighbors. In Paul's rhetoric, however, these submissions to disgrace are all for the sake of obedient service to God, hence a demonstration of Paul's piety and courage.

His final word in this ironic speech of self-commendation is to declare that he will only "boast with regard to the things of my weakness" (11:30), that he will "rather most gladly boast concerning my weaknesses, in order that the power of Christ may dwell upon me" (12:9). He thus returns to drive home the point he made at the beginning of their correspondence, namely that human strengths are merely a veil that blinds worldly eyes to the temporary and fading nature of this present age and all that belongs to it. The only boast that has any lasting value is a boast "in the Lord," in the knowledge that God's power is at work within, preparing one for the coming age and a share in God's honor. This can clearly be known, however, only in those places where displays of human "strength" do not interfere with one's view: "I am content, then, in weaknesses, in insults, in hardships, in persecutions and calamities, on behalf of Christ; for whenever I am weak, then I am strong" (12:10).

The question of the believers' evaluation of their apostles, and of the standards they used to measure honor and reliability, is ultimately tied to their understanding and embracing of the gospel itself. This accounts for why Paul urges so vehemently that honor must be redefined and reconceived. It is ultimately mandated first by Christ's example and the nature of his messiahship (cf. 1 Cor 1:17-25; 2:1-2; 2 Cor 4:7-18; 13:4). Viewed "according to the flesh" *(kata sarka)* he is "Christ crucified," an image of weakness and degradation; viewed by faith he is the "Lord Messiah" (1 Cor 12:3), the place where God's transforming power breaks into the perishing world. When one looks at Jesus with the eyes of the Spirit a veil is removed: the veil that covers the temporary, passing value of appearances and worldly achievements with a veneer of ultimate importance and reliability (2 Cor 3:16). Jesus—the Messiah who died on a cross, stripped, despised, worthless in the world's eyes—proves the unreliability of appearances. The one whom the world estimated as worthless was estimated in God's sight as of supreme worth. In obedience to God's purposes Jesus allowed himself to be deprived of all outward signs of acceptability and worth, valuing the approval of God rather than the approval of society. God's raising of Jesus proves that God's approval is of infinitely more worth than the world's, and to be pursued even at the cost of being evaluated as of no account by worldly standards.

The close relationship between Paul's approach to ministry and the revelation of God's power in weakness in Jesus emerges in the way Paul's transformation of his sufferings into a noble act reflect ways in which the early Church did the same with Jesus' sufferings. Recalling Matthew's reinterpretation of Jesus' experience of degradation as a noble achievement, we discover the declaration that it was endured to benefit others, that it was indeed the path to greater glory, and that it was a mark of Jesus' courage in remaining faithful to God's command. All these elements reappear in our discussion of Paul's interpretation of his sufferings above.

The redefinition of honor is mandated, secondly, by the temporary and fading nature of this creation and all that belongs to it. Paul's gospel is an apocalyptic message declaring the penultimate nature of this present reality and relegating it all to destruction. Strengths or claims to honor based on what belongs to the observable, physical world are all devoid of worth since their end is the grave (cf. 1 Cor 7:29-31; 1 Cor 15:43; 2 Cor 5:1-8). The present body, even if graced by poise, beauty, dramatic presence, and all manner of human achievement, is still mere nakedness. It is not until the resurrection that it will be fully clothed with a body of glory. This flesh is penultimate, subject to death and decay, looking forward to the day when what is mortal will be swallowed up by life (2 Cor 5:1-4). What real honor, then, can fleshly strengths bring? The only true claim to lasting honor is the transformation at work within the believer, the conforming of the believer to the image of Christ—and it is Paul, not the rivals, who bears that image in his body, who allows God's transforming power to be recognized (1 Cor 2:1-5; 2 Cor 1:8-9; 3:1-6; 4:7). The rivals mask God's power by holding up their own strengths, which are really no strengths at all since they are powerless in the face of death.

This also reveals why it was so important to Paul that he win the Corinthians back. It was not merely an attempt to reassert his authority and regain his power. Witherington observes from Dio Chrysostom (*Or.* 55.1, 3, 5) that disciples sought to imitate their teachers in all respects. Paul sincerely believed that the danger to the Corinthians' faith was great enough to warrant his spirited rebuttal. If they imitate the rivals they will not be discovering the transforming power of God, nor will they be given the life that transcends death, namely the life of the crucified and resurrected one within them. Their own commitment to their primary socialization in the dominant culture's standards for recognizing and seeking honor would keep them blinded to God's revelation and prisoners of this present age.

CONSTRUCTING AND ACTIVATING THE ALTERNATE COURT OF OPINION

We have seen how Paul's deconstruction of the "wisdom of the world" would contribute to the delimitation of the "court of reputation" whose verdict should concern the believer. These same passages could also threaten to place some of the believers, at least, within that court of reputation whose opinion is fundamentally flawed by error and ignorance of God's wisdom (and thus perhaps motivate them to pursue more vigorously their "secondary socialization" into the norms of the Christian culture). Paul also pays careful attention to constructing this alternate court of reputation more positively: as before in the Thessalonian correspondence God, Christ, and the Christian community form the essential components of this body of significant others whose opinion and grants of honor are alone important.

The supreme figures in the alternate court of reputation are, of course, God and Christ. God alone "will bring to light the things now hidden in darkness and will disclose the purposes of the heart" (1 Cor 4:5 NRSV), so that Paul cares nothing for the verdict of "any human court" (1 Cor 4:3). Indeed, "we must all appear before the judgment seat of Christ, so that each one may receive good or evil, according to what he has done in the body" (2 Cor 5:10 RSV). It is at this time that "praise will come to each person from God" (1 Cor 4:5) or the opposite, such that the main focus of living in this world must be "to please God" (2 Cor 5:9). This conviction emerges even in Paul's advice to the single, who have as their one advantage over married believers the possibility of undivided commitment to "pleasing the Lord" (1 Cor 7:32, 34). "Pleasing God" is ultimately the only true measuring rod of a person's honor (as opposed to the standards applied by the rivals in 2 Cor 10:12-16).

The other component of this court of reputation remains the Christian community, both the local chapter and the supra-local collective. Insofar as the believers evaluate using worldly standards their opinion is, of course, excluded. Insofar as they accept the measuring rod of christlikeness and of pleasing God they can become an important source of support and correction for the individual believer. The believers, first, need to honor one another: to reflect back to one another the honor that each member has received from God. The fundamental problem with the Corinthians' celebration of the Lord's Supper is their failure to do this very thing. Gerd Theissen has shown that the Corinthian Lord's Supper resembled the private banquets given at the homes of patrons for their friends of equal standing and their clients. The portions and kinds of food given out were calculated to replicate the relative honor of each guest. Thus the elites had a "private dinner" while the whole body shared the bread and wine (1 Cor 11:21). The community was called rather to reenact in their gatherings not their honor in this age but the honor God bestowed on each member. In short, their meals were to reflect the truth of 1 Cor 1:26-31, namely that God's choice of each bestows on each special honor. Similarly, 1 Cor 12:23-26 speaks of the necessity of bestowing honor on those members of the body who naturally possess less honor. The community must become a place where each believer enjoys affirmation and respect, all on the basis of God's election.

The community, however, must also work to keep each member in line with the values of the Christian culture. In the case of the incestuous brother (1 Cor 5:1-6) Paul orders the community to exercise the technique of social control known as expulsion or shunning. They are by such action to shame him, and indeed are to use similar pressure in the case of any brother or sister who flouts the morality of the new community: "I wrote to you in the letter not to have dealings or even eat with such a person as bears the name of brother or sister and is sexually immoral, greedy, an idolater, reviler, drunkard, or thief" (1 Cor 5:11). Paul is not concerned with "outsiders," but only with exerting social pressure on the "insider" who nevertheless refuses to live by the community's standards. What he advises in 5:1-6 specifically is one instance of this more general policy of using shunning or some other public act of imputing dishonor to reinforce community discipline.

The believers are also called to have a care for their reputation and honor within the supra-local Christian community. Paul's remarks in 2 Cor 8:1-7, 24; 9:1-4 concerning the collection use this concern for supra-local honor to reinforce his appeal for generosity and a quick completion of their part in the task. He urges them to excel in the collection as a means of gaining honor within the Church by being benefactors to their fellow churches (8:7). He stirs them to emulation by praising the generosity of the Macedonian churches (8:1-5). Moreover, the Corinthians' reputation for generosity—spread by Paul himself—is at stake. Before this supra-local court of reputation (8:24), and specifically before the emissaries of the Macedonian churches who are accompanying Paul to Corinth (9:1-4), the Corinthians will have to show reasons for their reputation for generosity (a noble and central virtue in a patronal society). They would be ashamed now to display less generosity than Paul has credited to them, since Paul has already praised them for this virtue.

PROMISES OF HONOR AND THE POWER OF SHAMING IN PAUL'S EXHORTATIONS

To close our investigation of honor discourse in the Corinthian letters we may briefly note how Paul uses the promise of honor and the power of shaming to motivate the Corinthians to pursue the course of action Paul perceives to be in the best interest of the Christian community. First, 1 Corinthians contains numerous examples of Paul's attempts to shame the Corinthian Christians into group-sustaining, unifying behavior. In 1 Cor 3:1-4 he questions their status as "spiritual" people and declares them to be mere children in the faith on account of the jealousy and quarreling among group members. In 1 Cor 5:1-2, 6 Paul censures the community for tolerating among them a vice at which even the nonbelievers would be indignant. In 1 Cor 6:1-7 he shames the believers (note 6:5: "I speak to your disgrace") for going to court against one another, presenting their cases to unbelievers for adjudication: indeed, he goes further to claim that the very existence of lawsuits between believers is already a mark of defeat, and therefore disgrace. Once again Paul censures the believers in 1 Cor 11:17-31 for their manner of keeping the Lord's Supper (11:17, 22).

While it is not overtly an attempt to shame the audience, Paul's attempt to reestablish a distinction between male and female appearance in worship, which has its roots in a conception of female honor as modesty (1 Cor 11:2-16) may appropriately be mentioned in this context. Paul's argument reflects the conviction that a woman's honor is embedded in the honor of some man ("woman is the glory of man," 11:7). The emphasis on a woman being "covered" in some way (either by a veil or by long hair, 11:5, 15) further reflects the distinctly female version of honor as modesty. Even the mention of the "angels" in 11:10 may recall the unholy union of the "sons of God" (the angels) with the "daughters of people" in Gen 6:1-4 (developed greatly through the intertestamental period in the Enoch literature), and so be linked with a concern for female honor as chastity and modesty (indeed, removal from the places of seduction and temptation). Intriguingly, Paul can finally offer no rationale for this save that it is the practice of "the churches of God" (11:16), to which the Corinthians should also conform.

Finally, Paul depicts certain activities as the way to honor, or the way to walk honorably, in order to motivate the believers to accept his directions. We have already seen that this includes becoming a fool in the eyes of worldly people (1 Cor 3:18-20), pursuing the way of love and mutual edification rather than seeking to establish precedence over one's brothers and sisters (1 Corinthians 8–9; 12–14), and being generous toward one's sisters and brothers in need throughout the Christian counterculture (2 Cor 8:1-7, 24; 9:1-4, 11-14). The believers are called several times to act honorably toward their divine Patron through loyalty, obedience, and a return of life for life. They are to honor God properly by not sitting at the table of God's enemies (demons, lurking behind idols), not compromising the patron-client bond, and avoiding any conflicts of interests in their loyalties (1 Cor 10:14-21); they are to bring honor to God through their obedient participation in the collection (2 Cor 9:11-14); most impressively, they are to live "no longer for themselves but for him who for their sake died and was raised" (2 Cor 5:15). The fulfillment of the obligation of gratitude demands nothing less than the commitment of their whole lives to obedient service (see Seneca, *Ep. Mor.* 81.27). Even if the pursuit of honor in God's sight means the experience of being dishonored by those who evaluate honor by worldly standards the believers must insulate themselves from such experiences with the assurance that any temporary disgrace is winning for them an eternal ascription of honor (2 Cor 4:16-18).

CONCLUSION

Investigation of honor discourse in the Corinthian letters takes the investigator to the central issues of the correspondence. Honor discourse is particularly important in these letters because Paul finds himself having to teach the Corinthians anew about the redefinition and recognition of honor in the new community. Many of the specific problems Paul must address in both letters radiate from the more basic issue of the believers' continued allegiance to their primary socialization. The gospel of the crucified Messiah, together with the apocalyptic message of the passing away of this present age and all that belongs to it, requires that the new community seek honor in the things that endure into the coming age and reject as valueless those human strengths that mask the true, temporary nature of all power and status in this age. The true apostle must present a paradigm of this new definition of honor, and it is precisely on this point that the rivals appear to Paul to be such a threat to the gospel itself. If the Corinthians continue to perceive honor and value in terms of the beauty, strength, and prowess of this world as the rival teachers lead them to do they will fail to perceive the true power that transcends this world's destruction.

Alongside these central issues we have observed honor discourse working in ways familiar from our study of Matthew, John, and the Thessalonian letters. Paul negates the value of the opinion of non-Christians in the strongest of terms, setting up an alternative court of reputation consisting of God, Christ, the supra-local church, and the local Christian community. He reaffirms his reliability and the reliability of his team members so that their ascriptions of honor and their censure will carry the necessary weight to guide the community. He seeks to activate this court of reputation by directing the believers to honor one another according to the standards of honor set by the gospel, and to use shaming where necessary to keep the wayward sisters and brothers true to the norms of the group. Finally, he sets them on the path to honor before God's court through mutual service and edification, directing them to distance themselves from the way the outside world (and their primary socialization) measures honor.

NOTES: CHAPTER 5

[1] I have attempted to demonstrate the literary and rhetorical unity of 2 Corinthians 1–9, especially attacking the problem of 2 Corinthians 1–7, in a series of articles: "Measuring Penultimate Against Ultimate Reality: An Investigation of the Integrity and Argumentation of 2 Corinthians," *JSNT* 52 (1993) 41–70; "Recasting the Moment of Decision: 2 Corinthians 6:14–7:1 in Its Literary Context," *AUSS* 31 (1993) 3–16; "Meeting the Exigency of a Complex Rhetorical Situation: Paul's Strategy in 2 Corinthians 1 through 7," *AUSS* 34 (1996) 5–22. The unity of 2 Corinthians 8 and 9 has been strongly supported by Stanley K. Stowers, "*Peri Men Gar* and the Integrity of 2 Cor. 8 and 9," *NovT* 32 (1990) 340–349. Excellent reviews of the strengths and weaknesses of the various arguments for partition and unity can be found in Margaret E. Thrall, *The Second Epistle to the Corinthians*. ICC (Edinburgh: T & T Clark, 1994) 3–49; Ralph P. Martin, *2 Corinthians*. WBC (Waco, Tex.: Word Books, 1986) xxxviii–lii; Paul Barnett, *The Second Epistle to the Corinthians*. NICNT (Grand Rapids: Eerdmans, 1997) 15–25.

[2] See especially Gerd Theissen, *The Social Setting of Pauline Christianity: Essays on Corinth* (Philadelphia: Fortress, 1982); Wayne A. Meeks, *The First Urban Christians* (New Haven: Yale University Press, 1983).

[3] Ben Witherington III, *Conflict and Community in Corinth: A Socio-Rhetorical Commentary on 1 and 2 Corinthians* (Grand Rapids: Eerdmans, 1995) 74, 84–87, 115; Stephen M. Pogoloff, *Logos and Sophia: The Rhetorical Situation of 1 Corinthians* (Atlanta: Scholars, 1992) 237–271. According to Barnett (*Corinthians* 27) factionalism continues to be a problem even in 2 Corinthians.

[4] Pogoloff, *Logos and Sophia* 175; see Seneca the Elder, *Controversies* 10.15 and *passim*.

[5] Paul's refusal to accept patronage, and hence enhance the honor of any of the elites within the congregation, was also a stumbling block in their relationship (cf. Witherington, *Conflict* 341).

⁶ Theissen, *Social Setting of Pauline Christianity* 145–174.

⁷ Witherington, *Conflict* 260.

⁸ It is unlikely that this mission should be identified with the "Judaizing" movement Paul encountered and combated in Galatia (cf. Victor P. Furnish, *II Corinthians*. AB 32A [Garden City, N.Y.: Doubleday, 1984] 50–54). Furnish rightly contends that despite certain similarities between Galatians and 2 Corinthians in terms of labeling the opponents the complete lack of the sort of argumentation one finds in Galatians—especially the lack of any reference to circumcision or other specific markers of "Judaizing"—renders it highly unlikely that Paul understands the particular threat of these rivals to be a "Judaizing" threat. The threat to the gospel is equal, but different. A recent attempt to revive the Judaizing theory can be found in Barnett, *Corinthians* 34–36. Barnett argues that the term "minister of righteousness" in 11:15 "when read with the contrast between the 'ministries' of the 'old covenant' (i.e., of Moses) and the 'new covenant' (i.e., of Christ/righteousness and the Spirit), suggests that their purpose in coming to Corinth was to 'minister' the 'righteousness' associated with Moses and the law . . . as opposed to the 'righteousness' issuing in 'reconciliation with God' based on Christ's death (3:9; 5:21), which was the ministry of Paul." The problem, of course, is that even in the contrast he addresses in ch. 3 "righteousness" is only lined up with the gospel: the old covenant is merely a ministry of death and condemnation. We will see that 2 Cor 3:7-18 serves a different goal for Paul than combating alleged Judaizers.

⁹ Witherington, *Conflict* 348.

¹⁰ Cf. 1 Cor 1:29, 31; 3:21; 4:7; 5:6; 9:15, 16; 13:3; 15:31; 2 Cor 1:12, 14; 5:12; 7:4, 14; 8:24; 9:2, 3; 10:8, 13, 15, 16, 17; 11:10, 12, 16, 17, 18, 30; 12:1, 5, 6, 9.

¹¹ So, rightly, Witherington, *Conflict* 74.

¹² On an individual's primary and secondary socialization see Peter L. Berger and Thomas Luckman, *The Social Construction of Reality* (New York: Doubleday, 1966) 129–147.

¹³ Cf. also 2 Cor 2:15-16, which draws the distinction between those who respond positively to the message housed in the messengers of the gospel (Paul and his team) and those who reject it, also using the terms "those who are being saved" and "those who are perishing."

¹⁴ Seneca, *Const.* 11.2; cf. also 13.2, 5; 16.3; Epictetus, *Diss.* 1.29.50-54; 4.5.22; Dio, *Or.* 77/78.21, 25. These are discussed in David A. deSilva, *Despising Shame.* SBL.DS 152 (Atlanta: Scholars, 1995) 81–99.

¹⁵ As Witherington (*Conflict* 155) perceptively comments: "Paul is not in the business of simply baptizing the cultural values of Roman society. To the contrary, he undermines many of the most cherished values and redefines what real status amounts to, namely being in Christ or being sons and daughters of God."

¹⁶ The Greek word frequently translated as "glory" *(doxa)* has a range of meanings in large part consonant with considerations of honor. It may mean "opinion" or "reputation," or be used as a synonym for the word "honor" *(timē)*, or may indicate the visual display that replicates the honor of the individual, such as the trappings of a human king (cf. LXX Esth 15:1-6).

¹⁷ Again Witherington *(Conflict* 97) displays a special sensitivity to considerations of honor in the Corinthian church: "The great danger for the gifted convert is to use one's gifts as a tool for self-aggrandizement and public display. This was an especially great danger in Roman Corinth, where public display, boasting, and the like were considered a necessary and indeed good part of normal life, especially if one wanted to succeed in life. Humility was seen in Greco-Roman culture not as a great virtue but as acting in a servile manner. But Paul scandalously will urge his converts to follow his and Christ's examples of self-sacrificial behavior, going against the whole directional flow and social value system that was well established in Corinth."

¹⁸ Victor P. Furnish, *II Corinthians* 53–54, on Peter Marshall, *Enmity at Corinth: Social Conventions in Paul's Relations with the Corinthians* (Tübingen: J.C.B. Mohr, 1987) 331–336, 525–526, 618.

¹⁹ This is not to say that Paul did not give a thought to rhetoric (vs. J.A.D. Weima, "What has Aristotle to do with Paul," *Calvin Theological Journal* 32 [1997] 458–468, at 466). Even this disclaimer of refusing to use the flashiness of presentation to awe an audience and focusing instead on the content of the message is not without parallel in the writings of the great orator Dio Chrysostom *(Or.* 32.39): "My purpose is . . . neither to elate you nor to range myself beside those who habitually sing such strains, whether orators or poets. For they are clever persons, mighty sophists, wonder-workers; but I am quite ordinary and prosaic in my utterance, though not ordinary in my theme. For though the words I speak are not great in themselves, they treat of topics of the greatest possible importance."

²⁰ Barnett, *Corinthians* 38.

²¹ These "hardship catalogs" *(Peristasenkataloge)* are a literary form shared by Paul and the Stoics. Furnish *(II Corinthians* 281) cites the following examples: the Stoic "is not impeded when confined, and under no compulsion when flung down a precipice, and not in torture when on the rack, and not injured when mutilated, and is invincible when thrown in wrestling, and is not blockaded under siege, and is uncaptured while his enemies are selling him into slavery" (Plutarch, "The Stoics Talk More Paradoxically than the Poets," *Mor.* 1057E); the Stoic is "sick and [yet] happy, in danger and happy, dying and happy, condemned to exile and happy, in disrepute and happy" (Epictetus, *Diss.* 2.19.24). One striking difference between Paul's usage and that of the Stoic authors is that Paul appears to be describing his own experiences and not the theoretical imperviousness of the true philosopher to external circum-

stances. Further, Paul uses these catalogs to demonstrate not his imperviousness to injury or anxiety but his sincerity and dedication to the commission God has given him and the power of God at work in delivering him from such dangers (cf. Furnish, *II Corinthians* 281–282).

[22] On the relationship of Paul's endurance to topics of "courage" see J. T. Fitzgerald, *Cracks in an Earthen Vessel* (Atlanta: Scholars, 1988) 87–90.

[23] Cf. Furnish, *II Corinthians* 48: "The rhetorical device of *comparison*, already present in 10:12-16, is further evident in 11:5-6, 21b-23a; 12:11b, and is implicit throughout 11:23b–12:10. The catalog of hardships in 11:23b-29 and the escape narrative in 11:32-33 have formal parallels in the ancient literature of *self-display*. *Irony* is extensively employed, as in 11:19-21a, but especially when the apostle insists that he will boast only of his weaknesses (11:30; 12:5, 9b-10). And there is also an element of *parody* involved in all of this." Witherington (*Conflict* 432) also notes that Paul "in fact *parodies*" the "ancient conventions involving matters of honor and shame, boasting and self-promotion."

[24] "As agent of God, Paul boasts that he has been proven a loyal and steadfast agent, in fact, more loyal and more honorable because of his faithful service through 'far greater labors, far more imprisonments, with countless beatings, and often near death' (v. 23)." Bruce J. Malina and Jerome H. Neyrey, *Portraits of Paul: An Archaeology of Ancient Personality* (Louisville: Westminster/John Knox, 1996) 57–58.

6

Honor Discourse in the Epistle to the Hebrews

The epistle (or perhaps better, sermon) "to the Hebrews" only reluctantly yields information about the circumstances that have arisen in the congregation and that arouse the author's concern. Scholars have therefore met with difficulty in determining precisely what challenges the congregation faced and what the author hoped to effect by writing this letter. Many commentators have sought some pressing crisis behind the writing of Hebrews, as if some new, bloody persecution or an imminent reversion to Judaism occasioned the letter. As with the Thessalonian correspondence, attention to honor discourse can again shed new light on the situation of the addressees and the rhetorical strategy of the author.[1]

We will approach honor discourse in Hebrews first in a more rhetorical vein. Two features of Hebrews, namely its repeated warnings (2:1-4; 3:7–4:13; 6:4-8; 10:26-31; 12:25) and extended series of examples (10:32–12:3), especially command attention. The warnings are all predicated on the danger of dishonoring the community's divine patron (God) or broker (Christ) through neglect of the gifts or disloyalty to the giver. These sections are particularly rich in the vocabulary of honor and dishonor, as well as the emotions frequently related to honor and dishonor (see the discussion in Chapter One concerning the relationship of fear and anger to honor, with examples drawn from Heb 10:26-31). The series of examples, we recall from the discussion of epideictic rhetoric in Chapter One, would be expected to appeal to the hearers' desire for a similar praiseworthy remembrance and hence rouse them to emulation. What course of action is the author positing as honorable, and what course leads to dishonor? As we unravel the use of honor discourse in what are essentially appeals to *pathos* we will get a clearer picture of the challenge the community is being called to overcome and how the author's sermon is rhetorically crafted to meet this challenge.

Finally, we will return to a number of questions that have become familiar especially from our investigations of Matthew and the Thessalonian letters. How does the author enable the believers to reinterpret their experience of rejection and dishonor at the hands of the dominant culture? How does the author affirm the believers in the honor they enjoy through their Christian commitment, thereby encouraging continued participation in the life of the group? How does the author seek to motivate support within the alternate court of reputation, the Church, for the continued commitment of individual members? Such questions again take us to the text not as a repository of theology alone but as a resource for maintaining the distinctive *ethos* of the Christian culture within a non-supportive society.

THE AUDIENCE'S PAST EXPERIENCE AND PRESENT CHALLENGE

The anonymous author gives very little information about the audience's past experience. The community was formed as a result of the proclamation of the witnesses of Jesus: the author writes that the message of salvation "was declared at first through the Lord, and it was attested to us by those who heard him, while God added his testimony by signs and wonders and various miracles, and by gifts of the Holy Spirit, distributed according to his will" (2:3-4 NRSV). This places the author outside the circle of apostles and paints a picture very much like the early period of the church in Galatia or Corinth, where also an awareness of the power of God's Spirit accompanied the reception of the message. The converts apparently enjoyed a detailed period of instruction, including the basic points of "repentance from dead works and faith toward God, instruction about baptisms, laying on of hands, resurrection of the dead, and eternal judgment" (6:2-3 NRSV). All of this points more toward a Gentile or mixed audience than a strictly Jewish audience, as the latter would have been familiar with these subjects.

Those who committed themselves to Christianity inherited Judaism's restrictions on participation in the Greco-Roman world. Because of their exclusive devotion to the One God and the accompanying refusal to acknowledge any other deity most Christians avoided any setting in which they would be exposed to idolatrous ceremonies. Since some form of religious worship formed a part of almost every political, business, and social enterprise in the Greco-Roman world[2] Christians adopted a lifestyle that in the eyes of their pagan neighbors would have been considered antisocial and even subversive.[3] Loyalty to the gods, expressed in pious attendance at sacrifices and the like, was viewed as a symbol for loyalty to the state, authorities, friends, and family. Because they abstained from the former, Christians (like Jews) were regarded with suspicion as potential violators of the laws and as subversive elements within the empire. The Christians were subjected to prejudice, rumor, insult, and slander, and were even made the targets of pogroms and local legal actions. It was thus both dishonoring and dangerous to be associated with the name of "Christian."

At some point in this earlier time the believers were indeed the victims of society's social control techniques exercised to bring them back in line with its values. Formerly good citizens were now pulling back from participation in the traditional religion and were withdrawing from social, civic, and business duties where those traditional gods were celebrated, all in favor of their attachment to this foreign sect of a crucified redeemer. The society, therefore, acted to deter any further defections to this group and to bring the believers to their senses, if possible. The one experience of the community most fully described by the author concerns the loss of status and dignity by these Christians as a result of their confession. This passage is all the more significant given the author's reticence in providing details about the community's history:

> But remember the former days in which, having been enlightened, you endured a hard contest with sufferings, in part being publicly exposed to reproaches and afflictions, in part having become partners of those being thus treated. For you both showed sympathy to the imprisoned and accepted the seizure of your property with joy, knowing that you possessed better and lasting possessions (10:32-34).

While we do not know how long ago the events of the "former days" transpired, we can say that the author perceives that the community must recover the same dedication and endurance that they displayed then but lack now. This description, moreover, shows that what was chiefly at stake was the honor of the Christian community (both collective and individual).

The experience is described in terms of a public show: some portion of the Christian community was subjected to being reviled and held up to ridicule and shame.[4] The term used to describe it evokes the image of the theater (arena), where games, contests, and public punishments occurred. Through the public imposition of disgrace the society sought to dissuade the afflicted from continuing in, and others from joining the Christian counterculture. The Christians were subjected to "reproach" and "affliction" *(touto men oneidismois te kai thlipsesin)*. The first term suggests verbal assaults on honor and character, an experience shared by many early Christian communities.[5] Shaming and reviling were the society's way of neutralizing the threat Christians posed to its view of the world and constellation of values and allegiances as well as attempting to retrieve the deviants. John Chrysostom—much closer to the culture of Hebrews than the modern reader—notes in his comment on this verse the power of such disapproval and grants of dishonor to affect judgment: "Reproach is a great thing, and calculated to pervert the soul, and to darken the judgment. . . . Since the human race is exceeding vainglorious, therefore it is easily overcome by this" (*NPNF*[1] 14:461; Migne, *PG* 63.149). The society added physical punishment to the verbal "correction," which meant not only the inflicting of physical pain but reinforcing the degradation of the person. We recall from Chapter One that a person's honor and the treatment of that person's body are closely connected, to which Philo of Alexandria bears witness when he speaks of the physical punishment suffered by the Jews in a riot there as a "disgrace" or "insult" *(hybris)*.

The believers, however, ably resisted these attempts to pull them away from the minority group. Far from being concerned for the opinion of outsiders, the Christians who had escaped being singled out for this public punishment went so far as to demonstrate their solidarity with those who were subjected to public humiliation, thus voluntarily becoming "partners with those thus treated," partners with the disgraced. This manifested itself in the care given by the community to those members who were imprisoned and who were thus in great need of both moral affirmation and physical relief from their free sisters and brothers. Rather than be concerned for what the unbelieving society would think of those who identified with such criminal deviants, the believers consistently supported and maintained their bonds with their sisters and brothers who were in prison or suffering society's other "correctional" procedures.[6]

A final component of the addressees' experience alluded to by our author is the confiscation of the believers' property. The Greek term used refers most often to plundering, the looting to which abandoned properties often fell victim.[7] Even an officially sanctioned act, however, could be regarded as "plundering" by those suffering the loss.[8] It is also difficult to discern from this passing reference what sort of property was taken. A court or local official might have ordered the seizure of land and house, or simply the imposition of a fine; unofficial plundering (while the believers were involved in trials or imprisonments) would involve the loss of movable property, but might nevertheless represent a substantial loss of wealth. "Plundering" could also indicate driving people from their homes in the context of a riot or pogrom.[9]

Whether the loss of property was occasioned by official or unofficial seizure the loss of material wealth translates into a loss of honor and status. When one lost material goods one also lost the raw materials for building prestige. Such loss would further provoke contempt from others if the victim had brought the loss on himself or herself.[10] This would have been the case for the Christians in Heb 10:32-34: through their own neglect of their obligations to society, state, and gods they had justly earned their misfortune. This loss of property could also have put the believers in an uncomfortable economic position. Further, as part of a disgraced "subversive" culture they could not expect to regain the security of wealth through partnerships with non-Christian partners or benefactors.

In summary, the former experience of the community to which the author calls attention was one of humiliation, rejection, and marginalization. The Christians lost their place and standing in the society, stripped of their reputation for being reliable citizens because of their commitment to an alternate system of values, religious practices, and social relationships. While the society intended this experience to draw the deviants back into line with the dominant culture, the believers remained steadfast in their loyalty toward God and the group, not allowing society's means of social control to deflect them from their faith.

Between that former time and the time of the author's writing, however, the situation appears to have changed. Those who were formerly bold and energetic in Christian witness and solidarity have become "sluggish" (6:12). Some are already in the habit of neglecting the group's meetings (10:25). Some believers are in danger of "drifting away" (2:1), neglecting "so great a salvation" (2:3), having "unbelieving hearts" (3:12), "falling through such disobedience" as the wilderness generation's (4:11), wavering in the "confession of our hope" (10:23), being numbered among "those who have trampled underfoot the Son of God, treated as profane the blood of the covenant by which they were consecrated, and insulted the Spirit of favor" (10:29), "growing weary and losing heart" (12:3), and "selling [one's] birthright" for short-lived temporal benefits (12:16). The author gives them the titles belonging to the heirs of the promise, but they can only keep them if they "hold firm the boldness and claim to honor that belong to hope" (3:6), hold their "first confidence firm to the end" (3:14 NRSV), and find the necessary "endurance" (10:36).

What danger does the community face, that they are wavering in their commitment and perhaps on the verge of turning back from following Jesus? What is pushing some believers to renounce their devotion to God and their hope for God's promises? When trying to determine what the believers addressed by Hebrews must *endure* in order to attain the goal one is struck by the lack of mention of new, dramatic developments or any strong foreshadowings of increasing hostility (such as one finds in the Revelation of John, for example). Rather it appears that the danger of falling away stems from the lingering effects of the believers' loss of status and esteem in their neighbors' eyes and their inability to regain a place in society or approval from the outside world by any means that would allow them to remain rigidly faithful to Jesus and the One God. The believers have experienced the loss of property and status in the host society without yet receiving the promised rewards, and so are losing hope in the promise that God would overturn their disgrace.

As time passes without improvement, believers begin to feel the inward pressure for their society's affirmation and approval. The fervor and certainty of their earlier life in Christ has cooled with their prolonged exposure to the pagan witnesses of their degradation, who no doubt continued to disparage the believers and regard them as subversive and shameful. They have begun to be concerned for their reputation before society. Though they were able to resist it at the outset, the machinery of social control is in the long run wearing down their resistance. While they could accept their loss in the fervor of religious solidarity, living with that loss has proven difficult. Some of the addressees, desirous of returning to a lifestyle that receives society's approval, feeling too strongly the loss of their honor and place in the dominant culture, are motivated to renounce their connections with Jesus and the Christian community (10:25; 2:3; 3:12; 6:4-6; 10:29). In the eyes of society, and perhaps increasingly in the eyes of some believers, renouncing the "confession" that had first alienated them from the dominant culture might be accepted as a step toward "recovery."

THE AUTHOR'S RHETORICAL STRATEGY

The author meets this challenge with a well-orchestrated strategy of appeals to honor. First the author presents a series of alternating expositions and exhortations (and admonitions) setting forth the incomparable honor of Jesus and the supremacy of his mediation of divine favor. This brings the hearers to the intersection of honor and patronage scripts: those who honor their mediator will enjoy God's patronage and look forward to the benefactions God has promised to give those who remain faithful clients to the end, including a share in Christ's honor; those who bring dishonor upon Jesus through distrust and disloyalty, preferring the approval of the outside world, show contempt for the gifts of God gained at such cost to Jesus himself, and so, for the sake of temporary gain, will be disgraced and punished before the court of God, whose verdict is eternal.

Second, the author holds up as praiseworthy and urges the believers to imitate "those who are inheriting the promises through faith and patience" (6:12; cf. 10:32–12:3). The composite portrait of these noble figures depicts those who have willingly left behind their status and esteem in the unbelieving society, choosing disgrace and downward mobility in the eyes of the world, in order to move toward the honor and inheritance promised by God. Even in the climactic example of Jesus (12:1-3) the emphasis falls on disregarding society's evaluation of one's behavior, ideals, and values—"despising shame" (12:2)—in order not to be distracted from attaining the prize God sets forward. Looking to the approval and esteem to be enjoyed before God, the community of the redeemed, and the host of witnesses throughout the ages enables one to set aside as valueless the negative opinion of outsiders. Indeed, the endurance of these painful experiences of loss and scorn becomes a noble contest in which the believers compete (10:32; 12:1-4), and a sort of parental discipline by which God fits the believer for holiness—hence a proof of the believers' having been adopted as God's daughters and sons (12:5-13).

Third, the author seeks to stimulate the believers to encourage one another to endure in faith, to hold on to their hope, to continue to practice acts of love and service toward fellow believers. Each is to look after his or her brothers and sisters, to make sure that no one is falling away from the group's values, succumbing to society's pressures to return to its values and serve its ideals. In effect, the author encourages them to intensify their efforts to counteract the negative messages the unbelieving society sends the Christians in so many ways, from insults and jibes to physical abuse and confiscation of goods. They are to reassure each other of their worth in God's eyes and in the eyes of the community, to reinforce the values learned from Jesus, to call each other to account where sensitivity to the world's opinion is leading individuals away, jeopardizing their attaining the reward. Since society will not affirm their worth, as they do not play society's game, the believers are to work especially hard affirming one another and supporting one another. We will look at each of these aspects of the author's strategy in turn.

A. The Honor Due the Divine Patron and the Preservation of One's Own Honor

The first-century person was not only concerned with his or her own honor and how to preserve or augment it, but also with the honor due to another and the consequences of failure in that regard.[11] Discussion of Jesus' honor, particularly in conjunction with discussion of how Jesus has used his position to benefit the believers, would be understood to place a claim upon the hearers. Appeals to *pathos* (especially "fear" and "confidence") figure prominently in the author's demonstration of the honor due to God and the danger facing the one who chooses to dishonor Christ.

The author develops the honor of Jesus by discussing his divine Sonship, his exaltation to the high priesthood of the "better" sanctuary, and his sitting at the "right hand of God." All these attributes are grounded in the author's Christ-centered reading of Psalms 2 and 110. That Jesus is declared to be God's Son (1:5; cf. 4:14; 6:6; 10:29) demonstrates that his honor is embedded within and protected by the honor of God. Recalling our discussion of ascribed honor we remember that in the ancient world the starting place for one's own honor is the honor of one's parents and one's ancestors. Dio, for example, claims respect purely on account of his illustrious father and grandfather (*Or.* 46.3-4); the Jewish sage Ben Sira claims that "a person's honor springs from the father's honor, and a mother in dishonor is a cause of reproach to her children" (3:11). The superior status of Jesus as "Son" is then developed through comparison with the angels (1:5-14) and Moses, the "servant in God's house" (3:1-6). Jesus is the "reflection" or "effulgence of God's glory" *(apaugasma tēs doxēs)*, that is, Jesus shines with the honor and status with which God has invested him. The comparison with Moses, like that with the angels and the Levitical priesthood, does not imply a polemical purpose: rather the author builds up the honor of Jesus through the technique of *synkrisis*, "comparison," an essential part of ancient encomia (cf. Aristotle, *Rhet.* 1.9.38-39). The author relies on a high regard for Moses (cf. Sir 45:1-3) as the foundation for his claims about Jesus' superior dignity.

The author also demonstrates Jesus' honor when he speaks of Jesus' placement in the court of God as being "seated at the right hand of the majesty on high" (1:3; 8:1; 10:12; 12:2; Ps 110:1). We recall again how in the ancient world relative dignity was symbolized in visible and physical ways such as seating order at a feast (cf. Luke 14:7-11) or at a court (cf. Esth 1:14; 3:1), in physical gestures and salutations (e.g., bowing; placement at the feet of another), and in rituals or symbols concerning some part of the body (e.g., crowning or anointing). The author of Hebrews brings together all three physical representations of honor to enhance Jesus' honor: his head is crowned and anointed by God (1:9; 2:7-9); he is seated "at the right hand" of God whence he awaits the subjection of his enemies and all things (1:13; 2:8). The angels are called to offer the *proskynēsis* (1:6) as an acknowledgment of Jesus' greater honor.

God's appointment of Jesus to the high priesthood is also explicitly named as a feature of Jesus' ascribed honor (5:4-5; cf. the appearance of the title in 2:17; 3:1; 4:14; 6:20). The office of high priest carried with it great esteem. Josephus (*Bell.* 4.164), for example, calls the title of "high priest" the "most honored of revered names," and speaks of the office as "the highest dignity" (*Bell.* 4.149). Philo of Alexandria shares this high regard for the office (cf. *Vit. Mos.* 2.142), even claiming that "the law invests the priests with the dignity and honour that belongs to kings" (*Spec. leg.* 1.142). The special dignity of the high priest derives from his role as mediator of God's good will and benefits: the high priest, like any broker of the favor of another patron, is to be honored in accordance with the value of the gifts he procures on behalf of the people.

The author emphasizes Jesus' honor to make two related points: the value of having such an exalted figure as one's personal patron is incomparable; the danger of failing to honor such a patron with the proper loyalty and obedience is also incomparable. The author appeals to the virtue of justice, which insists that the believers return the proper honor to the One who occupies a place of supreme status in the Jewish-Christian cosmos; second, the author appeals to the obligation of gratitude, since Jesus has made use of his exalted position for the benefit of his clients, securing God's favor and benefaction *(charis)* as their mediator. Within the argument of Hebrews one either honors and obeys God at the risk of dishonoring and provoking the world or one honors and conforms to society at the risk of dishonoring and provoking God. Stated another way, one either seeks to gain security through seeking friendship with the representatives of the unbelieving society or one attaches oneself to God and enjoys the benefits gained through Christ.

Given the prevalence of the system of patronage in the Mediterranean world it is fitting that the author of Hebrews should present Jesus as the patron of the Christian community. Elsewhere in the Greco-Roman world relationships with the divine are imagined in terms of patronage, so that we find talk of "patron deities" by individuals and groups (e.g., guilds or cities). It was, indeed, most desired that human beings find a divine patron who could afford the protection, security, and eternal benefactions human patrons could never provide. The slave-turned-philosopher, Epictetus, speaks of the search for the best patron under whose aegis to travel through life—one who could provide security against all assaults and in whom one could rely utterly not only for today but also for tomorrow. His search leads finally and only to God: "Thus [the searcher] reflects and comes to the thought that, if he attach himself to God, he will pass through the world in safety" (*Diss.* 4.1.91-98). When the author of Hebrews speaks, therefore, about Jesus' exalted status and successful mediation, he is appealing to the promise of great benefaction and advantage for those who make themselves clients of the Son.

The author's language emphasizes the patronal role of Jesus: he "helps *(epilambanetai)* the offspring of Abraham" (2:16)[12] and comes "to assist *(boēthēsai)* those who are tempted" (2:18). He is thus the one to whom Christians are to look to supply what is wanting in their own resources, which places him in the role of the patron, who provided assistance in many forms to clients. Christians, indeed, have been brought into God's household (3:6) through their clientage to the Son, thus under God's protection and provision.

The author speaks of Christ's death in terms of the numerous benefits this selfless act brings to those committed to Jesus. Because of God's grace Jesus' death became a tasting of death on behalf of all (2:9); his death also freed those who "were all their lives subject to slavery because of their fear of death" (2:14-15). The greatest benefit of Christ's death for our author derives from Jesus' appointment as "high priest in the order of Melchizedek," through which "he became the source of eternal deliverance for all who obey him" (5:9). In this capacity Jesus affords access to God. He is the broker, the mediator (*mesitēs*, 8:6; 9:15; 12:24) who secures favor from God on behalf of those who have committed themselves to Jesus as client dependents.

The emphasis placed by the author of Hebrews on Jesus' "Sonship" (cf. 1:1-6) has itself important implications for Jesus' efficacy as a mediator of God's beneficence. In the ancient world the close relatives of the emperor, especially his sons, were sought after as mediators of the emperor's favor; their close, familial relationship to the patron of the empire gave great hope of success.[13] Thus when the author of Hebrews presents Jesus as "Son" in 1:2 and constructs a comparison of Jesus with the angels in 1:4-14 the aim appears to be to emphasize the greater proximity of Jesus to God as mediator of divine favor. The angels, as God's servants, are familiar to the first-century Judeans and Christians as mediator figures, but they are strictly a second order of brokers when compared to the Son. Moses, as a valued servant in the household of God, would provide a certain level of access to the Patron of the house, but this pales in comparison to the hope given to those who have the Son in God's house as their advocate (3:1-6).

The heart of the letter (7:1–10:18) is devoted to a lengthy argument that stresses that the benefit of such access to God cannot be attained through the mediation (brokerage) of the Levitical priesthood. As with the earlier comparisons with Moses and the angels, this comparison continues to enhance Jesus' honor, but it is also calculated to heighten the value of Jesus' mediation of divine favor for the community. The choice of the Levitical priests as the point of comparison continues the author's interest in contrasting Jesus' efficacy as mediator with established figures in the history of revelation. Within the scriptural tradition and the practice of Second Temple Judaism the Levitical priesthood figures prominently in its claim to broker access to God. The author therefore increases the value of Christ's mediation by showing the limitations and ineffectiveness of the only alternative sanctioned by scriptural tradition. The "priestly" or "religious" tone of this central section of Hebrews should not obscure the fact that divine-human relationships are still being conceptualized in terms of patron-client relations. There was a widespread tendency to use existing social and political structures to give shape to beliefs about the divine and how one might relate to the divine and, as the larger argument of Hebrews makes clear, what is at stake is access to God's favor and benefits.

The author criticizes the Levitical priesthood because of the severe limitations it placed on access to God. This was demonstrated spatially in the layout of the tabernacle: the people remained in the outer courts, the priests could go only as far as the holy place, and the high priest alone enjoyed face-to-face access to the divine patron (9:1-3, 6-7). This access, however, was further limited temporally: on only one day out of the liturgical year could the high priest enter the Holy of Holies to engage in this face-to-face audience (9:7). The Levitical priesthood was unable to broaden access to God for, our author argues, it could not take away the sins that polluted the conscience and prevented the people from standing before the holy God with confidence for benefaction (9:9; 10:1-4). The offering for sin on Yom Kippur, far from removing the obstacle that stands in the way of forming a patron-client relationship with God, calls attention to the obstacle, providing only a reminder *(anamnēsis)* of sins (10:3).

The failure of the Levitical priests sharpens the perception of Christ's success and of the uniqueness of the benefit made available by him to those committing themselves to him. Before Christ's ministry one only had recourse to the ineffective brokers established by the Law; now after his death there is the possibility of unrestricted access to God following the perfection of the worshipers who draw near through Christ. The "second order resource" of direct access to God would have been especially valued in a patronal culture where face-to-face contact with the patron was of special importance, giving one a greater hope of making a successful suit. Jesus has made the necessary purification for sins. Through the "sacrifice of himself" Jesus has decisively "put away sin" (9:26) and "established eternal redemption" (9:12; cf. also 1:3 and 2:17). Jesus' sacrifice, offered once for all (10:12), provides the cleansing of the conscience the worshipers required, such that they might have confidence before God and assurance of divine favor.

Having passed into the true sanctuary of heaven, Jesus does not leave his clients waiting outside without direct access to God. Rather, Jesus' passing into the heavenly sanctuary opens up the way for believers to know and approach God as benefactor and patron. Jesus has entered "as a forerunner for us" (6:20): the Christian pilgrimage ends as we enter the rest of the city of God, the heavenly homeland (11:14; 13:14). Such final access, however, follows upon the access that can be enjoyed now in this life:

> Having therefore a great high priest who has crossed through the heavens, Jesus the Son of God, let us hold on to our confession. We do not have a high priest who is unable to sympathize with our weaknesses, but

one who has been tempted in every way just as we are—without sin. Then let us approach the throne of favor with bold openness, in order that we may receive mercy and find favor for timely help (4:14-16; cf. 10:19-22).

Jesus' gift of access to God (4:14-16) affords the community access to resources for endurance in faith so that they may receive the benefactions promised for the future, to be awarded before God's court at the end of the age. The believers may draw near to God and expect to "receive mercy and find favor"—that is, the disposition of God to give assistance ("timely help," 4:16). This would be expected to engender confidence in the believers, giving them strength and hope for resisting hostility from outside.

Such a gift of confident access to God as one's personal patron in the here and now and the promise of the future gift of honor and citizenship in the city of God demand a response of gratitude in the fullest sense (12:28). This entails honoring the giver *and* witnessing to the gift in public testimony to the generosity and virtue of the benefactor:

> The greater the favour, the more earnestly must we express ourselves, resorting to such compliments as: . . . "I shall never be able to repay you my gratitude, but, at any rate, I shall not cease from declaring everywhere that I am unable to repay it" (Seneca, *Ben.* 2.24.2).

> Let us show how grateful we are for the blessing that has come to us by pouring forth our feelings, and let us bear witness to them, not merely in the hearing of the giver, but everywhere (Seneca, *Ben.* 2.22.1).

This is an incentive to Christian witness—evangelism—even in the face of a hostile and unsympathetic society. "Confession with the lips" is a mandate, and in the context of a patronal society we see this more clearly not as a confession of belief within the safe walls of the church, but a confession of the debt one owes God "everywhere," in the public space of everyday life. The response of gratitude also entails loyalty ("faith" [*pistis*]) and obedience. Nothing must be deemed more valuable than the relationship with the patron—not one's reputation, one's civic standing, even one's life. When the patron calls for some return of the favor nothing must impede the performance of it.

The severity of the author's warnings stems from his perception that at least some believers are in danger of making an improper response, indeed of violating the sacred bond of the patron-client relationship. They are in danger of outraging the Son of God, of relinquishing their enjoyment of present benefits (e.g., access to God) and hope of future benefits (e.g., entering the promised rest) in favor of provoking God's anger, bringing upon their own heads God's satisfaction for the affronts to the divine honor. They are in danger of encountering God as judge and avenger, of receiving punishment, and hence disgrace, before God's court at God's coming, when every enemy will be subjected to Christ. Turning away from the discursive sections that develop the comparison of Jesus with other mediator figures in the Jewish tradition we look now to the hortatory sections in which the author expatiates on the ill consequences that will attend the violation of the patron-client bond through distrust and valuing too little the divine *beneficia*, and urges them through repeated warnings to consider the honor due their benefactor.

In 3:7–4:13 the author develops the negative example of the wilderness generation (the people who went out from Egypt with Moses) in order to show the danger of wavering in one's trust toward one's patron. The psalm quoted by the author refers, in the Hebrew, to the complaints of the wilderness generation over the lack of water at Massah and Meribah (Exod 17:1-7 and Num 20:2-13): in the Greek version he uses, however, these place names (Massah and Meribah) are translated as "provocation" and "testing." This change focuses the psalm quotation completely on Numbers 14, where the people finally refuse to take possession of the promised land because they fear the inhabitants of that land. Despite God's continued provision from the deliverance from Egypt to the threshold of Canaan the Israelites refused to display "faith."

In common Greek usage the *pistis* word-group involves trust or reliability. *Pistis* refers both to the responsibility accepted by another to discharge some duty or provide some service and the affirmation of the reliability of that other by the person who awaits the fulfillment of the obligation.[14] *Pistos* describes the person who may be relied upon to carry out the obligation, who is "trustworthy." *Apistia*, "distrust," may either signify the untrustworthiness of a base person or the feeling that ascribed unreliability to another such that one neither entrusts that other with something nor trusts that other to fulfill an obligation.[15]

God had undertaken an obligation to bring the people into the land God promised to give them, and had provided many proofs of reliability ("they saw my works," Heb 3:9). In light of the spies' report concerning the might of the native inhabitants of the land, however, they wavered in their trust, that is, doubted whether or not God would be able to fulfill God's obligation (Num 13:31–14:4). In the Numbers story they ascribe to their patron the base motive of treachery—bringing them to this place to die (Num 14:3)—and abandon the prospect of the promise's being fulfilled by setting in motion a plan to return to Egypt (Num 14:4), thus negating all the benefits God had already given them. They completely negate the validity of God's promise by complaining, "our little ones will become booty" (Num 14:3, 31 NRSV). Such distrust is interpreted by God as a test of God's reliability and ability to provide, which is nothing less than a challenge to the benefactor, all the more inappropriate given the number of tests God had allowed in order to stimulate trust.

Because distrust derives from a low estimation of the honor and reliability of the person one distrusts, the wilderness generation's response of distrust displays their low opinion of God. Distrust, in short, is an insult, a provocation of the would-be patron. Insofar as they withdrew their trust from their benefactor they declared God to be unreliable and unable to fulfill the obligation God had assumed in their behalf; they declare God to be base, and so repay their proven benefactor with flagrant contempt and disobedience, thereby rejecting the right and authority of the patron to command obedience (an expected return for receiving benefits).

God's response is one of "wrath" or "anger" ("therefore I was angered with that generation," Heb 3:10) toward those who have been disobedient, who have trampled the promise and faltered in their trust. Aristotle has informed us that anger is the emotion felt by a benefactor who was not treated with the appropriate honor (*Rhet.* 2.2.1-8). This well describes the exchange in Numbers 14 to which the author of Hebrews refers. God's every act in the narrative has been to bring the people from a wretched into an enviable state, leading them from slavery to a land for their own possession. Those whom he desired to benefit, however, returned insult for favor, slighting God through their distrust of God's good will and ability. The result of God's wrath is the people's irrevocable loss of access to the promised benefit, for in this anger God swears the oath that excludes the rebellious generation from the promised land (3:11): "I swore in my anger, 'They will certainly not enter my rest.'" The author of Hebrews hopes that the audience will not repeat their disobedience and distrust (3:18-19), provoking their patron to exclude them from the greater rest (4:1-11).[16]

The example of the wilderness generation shows a group brought to the very border of their promised inheritance who at the last moment panic in the face of their estimation of the native inhabitants and withdraw their trust from God. They choose to act with fear and respect for the people over whom God had promised to give them victory rather than in fear and respect for the God who promised them a lasting inheritance. Changing the specifics, but not the dynamics, this also describes the situation of the addressees as perceived by the author. Having endured a period of wandering, as it were, in which they experienced the world's rejection and still held on to God's promise (10:32-34), some of the believers are wavering in their commitment at the very time when they are closer than ever to attaining what was promised. Some stand in danger of falling into distrust, of disobeying God by not continuing to assemble together to worship (10:25) and by dissociating from those in need (13:3), of regarding more the opinion and hostility of society than of the God who promises them an unshakable kingdom.

The author heightens the addressees' awareness of the danger through a number of stern warnings designed to arouse fear and dread in the hearers: fear of the consequences of pursuing any course that would provoke their patron. These warnings, while calling for and advising against certain actions, also aim at appealing to the emotions of the hearers and are thus an important part of the argument from *pathos,* an essential component of persuasion for the classical rhetorical theorists. We will focus on the more highly-developed warnings in 6:4-8 and 10:26-31, which explicitly draw on topics of patronage and the proper return for benefactions. We may note in passing, however, that 2:1-4; 3:12; 4:1; 10:35-38; and 12:15 also reflect the author's interest in drawing the addressees' attention to the honor of Christ and the favor of God, both of which stand to be violated should the community show a lack of "firmness" in their "loyalty."

One of the more troublesome passages in the history of theological interpretation is 6:4-8, which however becomes readily intelligible (although no less difficult) when read in light of the expectations of honor in patronage:

> For it is impossible to restore again to repentance those who have once been enlightened, and have tasted the heavenly gift, and have shared in the Holy Spirit, and have tasted the goodness of the word of God and the powers of the age to come, and then have fallen away, since on their own [better, to their own disadvantage] they are crucifying again the Son of God and are holding him up to contempt. Ground that drinks up the rain falling on it repeatedly, and that produces a crop useful to those for whom it is cultivated, receives a blessing from God. But if it produces

thorns and thistles, it is worthless and on the verge of being cursed; its end is to be burned over (NRSV).

While the author quickly encourages his audience after delivering these dire warnings that such could never be their fate his words cannot have failed to have their impact (as they have upon generation after generation of readers). Indeed, by again arousing fear of the dread consequences of falling away he helps assure that the faltering among the congregation will find the resources to persevere. The author claims, however, no more than what was required by the Greco-Roman ethos. Again Dio Chrysostom provides helpful background material (*Or.* 31.65): "those who insult their benefactors will by nobody be esteemed to deserve a favour." This lies behind both this passage and the even stronger warning in 10:26-31.

Hebrews 6:4-6 contrasts the benefits that have been enjoyed by the believer (6:4-5) and are full of promise for the future perfection of the gifts with the strikingly inappropriate response of "turning away" from the one who has gained these gifts for the believer and "holding [him] up to public scorn." The one who does not persevere in trust enacts contempt for the gifts gained at such cost to the patron and shows a striking lack of gratitude. After one has spurned the benefactor and rejected the only mediator who can gain access to this patron there can be no restoration. The one who "shrinks back unto destruction" (10:39) in refusing to endure what is required to keep these benefits has esteemed them too lightly. The agricultural maxim that follows this warning is actually quite apt. Rain is regarded as a benefaction of God (cf. Matt 5:45b) that here looks for a proper return in fruitful soil. God's gifts are to bring forth gratitude and loyalty toward God as well as useful fruits for the fellow believers (e.g., the acts of service and love commended and recommended in 6:10). Such a response will lead to the consummation of blessing. The improper response of breaking with the benefactor, indeed bringing dishonor to the name of the benefactor, leads to the curse and the fire, that is, exclusion from the promise and exposure to the anger of the judge.

The admonition of 10:26-31 (quoted above in Chapter One) presents the same severe result in even more heightened tone, seeking to augment the hearers' fear. The passage compares infraction of the Mosaic covenant with transgression of the new covenant: the "willful sin" of 10:26, a deliberate violation of the loyalty due the Patron who has struck up a better alliance with the people. Just as the dignity of Christ exceeds that of Moses (cf. 3:1-6), so violations of that dignity will incur a greater punishment than even the "death without mercy" that fell upon those who disregarded Torah.[17] This willful sin, a challenge to the honor of Christ, will lead to "punishment" *(timōria)*. Why should this punishment be necessary? Aulus Gellius (*Attic Nights* 7.14.2-4) specifically links it to the preservation of "the dignity and prestige of the one who is sinned against . . . lest the omission of punishment bring him into contempt and diminish the esteem in which he is held."

The one who assaults the honor of Christ, who should rather enhance the honor of the patron, becomes the target for divine satisfaction, the restoration of the honor of the Son. The one who fails to persevere in loyalty and obedience to Jesus manifests disregard for the gifts of God and for the patron-client relationship with God through Jesus. Thus the one who continues in sin (i.e., abandons the people of God, cf. 11:25-26) "has regarded as profane the blood of the covenant with which he or she was sanctified," the blood by which he or she has been given access to God as patron. The one who falters in trust and perseverance "has insulted the Spirit of grace." The contrast between "insult" and "favor" could not be more striking, and indeed meeting favor and the promise of benefaction with insult is at once highly inappropriate and foolish. Dio expresses the baseness of such a return, going so far as to call it "impiety" *(asebeia):* "to commit an outrage against good men who have been the benefactors of the state, to annul the honours given them and to blot out their remembrance, I for my part do not see how that could be otherwise termed" (*Or.* 31.14). Those who turn away from God's beneficence in Christ encounter God no longer as favorable patron, but as judge and avenger: "For we know the one who said, 'Vengeance is mine, I will repay.' And again, 'The Lord will judge his people.'" The threefold challenge to God invites God's response as vindicator of the honor of the Son and the worth of the gifts that have been scorned.

The author has designed these passages to lead the hearers to a feeling of deep dread, which he underscores explicitly in his text. He openly exhorts the addressees to "be afraid" (4:1); he claims that nothing remains for the apostate but "a certain fearful *(phobera)* prospect of judgment" (10:27); such a one will learn what a "fearful thing *(phoberon)*" it is "to fall into the hands of the living God" (10:31). The passage forms a climax to the part of the argument from *pathos* that builds on the "fear" of the audience. Aristotle (*Rhet.* 2.5.1) defines fear *(phobos)* as "a painful or troubled feeling caused by the impression of an imminent evil that causes destruction or pain." The author has provided the prerequisite for fear in his depiction of the coming of God as judge and avenger. Aristotle suggests (*Rhet.* 2.5.3, 5) that fear can be aroused also by signs of impending danger such as the "enmity and anger *(orgē)* of those able to injure us in any way . . . and outraged virtue *(aretē hybrizomenē)* when it has power, for it is evident that it always desires satisfaction." In showing contempt for the Son of God one knowingly incurs the wrath of God, as anger is the expected response to a slight (all the more when one is slighted by those whom one desired to benefit). Fear is again heightened by the declaration of the impossibility of restoration (10:26), for after one has rejected the brokerage of Jesus there remains no mediator who can regain God's favor for the transgressor.

Having aroused such fear in the audience, the author has prepared and motivated them to consider how to avoid the course of action that would offer such an affront to God and turn beneficence into anger. It is at this point that he reminds them of their former display of loyalty to Christ and to one another (10:32-34), and of the trust and hope they showed as their status and property in the world were stripped from them. Such a stance manifested the "boldness" or "confidence" *(parrhēsia)* that springs from commitment to the benefactor and to attaining the reward God promised. The admonition of 10:35 urges the addressees to hold on to precisely this stance as the means to retain the favor of the benefactor, and cautions against "shrinking back" as the act that would cause the loss of that favor. This brings us, then, to the author's use of examples of faith. The warnings have prepared the audience to listen and to follow the advice that will lead them away from returning insult for favor and incurring the just penalty. Recalling the "shrinking back" of the wilderness generation the believers will be more motivated to avoid this course as ultimately more dangerous than enduring society's hostility.

B. "Despising Shame": The Models for Emulation in 10:32–12:3

We recall from our discussion of ancient rhetoric that epideictic speeches—speeches that praise some figure or figures from the past—were intended to strengthen the commitment of the audience to the values embodied in those figures. Hearing others praised, they would be stirred to imitate the behaviors that led to such esteem in the hope of augmenting their own honor in the eyes of their group (emulation). Within deliberative speeches ancient orators would often include shorter epideictic sections expressing the honor achieved in the past by those who embrace a course of action similar to that promoted by the speaker. So it is with the letter to the Hebrews. The author is vitally concerned with renewing the addressees' commitment to the virtue of *pistis*, which we generally translate "faith" but have also seen to be closely related to "loyalty" and "reliability." He argues that the way for them to attain the inheritance God has promised them is through remaining loyal to their divine benefactor:

> You have need of perseverance, in order that, having done the will of God, you may receive the promise. . . . For yet "a little while, the coming one will come and not delay: but my righteous one will live by faith, and if he or she shrinks back, my soul takes no pleasure in him or her." But we are not characterized by shrinking back unto destruction but by faith unto the attainment of life (10:36-39).

The opposite course of action is also mentioned in these verses, namely "shrinking back" in commitment to Christ. This, we have seen, appears as a concern throughout the epistle. The author therefore fortifies his exhortation by including an encomium declaring the honor and approval before God's eyes attained by the exemplars of commitment (*pistis*) known to the community from the tradition of the Septuagint in order to stir up their waning zeal for honor before God and to reinforce the detachment of Christians from society's honor rating.

Acting faithfully leads to *martyria*, "attestation" (11:2, 4, 5), gaining for the faithful a lasting testimony to their worth and virtue. This term is used to speak of the endorsement given by Roman authorities of a person whom a local assembly wished to honor. The "witness" borne by these authorities was to the worthiness of the recipient of honors. This sense carries over into the New Testament where this word can carry the sense of "bearing favorable testimony" and thus "spreading a good reputation." The author creates an *inclusio* around the whole of ch. 11, using forms of the verb *martyreisthai*, "bear a favorable witness," in the opening verses of the litany of faith and again at the transition from encomium to hortatory peroration (11:39), indicating that the author wishes to drive home the assurance that the worth of God's clients will receive favorable attestation from the highest authority.

The chief models the author holds up for emulation in 10:32–12:3—the community, Abraham, Moses, the martyrs, and Jesus—all share a common feature. They have chosen to embrace a lower status in the eyes of the society in order to pursue the greater and lasting honor to be won through obedience to God. Renouncing the honor and approval that accompany success and integration into the unbelieving society, they have all borne witness to a hope for something greater—the eternal benefaction promised by God—and in their loyal obedience to this hope have accepted marginality with regard to human networks of honor and status.

The climax of the author's encomium on "faith" is the example of Jesus in 12:1-3, the "pioneer and perfecter of faith." As faith's pioneer Jesus is the one on whom the addressees must fix their gaze; as faith's perfecter[18] Jesus shows faith in its most complete expression. Jesus shows this faith by "enduring a cross, despising shame" (12:2); this same faith led to the honor that followed, when "he sat down at the right hand of God" (12:2). The phrase "despising shame" brings us to the heart of one of the main goals of the author, who seeks to detach his audience from placing value on society's approval or disapproval. Such concern for reputation in the eyes of non-group members, as we have seen, would pull believers away from the group and its values and lead them to assimilate back into the dominant culture.

The recipients of Hebrews, who had embraced the loss of honor and status in order to remain loyal to God and Christ in the "former days," would certainly be sensitive to the loss of honor and status Jesus endured on their behalf in order to secure for them the promised benefits of children of God. Jesus' humiliation begins with the incarnation (cf. 2:5-7; Phil 2:6-11) but climaxes in the crucifixion. The author speaks of the suffering of Jesus in 2:10, 18; 5:8, but only gives it the specific shape of a cross in 12:2, a death that occurs "outside the camp" (13:11), a place of dishonor and uncleanness. Closely connected with this death is *antilogia*. Generally translated "opposition" or "contradiction," this term recalls more specifically the insults and mocking Jesus had to bear during his trial and death.[19] This aspect of the passion will resonate deeply with the addressees' own experience of "reproaches and sufferings" (10:32-34).

The phrase "despising shame" (*aischunē kataphronēsas*, 12:2) points us toward the socially formative impact of Jesus' example. "Shame" (*aischunē*) here goes beyond the experience of disgrace; it signifies sensitivity to the evaluation of one's actions and commitments by others.[20] When one "despises shame" one sets aside concern for one's reputation and simultaneously places a negative value on the opinion of those who would judge one's actions as disgraceful. This corresponds to the philosopher's setting aside of the evaluation non-philosophers formed of his or her values, goals, and behavior. The person unacquainted with the truth was like a child, whose opinion counted for nothing (Aristotle, *Rhet.* 2.6.14-15; Seneca, *Const.* 13.2). Those who were dedicated to different ideals belonged in two different courts of reputation, which did not intersect. The phrase indicates Jesus' awareness that the society that held him in contempt was unaware of what was truly valuable and honorable in God's sight, and therefore their evaluation of him simply did not affect his true honor in the least—a conviction confirmed by his subsequent exaltation to God's right hand. This was also the way the early Church fathers read Heb 12:2; they also saw in Jesus a model for the believers' own approach to the opinion of nonbelievers.[21]

The author thus confronts the addressees, who were increasingly uncomfortable with the lower status they had fallen to on account of their commitment to Christ and in whom a sense of "shame" with regard to the opinion of unbelievers was beginning to return, with the example of Jesus. Jesus shows "faith," the virtue that leads to God's approval (10:38-39), in its most complete expression. Faith rejects the opinion of those who do not share the hope of the Christian and considers valueless society's evaluation of those acts that obedience to God required; the believers are called to imitate this faith in order that they may attain the promised reward and continue in their commitment to one another and to their divine benefactor. Jesus' exaltation, moreover, proves the error of society's evaluation by exemplifying the extreme: the one who suffered the most revolting and degrading death in the world's eyes attained the most exalted status in God's eyes.

Jesus' example brings into sharper focus the thread that unites the more prominent examples that precede his in 10:32–11:40. Abraham, Isaac, and Jacob are set forward prominently as examples of faith in 11:8-22. Their faith is summarized in their confession that they are "foreigners and sojourners upon the earth." Abraham and the patriarchs left their homeland and embraced the status of "foreigner" and "sojourner" while awaiting the promise, but in so doing they, like Jesus, despise shame. In the Greco-Roman world one's native land was the source of one's sense of identity and belonging. The fellow inhabitants of one's native country or city formed one's group of significant others, one's primary reference group.[22] Living away from one's native land, moreover, resulted in a loss of the status enjoyed in that native land (particularly that which came from the honor developed by the family over generations). This state of affairs was aggravated by limited access to acquiring honor in the foreign land. Indeed, sojourning was considered a state of humiliation (so Lucian, *My Native Land* 8) and the terms "exile," "foreigner," and "immigrant" *(ton xenon kai ton metoikon)* could be used as insults (Plutarch, *Exil.* 17 [*Mor.* 607 A]). The stranger or foreigner is usually barred from enfranchisement in the new location. Lacking citizenship and the rights and protection it afforded left one defenseless against insult, abuse, and assaults on property or honor.[23] Citizenship provided some measure of security, a comfortable "mooring" within society: lack of citizenship left one adrift.

The choice by Abraham and his family to embrace the life of "foreigners and resident aliens" (*xenoi kai parepidēmoi*, 11:13) would therefore have been heard by the addressees as a choice of a lower status liable to dishonor and danger, undertaken for the sake of obedience to God's call. The author has focused the recipients' attention on this aspect of Abraham's faith because it answers most nearly the condition of the letter's recipients (cf. 10:32-34). While they had not physically moved from their native land their rejection at the hands of their neighbors—expressed in the abuse and insult directed toward them—signifies their social dislocation. They had lost their former status and the dignity and security that status afforded them. The patriarchs are further praised in that they chose not to return to their native land and to the political safety and security that would bring, choosing rather to press on in their quest for a "better homeland, that is, a heavenly one" (11:16). This again mirrors the addressees' situation; they must choose between renouncing Christ (and thus regaining society's favor) and remaining exiles in their society for the sake of enrollment in the "city that is about to come" (13:14).

Just as the heavenly city founded by God carries greater value than earthly cities founded by human beings, so it confers on its citizens greater prestige than that enjoyed by the citizens of earthly cities. The people of God strive for honor in the heavenly city with the same vigor displayed by those seeking the fleeting honor of the transient cities of the world. Commitment to God, or "faith," manifests itself precisely in refusing to call any city in this world their home. In this regard Dio's claim (*Or.* 44.6) before his native city is informative. Having lived in exile for many years he avoided acquiring citizenship or land abroad in order to demonstrate his loyalty to his native Prusa, a dedication he expects will win him greater approval and honor where he most desires it. In the same way the patriarchs' refusal of earthly citizenship assures them of honor and approval—indeed, high civic standing—in the city God has established and will reveal. This grant of honor is expressed in God's willingness to have the divine Name associated with them (11:16). By this

God reveals their true worth (they are worthy to be associated with God) and pledges to preserve their honor as an extension of God's own honor.

A second prominent example in Hebrews 11 is Moses, who as "a son of the daughter of Pharaoh" (11:24) occupies a position of very high social standing. The author focuses not on Moses' part in giving the Law; instead, central to Moses' faith is his renunciation of status and honor in the sight of the world and his adoption of the degraded status of the slave in order to bind himself to the people of God and share in their future enjoyment of God's benefactions. This pattern matches the community's past choices (10:33-34) and is called for in the community's present (13:3). Moses' honor rating by birth is very high, as he is endowed with noble ancestry and wealth (access to the "treasures of Egypt," 11:26). Faith expresses itself, however, not in achieving honor in society's eyes (the advantages of which are consistently described in the New Testament as "temporary," 11:25), but in achieving honor in God's eyes. He therefore chooses "maltreatment with the people of God" and joins himself to slaves, people of no honor in society's eyes and thus subject to insult and physical outrage.

Moses is able to make this choice because he understands that before God's court of reputation and in light of God's promised reward (11:26) the "reproach of Christ" is of greater value than the "wealth of Egypt." The phrase "reproach of Christ" (*ton oneidismon tou Christou;* cf. LXX Ps 88:51-52) connects Heb 11:24-26 with 13:12-13, which exhorts the addressees to choose to bear Christ's reproach: "Therefore even Jesus, in order that he might sanctify the people through his own blood, suffered outside the gate. Therefore let us go out to him outside the camp, bearing his reproach" *(ton oneidismon autou pherontes).* Knowledge of God's reward—citizenship in the abiding, heavenly city (13:14)—relativizes both the sting of temporary disgrace and the incentive to pursue worldly honors, allowing Moses, like Abraham, to leave his native land (11:27) and join the people of God in their pilgrimage toward the promised reward. Moses' choice of solidarity with the people of God, even under the conditions of experiencing society's shame and reproach, was a pattern of faith replicated in the community's past when they "became partners" with those who had been imprisoned or shamefully treated for their confession (10:33-34a), and a pattern held up for the community's imitation for the future, as the author will exhort them in 13:3: "remember those who are in prison, as though you were imprisoned with them; those who are being tortured as though you yourselves were being tortured" (NRSV). Following

Moses' pattern the recipients are called to "draw near" (10:22) to God in fellowship with one another as the mutually reinforcing community of believers (10:24-25) who also choose "ill-treatment with the people of God" as the path of confidence in God (10:32-35).

The author of Hebrews presents another group of low-status examples in 11:35b-38. Those who "were tortured, not accepting release so that they might attain a better resurrection" are clearly the martyrs of the Hellenization crisis of 167–164 B.C.E. Second Maccabees 7 and 4 Maccabees 8–9 portray these martyrs refusing enfranchisement in an ungodly society, choosing to persevere to the end because of their hope in receiving a new life from God: a "better" resurrection in that it brings the faithful into the life of the heavenly realm. The author of Hebrews shares the basic convictions of these martyrs, namely that the benefits of honoring God through obedience and the dangers of dishonoring God through disobedience outweigh any benefits or dangers society can offer or threaten. Despising the society's system of evaluation of what is honorable and what is shameful follows as a matter of course.

Along with the martyrs the author of Hebrews holds up other examples of those who have suffered society's disgrace (in the form of physical abuse and torture) and censure. By society's standards this constitutes a list of sorry examples, a parade of those who were utterly disgraced and had no honor within society. In the middle of this list of those who are dishonored by society's standards the author introduces the striking remark that "the world was not worthy of them" (11:38). This encapsulates the reversal of evaluations of honor and disgrace that undergirds the author's exhortation. Here again he turns the norms of society upside down, affirming that the faithful person's true worth is not measured by the standards of the dominant Greco-Roman culture. On the contrary, it is the society that will be measured by the standard of the faithful. The world's rejection and negative evaluation of the faithful is in fact a judgment on the world.[24] This set of examples encourages the addressees once more to accept having no place in society (cf. the example of those who "were wandering about in deserts and hills and caves") and to accept the negative judgment of the public court of opinion (even its physical abuse) rather than shrink back in fear of such disgraces and lose the greater reward. Even if society ascribes disgrace to the believers they are to despise a disgraceful reputation for the sake of gaining the honor and citizenship that God ascribes.

The author prefaces these examples of despising society's negative evaluations for the sake of a positive evaluation by God with a depiction of the addressees' own past conduct as exemplary in 10:32-34. Using a group's own successful past experience was a powerful source of encouragement to repeat an enterprise, seen often in speeches on the threshold of a decisive battle.[25] The believers' former conduct—their endurance of reproaches and suffering, their show of solidarity with those thus treated, and their joyful acceptance of the loss of status markers such as property—is precisely that in which the author wants them to continue. Rather than shrinking back, as manifested in those who have ceased to assemble with the gathered church, the addressees are challenged to continue to bond actively with other believers, whether through encouragement in service (10:24) or service itself (10:33-34; 13:3). Their continued "boldness" and "endurance" will lead them to receive the "reward" and the promises. Their continued rejection of the quest for honor by society's standards will free them to pursue and achieve honor in the sight of God and of the believing community.

An essential part of the author's response is therefore the rousing of emulation and imitation through the praise of the exemplars of "faith," particularly those who have "despised shame" in one way or another. Sensing the addressees' growing sensitivity to society's opinion of their worth and their reawakening ambition to regain their lost status in their neighbors' eyes, the author seeks to direct their attention back toward the alternate arena of honor where so many have successfully competed and attained a lasting praiseworthy remembrance before God. He hopes to spur them on to complete their race for honor before that court, while insulating them from society's means of enforcing adherence to its own self-preserving values and goals—that is, by reinforcing their ability to "despise shame." The path of faith remains the way of honor, no matter what opinion society has of, or what dishonor society shows, the believers. Ultimately God will vindicate God's clients before the eyes of the unbelieving world, when God shall "put all things under [Christ's] feet" (2:8; cf. 1:13; 10:13). On that day God will rule the court of human opinion out of order and overturn its former verdicts.

C. Reinterpreting the Experience of Disgrace

From within the framework of the Christian counterculture the author is able to reinterpret the believers' experience of disgrace at the hands of the dominant culture. By attaching positive significance to these experiences from within the alternative culture the author hopes not only to undermine the force of society's attempts at social control (i.e., by shaming the "deviants" back into conformity with the norms of the dominant culture) but even make these same experiences an occasion for strengthening commitment to the minority culture by turning the experiences of disgrace into tokens of honor and promises of greater reward.

First the author recasts the believers' experiences of ridicule, trial, loss of status and property, and endurance of continued reproach as the training or discipline by God of God's adopted children. The community's endurance of society's rejection and censure in fact turns out to be the token of God's acceptance and discipline (12:5-11) whereby the addressees are fitted to receive their birthright and to enjoy the honor toward which God leads them (2:10):

> You have forgotten the exhortation that speaks to you as sons and daughters: "My child, do not think little of the Lord's training, nor lose heart when being chastened by him. The one whom the Lord loves, he trains, and he disciplines every son or daughter whom he welcomes." Endure for the sake of your training—God is treating you as sons and daughters. For what child does a father not discipline? If you do not experience the training that all share, then you are illegitimate children and not true children. Since we had our biological parents for trainers and submitted, shall we not all the more be subject to the father of our spirits and live?

The believers' struggle to hold on to their confession in the face of society's hostility and censure is their endurance in *paideia,* the "education" by which all parents mold the character of their children. What society intends, therefore, as an experience of disgrace aimed at bringing the deviant back into line with the values of the dominant culture becomes the proof of the believers' adoption into God's family and a powerful encouragement to persevere in their commitments to the minority group. Only those who have shared in discipline (12:8) will also share the rewards as "partners of Christ" (3:14), who also learned obedience through suffering (5:8-10), and "partners in a heavenly calling" (3:1). The believers may even cherish their marginalization and censure by society as a process by which their character is tried and proven, and that guarantees their future honor and vindication.

Second, the author uses the image of the contest *(agōn)* to speak of the traumatic experience of public disgrace and social and economic disenfranchisement suffered by the believers (10:32-34). The author sums up this experience as a "competition," the rhetorical force of which was to set their endurance of hardships in the context of competition for an honorable victory. A more extended use of this image appears in the exhortation built around the example of Jesus in 12:1-4:

> Therefore, since we indeed have so great an encircling cloud of witnesses, laying aside every weight and the entanglements of sin, let us run with endurance the race *(agōna)* set before us, looking away to Jesus the pioneer and perfecter of faith, who for the joy that was set before him endured a cross, despising shame, and sat down at the right hand of the throne of God. Ponder the one who endured from sinners such reviling against himself, in order that you may not tire or become weary in your souls. In your contending with sin you have not yet resisted to the point of blood.

The heroes of faith are not only "witnesses" to God and the promised reward: the image of the "encircling cloud of witnesses" conjures up the image of the spectators of competitions or games, from whom the competitors seek honor and esteem. Like those who compete in races the believers are to "lay aside" everything that might impede their running: they are to set aside "sin" as if it were a clinging garment that restricted their movement toward the prize. Sin—the temptation to yield to society's pressures—is also their antagonist (12:4) in this contest (12:1). Finally, as runners clear their minds of all distractions and set their eyes wholly toward the goal, so the believers are to fix their gaze on Jesus, who has run ahead to the victory in which all may share (12:2).

We will recall from Chapter One that many minority cultures used the image of the athletic competition as a means of setting the disgrace and abuse suffered by their adherents (which parallel the rigors of athletic training) in the light of an honorable competition for victory. The author of Hebrews thus applies a firmly established tradition to the needs of his audience. Moreover, interpreting the addressees' experience as a contest allows the author to harness the widely praised virtue of courage, and to define it as perseverance or "endurance" in Christian community and activity. The community's experience of disgrace and rejection at the hands of the unbelieving society, far from being a sign of their lack of honor and their deviance, becomes a source of assurance for their worth and future reward. Their perseverance in the face of society's means of social control (e.g., dishonor and rejection) is in fact a noble contest in which the believers compete for a heavenly prize, and a sign of their adoption by God and the training by which they are fitted to be God's children. It is the path to honor pursued by Abraham, Moses, the martyrs, and Jesus himself; those who walk such a path need fear no disgrace, for their honor is assured by God and God's Son.

D. Sustaining the Alternate Court of Opinion

An essential counterpart to the author's attempt to separate the believers from sensitivity toward the evaluation of outsiders is a an effort to strengthen the mutual interaction and reinforcement within the group. The author speaks of the believers as "partners of Christ" (3:14) and "partners in a heavenly calling" (3:1). As such they are to look after one another as would partners in any joint venture.

They are called to look out for the straying, those succumbing to society's pressure to conform: "Watch out, brothers and sisters, lest there arise in some of you a base, distrustful heart, expressing itself in turning away from the living God. Rather encourage one another daily, as long as it is still called "today," in order that none of you be hardened by sin's guile" (3:12-13). Near the end of the sermon the author adds: "See to it that no one fails to obtain God's gift" (12:15), making each believer aware that he or she must take some responsibility in keeping his or her fellow believers on track. In the face of unbelievers' encouragements to join in the life and values of the Greco-Roman society the Christians are to double their efforts with encouragements of their own, calling back the wavering, reinforcing the values of the group and the rewards of perseverance and loyalty.

The author seeks to make encounters between believers more frequent and more meaningful, to offset the impact of outsiders and hold up behaviors that support the community as honorable and praiseworthy: "let us ponder how we may incite one another to love and good works, not neglecting our common assembling, as is the habit with some, but encouraging one another, and so much the more as you perceive the approaching day" (10:24-25). The author acts personally as part of this alternate court of opinion, censuring the addressees for their waning fervor and lack of zeal (5:11-14), praising them for their displays of love in service (6:9-10) and for their former demonstration of commitment even at great cost (10:32-34). The community leaders will also function as an important part of this alternate court, ascribing honor to the obedient and committed, rebuking the half-hearted.

Further, this encouragement is to extend to material support and acts of service so that each helps one's fellow Christians feel their losses less. The apparently unrelated exhortations of ch. 13 continue the author's interests in maintaining a strong group culture. The writer urges that "fraternal love" (*philadelphia*, 13:1) continue so that members of the community will go on regarding fellow believers as kin: as family, one's fellow believers will also be the primary source of one's identity and honor as well as the primary group to whom one owes one's first duty and allegiance. The exhortation to provide hospitality for traveling fellow believers (13:2) links the local Christian community to the broader Christian minority culture. The author urges solidarity with those whom society has targeted as deviants (13:3; cf. 10:32-34; 11:25): only the group that is willing to support its members under such conditions can maintain the loyalty and trust of its adherents and show that society's court is not, after all, the final adjudicator of worth. Their loyalty to and confession of Christ is thus joined, in the concluding exhortations, to loyalty and support for one another: "Through Jesus let us continue to offer a sacrifice of praise to God, that is, the fruit of lips confessing his name. Do not neglect doing good and sharing, for God is pleased with sacrifices of this kind" (13:15-16). The believers themselves are thus invited to exercise a sort of priestly service appropriate to the access they have to enter the Holy of Holies itself, before the very throne of God. This priestly service, however, expresses itself not only in liturgy, praising the patron through the mediator, and liturgical service, but also in the everyday activity of loving, encouraging, and helping one another.

Where believers take an active part in reinforcing for one another the convictions, values, and promises of the group, and where believers look to one another and to their leaders (13:17) for approval rather than to the unbelieving society, it is easier to disregard the many and forceful voices that call the believer back from deviance to normality, to a form of life that supports the existing society's values and structure. The believers will thus affirm one another's worth and honor as children of God, partners with Christ, full citizens of the city of God, and heirs of the better and lasting possessions. They may assure one another of the firm basis for their hope in the better covenant Jesus has established between God and human beings and spur one another on to endurance of the contest and discipline that, though painful for a time, lead to eternal honor and approval before God.

CONCLUSION

Looking closely at how Hebrews uses the language of honor and dishonor brings us closer to understanding the situation of the addressees and the strategic response to that situation formulated by the author. People who have lost their esteem in society's estimation on account of their response to the gospel, who are beginning to feel again the longing for a place of acceptance in the world, are encouraged to set aside as nothing the negative reactions they encounter from their former associates and unbelieving peers and to persevere in their quest for greater and lasting honor in the reign of God. People who have begun to desire reentry into the networks of patronage and to reclaim their access to goods, services, and advancement are directed to have a care for the honor of the patron they have acquired in God at such great cost to Jesus, the broker and mediator of that relationship. The only fitting and rewarding channel for the satisfaction of their longing for esteem and self-worth is in mutual love and service in the believing community and continued loyalty and gratitude toward their benefactor.

Hebrews thus also holds before us the importance of God's honor for the first-century believer, who is warned against taking disloyalty and disobedience lightly. The author shows that God's favor and wrath are not in fact two separate faces, a view reflected in the frequent contrasting of the God of the Old Testament and the God of Jesus by theologians and lay persons throughout the centuries. God's anger and grace are, rather, interrelated: precisely where God's favor, benefactions, and promises have been rejected in favor of the deceitful promises of the world and sin—where God's favor and gifts have been so lightly valued that one would choose the temporary pleasures of following the world's way over God's way—there favor is exchanged for wrath. The favor that was despised gives rise to anger and judgment. This does not limit God's freedom or undermine God's mercy; rather it restores the immense value of God's gracious favor, so often taken for granted and held as a cheap and readily available commodity. The author thus rests this appeal on the claim that the salvation and inclusion into God's family that cost the Son his life must be appropriately valued, so that loyalty to God, the Giver, and to Christ, the Broker, must always be faithfully maintained and enacted in the ways God directs, such as in acts of love and service to other members of God's family and in bearing testimony to God's purposes, values, and gifts.

Hebrews again reminds us about the need perceived by leaders and shapers of the early Church to be intentional about establishing and preserving Christian community. Through a judicious selection and shaping of praiseworthy examples the author connects disregard for the opinion of outsiders with preserving one's claim to honor before God's eternal court, and shows concern that the believers who are firm in their loyalty encourage those who are wavering, reminding them of the honor and favor that await those who persevere. The believers are to continue to gather together, to express love in word and in mutual help so that none will fall victim to pressure from outside the group to defect, or to pressure from within the individual to seek rather the honor that comes from the dominant culture's approval.

NOTES: CHAPTER 6

[1] For a more complete discussion of the identification of honor discourse in Hebrews and analysis of its rhetorical impact see David A. deSilva, *Despising Shame: Honor Discourse and Community Maintenance in the Epistle to the Hebrews* (Atlanta: Scholars, 1995) chs. 4–7.

[2] The pervasiveness of cultic activity throughout all aspects of life in Greco-Roman society has been demonstrated in such works as Ramsay MacMullen, *Paganism in the Roman Empire* (New Haven: Yale University Press, 1981) 38–39, 47.

[3] The connection of piety and civic order and duty can be seen from such texts as Isocrates, *Ad Dem.* 13; Cicero, *Nat. D.* 1.4; Plutarch, *Adv. Col.* 31 (*Mor.* 1125D-E). Criticisms leveled against the Christian group are attested in Tacitus, *Annales* 15.44; Pliny, *Ep.* X.96; 1 Pet 4:14-16; Origen, *C. Celsum* 8.75.

[4] Commentators have consistently recognized this aspect of the addressees' experience: cf. Harold Attridge, *The Epistle to the Hebrews* (Philadelphia: Fortress, 1989) 299; Ceslaus Spicq, *L'Epître aux Hébreux* (Paris: Gabalda, 1952) 2.329.

[5] Cf. 1 Pet 4:14-16 and Matt 5:11.

[6] The imprisoned were aware of the sacrifice made on their behalf, as both "Paul" (2 Tim 1:16) and Ignatius (*Smyrn.* 10) are aware that their visitors had to set aside the disgrace attached to the prisoners' bonds and risked further injuring their own reputation by associating with the prisoners. Such association could even lead to the sympathizers' falling prey to the same treatment, as it did for many Jews in the Alexandrian riots recounted by Philo (*Flacc.* 72).

[7] Cf. Lucian, *Peregr.* 14; Josephus, *Bell.* 4.168; Philo, *Flacc.* 5, 53-57.

[8] Melito of Sardis, in his "Petition to the Emperor Marcus Aurelius" (cited in Eusebius, *Ecclesiastical History*, trans. G. A. Williamson [London: Penguin, 1965] 4.26.5), bears witness to a sort of open policy for the pillaging of those denounced as Christians: "Religious people as a body are being harried and persecuted by new edicts all over Asia. Shameless informers out to fill their own pockets are taking advantage of the decrees to pillage openly, plundering inoffensive citizens night and day."

[9] 2 Esdras 16:70-73 includes such dispossession as part of the persecution of the righteous: "There shall be a great insurrection against those who fear the Lord . . . plundering and destroying those who continue to fear the Lord. For

176   *The Hope of Glory*

they shall destroy and plunder their goods, and drive them out of their houses." Philo, *In Flaccum,* attests to the same phenomenon.

[10] Jerome H. Neyrey, "Poverty and Loss of Honor in Matthew's Beatitudes: Poverty as Cultural, Not Merely Economic Phenomenon" (unpublished paper delivered at the CJA Seminar in October 1992) 7.

[11] Cf. Bernard A. O. Williams, *Shame and Necessity* (Berkeley: University of California, 1993) 80.

[12] The verb means literally "to lay hold upon," but it carries strong overtones of "helping" and "assisting," as its use in Sir 4:11 and LXX Jer 38:32 (MT 31:32) demonstrate.

[13] R. P. Saller, *Personal Patronage under the Early Empire* (Cambridge: Cambridge University Press, 1982) 59; cf. Fronto, *Ad M. Caes.* 5.34, 37.

[14] For example, Dio Chrysostom delivers an oration on *apistia* (*Oration* 74) in which he recommends distrust of other people as a path to safety in human affairs. The companion oration, *peri pisteōs,* speaks of the burdens of being entrusted with some charge or responsibility. Frederick W. Danker (*Benefactor: Epigraphic Study of a Graeco-Roman and New Testament Semantic Field* [St. Louis: Clayton Publishing House, 1982] 352–353) catalogues several inscriptions in which *pistis* refers to "that which is entrusted," such that "faith is required by the one who awaits fulfillment of the obligation that has been accepted by another."

[15] See Dio, *Orations* 73 and 74 ("On Trust" and "On Distrust").

[16] A second noteworthy negative example is Esau, who is permanently barred from his birthright once he trades it away (12:17). Esau's downfall is that he has no regard for God's promises and benefactions, represented here by his birthright as a son of Isaac, the son of Abraham. His incorrect evaluation manifests "a decisive contempt for the gifts of God" (William L. Lane, *Hebrews 9–13* [Dallas: Word Books, 1991] 488) that earns him exclusion from the promise.

[17] The warnings in 2:1-4 and 12:25 also build on a "lesser to greater" argument contrasting the danger of dishonoring the first covenant with the greater danger of showing contempt for the new covenant and its mediator.

[18] Many translations render this phrase as "perfecter of *our* faith," but this is without support in the Greek. Rather the author names Jesus as the one who most perfectly embodies the virtue of "faith" and who therefore serves as its best exemplar.

[19] So Chrysostom (NPNF[1] 14:494; Migne, *PG* 63.196): "The blows upon the cheek, the laughter, the insults, the reproaches, the mockeries, all these he indicated by 'contradiction.'"

[20] So Rudolf Bultmann (*"Aidōs," TDNT* 1.170): "Shame" is "fear of the *aischron* [shameful thing] and therefore of one's *doxa* [reputation]."

[21] Cf. Origen, *Fragmenta in Psalmos* 37.12.4-5; *Exhortatio ad Martyrium* 37.11-14; Gregory of Nyssa, *Contra Eunomium* 3.5; John Chrysostom, *Commentary on Hebrews* in NPNF[1] 14:493 (Migne, *PG* 63.194).

[22] Cf. Dio, *Or.* 44.1, on being held in honor in one's native land as the highest good.

[23] Cf. Dio, *Or.* 66.15; Philo, *Flacc.* 53–55.

[24] See the similar strategies employed in Epictetus, *Diss.* 1.29. 50–54; 3.22. 63–65.

[25] Cf. Tacitus, *Agricola* 33–34.

7

Honor Discourse in the Apocalypse of John

We have seen how analysis of honor discourse can be useful in illuminating the rhetorical goal and strategy not only of epistles, which are traditionally quite accessible to classical rhetorical analysis, but also of the gospels, which while less accessible to rhetorical analysis nevertheless are clearly texts seeking to persuade as well as inform. We turn now to the last major genre in the New Testament, the genre of apocalypse. This book also defies strict analysis in terms of its appeals to *logos, ethos,* and *pathos,* or in terms of its rhetorical *genos* (epideictic, judicial, or deliberative). Nevertheless, Revelation clearly has a rhetorical agenda. It seeks to persuade seven different Christian communities to take certain specific actions (seen most clearly in the seven oracles of Rev 2:1–3:22), as well as to engender a firm commitment to certain values in opposition to other values (reflected throughout the work).[1] Its visions articulate a world in which certain actions or alliances are advantageous and others disadvantageous (hence deliberative topics). John presents models of praiseworthy action for emulation and anti-models of those whose actions are censurable and lead to disgrace (epideictic strategies). Attention to John's use of honor discourse, as this has been defined and refined throughout this book, will assist in the discovery of the rhetorical strategy of this visionary work as we ask of it the same questions we asked of the gospels and epistles.

THE SETTING AND PURPOSE OF REVELATION

The questions of the authorship and date of Revelation continue to spawn much debate, and it is not the purpose of the present volume to enter into the intricacies of such issues. For the purposes of this discussion we will assume a date during the reign of Domitian (81–96 C.E.) and will make no claims based on the identification of John the Seer with any other John known from early Christian literature (e.g., John the apostle).[2] John writes to seven churches with whom he may have had intimate acquaintance, perhaps conducting a circuit ministry among them. The seven oracles in chs. 2 and 3, combined with other literary and archaeological evidence concerning the seven cities[3] and the churches in them (e.g., letters from Paul, his circle, or Ignatius of Antioch) provide a clear picture of the tensions and challenges facing these Christian communities. Indeed, one is immediately struck by the different life situations faced by the churches, and in many cases the different challenges present within a single congregation, such that the old paradigm of reading Revelation simply as comfort for the marginalized and persecuted will no longer hold. At best this corresponds only to the situation in Smyrna, and even there no deaths are mentioned. Pergamum has witnessed only one martyrdom at the time of John's writing.

Revelation is therefore not merely written to Christians in daily danger of being hauled before magistrates and sent to the arenas.[4] Some believers—those who are mainly in agreement with John and fully committed to their confession—are comforted and encouraged in the face of growing troubles; others, however, are in grave danger (from John's perspective) because they are in no danger of suffering for their faith. Revelation can thus be read from some situations as a word of encouragement but from others as a wake-up call to see that one's easy alliance with society is a partnership with the Whore of Babylon.

The honor of a number of Christian communities appears to have been challenged. The oracles to Smyrna and Philadelphia (2:8-11; 3:7-13) speak of the "slander" of Jews living in those cities directed toward the Christian community and of the promise of the vindication of the believers' honor in the sight of their detractors. Believers in Smyrna are exposed to "affliction" and stand in danger of imprisonment, both of which may be understood as replications of the society's rejection of them as deviants and attempts to shame them into a more "honorable" way of life. A number of believers are commended for not denying Jesus' name, a course that apparently led to the untimely death of one

Christian in Pergamum (perhaps by official action but also possibly the result of an unofficial lynching). There are clearly attempts being made to pressure believers into hiding or denying their association with the unpopular and subversive name of Christian. John envisions such pressure growing in the future, so that in Antipas the martyr one might see the shape of things to come.

Notably, however, the honor of the believers in Sardis and Laodicea is challenged not by their society but, in John's prophetic voice, by Jesus himself. Here are congregations that receive no encouragement from John, but instead a challenge to their claims to honor. Sardis has a reputation (a "name") for being alive, but is really dead (3:1); Laodicea's claims to wealth and prosperity are rejected as self-deception (3:17). These congregations, together with some percentage of the believers in Pergamum and Thyatira, suffer from being too well adjusted to the ethos and demands of the dominant culture. The external pressures and the internal propensities to conform constitute, from John's perspective, a grave danger to the believing communities.

We have seen earlier in our discussions of Hebrews and the Thessalonian letters the importance of imperial cult and the cults of the traditional gods for the majority of the inhabitants of the Greco-Roman world.[5] By withdrawing from cultic expressions of solidarity with the citizenry and loyalty and gratitude toward those who secured the well-being of the city, Gentile Christians especially were at risk of being viewed as subversive, unreliable, and even dangerous elements of society.[6] An in-church movement John labels the "Nicolaitans" appears to have been gaining some ground in Asia Minor, speaking to this very issue. The Nicolaitans, those "who hold to the teaching of Balaam," and the followers of "Jezebel, who calls herself a prophetess," are all depicted in similar terms: they "eat food sacrificed to idols and commit fornication" (Rev 2:14, 20 NRSV) and teach others to do so as well. They present an alternative interpretation of the gospel and therefore an alternative response to the social order, vying with John's for acceptance as the "faithful" response. For John they represent a present and persuasive threat to the boundaries and definitions of the communities.

John labels (and censures) his opponents using figures from the Jewish Scriptures, casting them as enemies of the people of God. The Nicolaitans are cast as disciples of Balaam (Balaam means in Hebrew what Nicolaus means in Greek, namely "conquering" or "wearing down the people").[7] Balaam is remembered in Jewish tradition for leading Israel astray at Baal-Peor, a story recounted in Num 25:1-3. Balaam's responsibility in this incident is recorded in Num 31:16. At Baal-Peor the Israelites "began to play the harlot with the daughters of Moab," with the consequence that they accepted the Moabites' invitation to bow down to their gods and eat of their sacrifices. Balaam thus became a figure for the false teacher of apostasy and is particularly connected with teaching the Midianites to convince the Israelites to "eat food sacrificed to idols and practice immorality." The danger associated with this is loss of Israel's identity as the "people of God," becoming indistinguishable from the nations around them.

When John casts the Nicolaitans as "disciples of Balaam" and highlights "eating food sacrificed to idols" the main issue appears to be whether or not one can, as a Christian, participate in the religious life of the Greco-Roman society.[8] There are obvious advantages for doing so: it eliminates all the tension between Church and society if one can again go out in public and show oneself pious and reliable through participation in the cults of the traditional gods and emperors. If it could be shown that "an idol is nothing" and that these empty rituals could not offend God why should the Christians suffer society's hostility unnecessarily? In this context it is better to read the second charge—committing fornication—metaphorically, especially in light of the history of depicting God's relationship with God's people Israel as a marriage (with frequent infidelity on the part of the bride).[9] Following the Nicolaitans' compromising position amounts to forsaking a faithful relationship to Jesus. "Jezebel," known from the Hebrew Scriptures as a patroness of the prophets of Baal in Israel, may be a woman of prominence who has opened her house to the Nicolaitan prophets, supporting them in the same way as others supported John in his itinerant ministry. For both theological and economic reasons she, too, advocates the stance preached by the Nicolaitans concerning how to relate with the pagan society and its pressures for the sake of the survival of the community.[10]

Another sort of internal compromise is to be found in the issue of wealth in Laodicea. Achieving and maintaining wealth in the Roman province was closely tied to partnership with Rome, presented in Revelation 18 as the image of wealth and conspicuous consumption. The road to riches was the way of accommodation and compromise. When the boundaries of the community could be abrogated the members of the community could freely participate in the pagan economy, in league with Babylon, as it were, and share in her prosperity. Perhaps even more insidious, they might believe in the myth of her prosperity, encapsulated in the ideology of *Roma Aeterna*. It was, however, a tainted prosperity because on the one hand Babylon was already drunk with the blood of God's servants (who held to a different system of values), and on the other hand material prosperity had been purchased at the expense of maintaining "the testimony of Jesus." That wealth was tainted for John because it meant cooperation with and participation in an unjust system is seen both from the negation of the Laodiceans' wealth as being in fact poverty, and from the affirmation of Smyrna's poverty as being, in God's sight, wealth.[11]

The setting of the addressees of Revelation is thus varied and multifaceted. Some believers need encouragement that they have chosen the path that will lead them to true and lasting honor; others, however, need to see that a compromise with the dominant culture may bring graver danger and loss than it averts. In Revelation John calls each reader and each community of readers to seek out the path of faithfulness to God and the Lamb and to respond to the challenge to reject the enticements of participation in or peace with an impious and unjust social order. Here his use of honor discourse becomes an essential part of his rhetorical strategy. He must move the audience to construe advantage in terms of the "larger picture" of the Christian worldview and eschatology.[12] He must set token expressions of honor toward the gods of the society against the background of the exclusive claims to worship made by the One God.

REVELATION AND THE QUESTION OF WHOM TO HONOR

Many who have read Revelation as "prophecy" only in the sense of eschatological prediction have missed a critical aspect of the book's message. John's driving question from beginning to end is not simply about the course of events leading up to the end but about whom to honor and at what cost that honor is to be preserved.[13] Those scholars who see in Revelation a work fundamentally interested in worship and liturgy[14]—the right worship of God and the Lamb standing in opposition to alternative, idolatrous worship settings—come closest to the heart of John's vision (as long as this understanding of "worship" is not limited to cultic activity). John thus manifests most strongly what is a concern for almost every New Testament author, namely the claim that God has to be honored, and the need to choose the course of action that shows God the honor that is God's due.[15] This was a prominent aspect, for example, of the rhetorical strategy of Hebrews, where the role of God and Jesus as patrons of the new community demanded the proper return of honor and loyalty. Any course of action that might bring dishonor to the name of Christ was to be rejected outright as an expression of rank ingratitude that would result in the punishment of the offender.

John's encouragement and challenges to the seven churches, and his denunciation of the non-Christian world, are motivated by his vision of the honor due God and the violations of that honor that are rampant in his world. He prescribes as a path to honor the way of life that at any cost refuses to share the honor of God (or of God's Anointed) with another; he repeatedly insists that the failure to reserve divine honors exclusively for God and the Lamb, while it may result in temporary advantage, is ultimately the path to greater disadvantage. The hearers of Revelation are thus invited into a deliberative arena in which they are directly advised by the seven oracles and indirectly by the visions that follow. In both types of appeal Revelation gives evidence of a well-orchestrated implementation of honor discourse in the service of its rhetorical goals.

Quintilian (*Inst.* 3.8.33) writes that "at times we have to choose between two advantageous courses after comparison of their respective advantages" (cf. Aristotle, *Rhet.* 1.7). As the Nicolaitans have already gained some hearing for their case that participation in the cultic expressions of loyalty toward the Roman order brings the advantage of lessening hostility from outsiders toward the group, John must demonstrate that the course of renunciation of partnership with the Roman order is indeed the more advantageous course of action. His use of topics of justice and courage throughout the book (depicting the path of loyalty to Christ as the way to express these virtues in the present) suggests that the eschatological punishment of the unfaithful and reward of the faithful, while an important part of his deliberative strategy, is not the only motivating factor he employs.

The chief themes of this orchestration are concentrated in Rev 14:6-13, the messages of the three angels and the makarism that closes the episode, which we will use as a starting point for an examination of the broader literary context. The messages of the three angels represent the most extensive and closest approximation of direct exhortation after the opening of the visionary experience in Rev 4:1, and so it is perhaps not accidental that these should point most strongly to the pillars of John's rhetorical strategy and his use of honor discourse.

A. "Fear God and give God glory": Respect for and Challenges to God's Honor

The first angel proclaims a message of good news with a loud voice "over those sitting on the earth, over every nation and tribe and language and people," calling them to "fear God and give honor to him, for the hour of his judgment came; and fall down in worship before the one who made heaven and earth and sea and fountains of water" (14:6-7). As John looks out upon "every nation" he sees that the majority of humankind is engaged in the worship of gods other than the one recognized by Israel. These idolaters are guilty of failing to honor the One God, sharing the honor due God with false gods and demons (cf. 1 Cor 10:14-21; Rev 13:4). The angel summons them to give honor where it is due, to the God who created all things and thus claims the gratitude and reverence of all living as the divine patron of all. Moreover, God's day of judgment approaches: the day on which God will mete out honor and dishonor, reward and punishment. Those who have honored God in their lives may anticipate approval on that day, whereas those who have failed to honor God may anticipate becoming the objects of God's vindication of God's honor.

Many readers stumble over the command to "fear" God, finding "love" to be a more appropriate orientation toward the Deity. Indeed, Revelation has been criticized as an inferior expression of theology on account of its emphasis on "fear" and "wrath."[16] We have seen, however, that "fear" is not an expression of a servile attitude, but rather one of respect for the honor of God. It is the awareness of the greatness of God's honor and the value of God's favor, such that one would do nothing willingly to violate these but rather choose those actions that expressed one's acknowledgment of God's honor and one's debt of gratitude to God for life itself. We have also seen that "glory" *(doxa)* signifies the visible representations of one's honor (cf. the description of Jesus in 1:12-20), here in the postures and words of those who acknowledge God's honor. John calls his audience (and indirectly their non-Christian neighbors) to recognize God's claim to reverence and gratitude and to weigh all their actions and choices in light of that claim.

The first angel's message recalls the opening scene of John's vision, namely the heavenly liturgies of chs. 4 and 5. Here the various orders of angels render to God and to the Lamb the honor they deserve, and their hymns teach John's audience the grounds for such honor and gratitude. God sits on the throne, the symbol of God's rule and authority, surrounded by concentric circles of worshiping beings: the four living creatures (reminiscent of the seraphim of Isaiah 6), the seven spirits (corresponding to the seven archangels or angels of the presence in other Jewish texts, cf. *T. Levi* 2–5), and the twenty-four elders on their thrones (perhaps corresponding to the angelic order known as "thrones" in Col 1:16; again cf. *T. Levi* 2–5). These figures are engaged unceasingly in giving honor to God, affirming that God is "worthy . . . to receive honor and respect and power, because you created all things, and according to your will they began to be and were created" (4:11). As the creator of all things and source of all living God has a unique claim to honor and to the gratitude of all people (cf. Rev 14:7). Those who fail to render to God the appropriate return of gratitude show themselves to be dishonorable clients, and this ingratitude in the face of the gift of life itself is especially shameful.[17]

As the heavenly liturgy continues John's attention turns to the figure of the Lamb who also has a unique claim to honor. Of all "in heaven or upon earth or under the earth," the Lamb alone is worthy to open the seals of a certain scroll held in God's right hand. The Lamb's surpassing worthiness derives from his own beneficent acts toward humanity: "You are worthy to take the scroll and to open its seals, for you were slaughtered and by your blood you ransomed for God saints from every tribe and language and people and nation, and you have made them to be a kingdom and priests serving our God, and they will reign on earth" (5:9-10 NRSV). The career of Jesus is summed up in his death on behalf of others (recall the interpretation of Jesus' death in Matthew and John). By this death people from every nation have been ransomed from a servile status and ascribed an honorable status: that of priests serving God, enjoying the honor of face-to-face access to the Divine Patron. The angelic orders are joined by "every creature which is in heaven and upon the earth and under the earth and in the sea" (5:13) in the recognition of Jesus' achieved honor, as the whole of creation unites in acclamations honoring their divine patrons for creation and redemption. John thus attempts to catch his audience up in the sense of gratitude and the immensity of the honor of God and the Lamb (an implicit appeal to *pathos*) so that each believer, within each of the different settings of the seven churches, will seek to find his or her place in these concentric circles of worship that extend to all creation. They are summoned to live from their acknowledgment of their debt of gratitude to Jesus and the One God, and thus to resist internal enticements to compromise or external pressures to deny the name to which they are to bear witness as faithful recipients of a patron's favor.

Revelation 7:9-12 provides another such scene of people "from every nation, from all tribes and peoples and languages" (7:9 NRSV) honoring God and the Lamb, again because of the salvation provided by these figures. Later scenes of giving honor to God, however, reflect the second cause for "respecting God's honor" introduced by the angel of 14:6-7, namely God's ability to hold the world accountable before God and to exact satisfaction from those who have slighted God through disregard of God's honor and mistreatment of God's loyal clients. After the sounding of the seventh trumpet the inhabitants of heaven again worship God on account of God's taking of the reins of the government of the world, particularly for the enacting of God's wrath against the nations, judging them, rewarding God's servants and "ravaging the ravagers of the earth" (11:18). A second hymn, sung now by those human beings who have remained loyal to God, declares that the enacting of God's judgments must surely result in all fearing and honoring God's name (15:3-4).

John's opening vision of all creation honoring God and the Lamb, however, soon shows itself not to be a representation of things as they are. Rather, chs. 4 and 5 portray the cosmic order as it ought to be if all were to acknowledge God's just claim to honor. Even within that vision the hearer is told of the Lamb's work redeeming a kingdom for God "from every nation," an expression that is echoed in the song of the redeemed in 7:9-12 where again the body of those ransomed are presented as a partial representation of humanity. There are other centers of worship in John's world, most notably the cults of the traditional Greco-Roman pantheon and the cult of the emperor and the goddess *Roma*. The first angel's message, with which we began this section, itself follows closely upon the description of the emergence and enforcement of imperial cult (13:4, 8, 11-18). There is little evidence for a centrally-organized enforcement of this cult during the reign of Domitian, and it appears that Pliny the Younger (governor of Bithynia under Trajan in 110–111 C.E.) was the first to use participation in the imperial cult as a test of loyalty in the trial of Christians.[18] Nevertheless we have seen how significant pressure could be brought to bear on individual Christians by their neighbors to return to the cultic expressions of solidarity and loyalty that marked the solid citizen of the province. John seeks to defuse the force of such pressures in light of God's exclusive claim to honor and God's unique ability to enforce that claim. Here we enter into John's demarcation of the "court of reputation."

After several episodes of divine judgment in chs. 8 and 9 John introduces those who are especially the targets of God's wrath:

> The rest of humankind, who were not killed by these plagues, did not repent of the works of their hands or give up worshiping demons and idols of gold and silver and bronze and stone and wood, which cannot see or hear or walk. And they did not repent of their murders or their sorceries or their fornication or their thefts (9:20-21 NRSV).

The majority of people in Greco-Roman society would have been regarded by John as idolaters (or worshipers of demons: in 1 Cor 10:19-20 Paul argues that the worship of idols is synonymous with the worship of demons). Jews and Christians, who opposed the worship of idols, formed a distinct minority in the empire. As John's vision evolves, however, it is the worshiper of idols who is in the minority. All the host of heaven and "every creature which is in heaven and upon the earth and below the earth" know where the true center of the cosmos is, and thus where worship and adoration are properly directed. Contrary to what the public "knowledge" about the cosmos and the virtue of piety posits as true, the worship of the Greco-Roman divinities does not bring one in line with the cosmic order. Such worship points one away from the center so that one is no longer acting in accord with the hosts of heaven or the rest of creation. Moreover, such a one becomes a source of disorder, a disruptive force within society working murder, sorcery, fornication, and theft. Such subversive and vicious acts were also attributed to Christians as part of the dominant culture's attempt to marginalize the group as "deviant." Pliny the Younger, for example, expressed surprise when he failed to uncover even through torture the sorts of crimes he had been led to expect from Christians, such as cannibalism and orgiastic gatherings.[19]

In John's vision, however, it is this powerful majority who are the deviants and who are shown to be in fact powerless when faced with the wrath of God and the Lamb (cf. 6:15-17). Those who refuse to honor God as God deserves are themselves shown to be dishonorable on account of their impiety and injustice. John directs most of his attention to the dismantling of the imperial cult. In the "public discourse" the emperor was a model of piety and an object of reverence (both aspects are held together in the title *Augustus* or, in Greek, *Sebastos*). He was the *Pontifex maximus*, the chief priest of the empire who mediated the favor of the gods. In John's vision the divine names that adorned the emperor were in fact "blasphemous names" (13:1); his speech was a constant affront to the honor of God and the inhabitants of heaven (13:5-6). He is the instrument of Satan, the enemy of God and deceiver of the earth (12:9; 13:4).[20]

Those who participate in the emperor cult and the cults of the traditional deities are, in fact, offering worship to Satan (13:4) and have fallen victim to the deceptions of his agents (13:14). They, and not the Christians, are ignorant of the knowledge of whom to honor, which is dishonorable. They, and not the Christians, are "deviant" when set against the cosmic order envisioned in Revelation 4 and 5. Moreover, as the visions continue they are shown to be recalcitrant (9:20-21; 16:9, 11, 21), refusing, even after God's judgments begin to be revealed, to acknowledge their error and give God the honor due God. They are committed to error and impiety, cursing the name of God with their dying breaths (16:21). Since they lack essential virtues such as piety and justice, and will remain committed to vice, they are censured as dishonorable.

The Christian addressees of Revelation, therefore, must reevaluate their opinion of such people. How can the believer desire to conform to what such people affirm as "honorable" behavior when they are shown to be ignorant of what is truly honorable? How can the believer yield to the pressures of his or her deviant society when such acquiescence can only mean a share in God's wrath? John thus excludes the unbeliever from the "court of reputation," leaving the believer to seek above all else the approval of God and Jesus, whose opinion of one's life matters most. The glorified Christ is the one to whom the churches must answer, and not society. The seven oracles make this abundantly clear: believers are themselves called to take responsibility for deviancy in their midst (cf. 2:14, 20) and to exercise pressure within the group to motivate adherence to the group's norms.

As judge of the world God is indeed able to preserve God's honor and the honor of God's loyal clients. God's vindication of the witnesses is an important episode in this regard (11:3-13). These two unnamed witnesses are vested with divine authority and power, and call the inhabitants of the Greco-Roman world to repentance. Their relationship to the society can only be described as antagonistic, and the people breathe a great sigh of relief when the Beast strikes the witnesses down. Indeed, they "gloat" over their unburied corpses, celebrating with one another even as they subject the bodies of the witnesses to the most profound shame, namely to lie unburied (11:9-10; cf. Sophocles' *Antigone*). The verdict of the dominant culture, however, is not the final word on the honor of the witnesses, for God raises their dead bodies to life and exalts them to the heavens "while their enemies watched them" (11:12 NRSV). This assurance of public vindication in the sight of one's detractors is crucial. Notably, God's vindication of the honor of the servants of God is intimately linked with God's establishment of God's own honor, for the sequel shows the onlookers struck with fear and giving "honor to the God of heaven" at last (11:13).

Following the episode of the two witnesses is the hymn offered to God at the sounding of the seventh trumpet, which again shows how the manifestation of God's "wrath" and the meting out of punishments to God's enemies and rewards to God's "servants, the prophets and holy ones and all who revere [God's] name" is linked to God's reception of honor (11:15-18). Honoring God leads to honor on that day when God's wrath is poured out. We should recall at this point the intimate relationship between wrath and honor as found, for example, in Aristotle's *Rhetoric* (2.2.1, 3, 8). God's wrath in Revelation is the anger of a slighted benefactor whose favor met not with gratitude but with rejection and affront, both in the form of idolatrous worship and in the form of violence against God's loyal clients. Hence the manifestations of God's wrath in the form of judgments (the plagues of Revelation and so forth) are expected to result in the acknowledgment of God's honor: "Lord, who will fail to revere and honor your holy name? . . . All the nations will come and prostrate themselves before you, because your judgments have been revealed" (15:3-4). The final, celebratory hymn honoring God in 19:1-8 shows how God's judgment of the social order of Rome upholds God's honor and reliability—honor because God has not tolerated the affronts of an idolatrous and self-glorifying regime, and reliability because the clients of God, who entrusted their honor to God as they fell victim to society's machinery of social control, are at last vindicated.

These assurances of God's care for the honor of the believer appealed to the confidence of those Christians in danger of shameful treatment or worse at the hands of the dominant culture. As the tension between Church and society escalated (as it assuredly would if John's advice were followed rather than the preaching of the Nicolaitans) believers would be enabled to endure society's verdict upon their lives as dishonorable or even worthless in the knowledge that God's own honor demanded that God vindicate God's clients. The final vision in Revelation, that of the New Jerusalem, the place where God's servants receive their full honor and reward, is also of the place where God's servants will worship God face to face (22:3-4). Citizenship there, however, is enjoyed only by those whose first thought in this life was concern for God's honor rather than for their safety or comfort within the dominant culture (the latter being the "cowardly" and "unreliable" clients of 21:8, who are explicitly excluded). John thus weaves into his vision the dual considerations of concern to live so as to preserve God's honor and of assurance of God's care for the believer's honor: both are pillars of his rhetorical strategy, supporting his call to remain faithful to the minority culture's values and preserve its identity.

B. "Fallen, fallen is Babylon": The Censure and Future Degradation of Rome

The message of the second angel consists in the declaration that "Babylon the great is fallen," attributing her demise to her censurable behavior: she "has given the nations a drink of the wine of her adulterous passion" (14:8). We have seen how John censures the behavior of those who engage in idolatrous worship; with the message of the second angel we turn to John's censure of the Roman order itself. Rome laid claim to (or rather the spokespersons of the dominant culture claimed for Rome) a highly honorable position in the divine scheme. Rome was the city selected by the gods to rule forever, to usher in a new Golden Age of peace and prosperity, to extend law and order to the far reaches of the known world.[21] John challenges Rome's claim to honor at every point, protesting to the contrary that the Roman order was a dishonorable and vicious order diametrically opposed to virtue as embodied by God's standards.

Prominent among the charges leveled against Rome is that of wanton violence against God's servants. The goddess *Roma* is presented as a polluted whore, "drunk from the blood of the holy ones and the blood of Jesus' witnesses" (17:6). In her was found "the blood of prophets and of holy ones, and of all those who have been slaughtered upon the earth" (18:24), a fact that calls out for divine vengeance (18:20; cf. 6:9-11; 16:5-7). She is not the sustainer of peace but the source of violence and unjust bloodshed.[22] Rome claimed honor ("she glorified herself," 18:7) beyond what was rightly hers to claim; she spent on herself wealth in proportion to a status that did not belong rightly to her (her "luxury," 18:3, 7). She is censured for assuring herself and her subjects of her perpetual well-being in the ideology of *Roma Aeterna* ("I sit as a queen, I am not a widow, and I will certainly not see grief," 18:7), a form of arrogance violating God's power to allot kingdoms their periods and their ends (cf. Dan 2:21; 4:26; 5:21). Rome sits as "the great city which has authority over the kings of the earth" (17:18), exercising that rule, however, in opposition to the rightful claim of Jesus as "ruler of the kings of the earth" (1:5). Ultimately it is not the Christians who act seditiously in opposition to Roman imperial ideology but the supporters of Rome who rebel against the rule of the Most High and his Anointed.

Rome extends its power and influence not through enlightened policy but through deception (18:23), through the intoxication of the ignorant (17:2). Partnership with Rome is a sign again of being "taken in" by the agents of Satan, of being kept ignorant of the truth. Such ignorance was regarded by Greco-Roman philosophers, at least, as a dishonorable, servile state.[23] John thus invites the believers once again to assess the activity and opinion of the majority of their neighbors. He wants the believers to see them as deceived, aberrant individuals, whose hostility toward the Christian confession should be understood as an expression of their error. Connection with Rome, moreover, is labeled "fornication" and pollution (17:2, 4; 18:3; 19:2). It brings defilement, a stain upon one's honor, rather than opening the door to the acquisition of things honorable.[24]

John avers that Rome is not the "eternal city" chosen by the gods to rule forever, but rather stands under God's imminent judgment, sentenced already to destruction. God's wrath and vindication of the honor of the "apostles, holy ones, and prophets" against the city that made lofty but false claims to honor and affronted God through her "sins" is certain. This must change how the hearers weigh "advantage" and "security": if they accept John's message these are clearly not to be found in alliance with Rome or the dominant culture. The Roman order is itself censured as a dishonorable, vice-ridden system, connections with which mean pollution and defilement rather than enfranchisement and profit. Whatever smacks of seeking peace with Rome becomes a partnership in her sins (18:4) and in the punishments that must ensue. The path to advantage and safety is the path of separation from her sins even if that should bring marginalization or worse in the present.

C. "Those who worship the beast and its image": The Path to Dishonor in Revelation

The third angel is given a disproportionately long message, one that may therefore have been of special importance for the hearers of Revelation:

> Those who worship the beast and its image, and receive a mark on their foreheads or on their hands, they will also drink the wine of God's

wrath, poured unmixed into the cup of his anger, and they will be tormented with fire and sulphur in the presence of the holy angels and in the presence of the Lamb. And the smoke of their torment goes up forever and ever. There is no rest day or night for those who worship the beast and its image and for anyone who receives the mark of its name (14:9-11 NRSV).

Not only is the worshiper of the beast subjected to physical punishment (itself an expression of dishonor), but the disgrace of such punishment is highlighted by the presence of an honorable audience: the holy angels and the Lamb bear witness to the degradation of the idolaters, and the public nature of this punishment makes the disgrace all the more bitter. The rhetorical impact of such a message on the hearers is clear: participation in the imperial cult, whatever benefits it might bring in terms of relieving tension between Church and society now, would ultimately lead to disgrace and disadvantage.

The believer faced, and would increasingly face throughout the second century, pressure from members of the dominant culture to participate in the imperial cult. John acknowledges that refusal to participate would remain a threat to the believers' temporary safety and honor. Revelation 13:7 speaks of the beast's power to make war on God's servants and kill them; in 13:15-17 economic disenfranchisement and execution are posited as the result of noncompliance with the demands of the dominant culture; in 20:4-6 the hearer encounters a large company of "those who had been beheaded for their testimony to Jesus and to the word of God," who "had not worshiped the beast or its image" (20:4 NRSV). In light of the milder pressures faced by the recipients of Revelation and this prospect of increasing pressure from outside the Nicolaitans' proposal of a Christianity that allowed for "eating food sacrificed to idols" might have seemed to many an advantageous course of action.

John responds to this sort of proposal, however, with a stark picture of the greater disadvantage that would accompany the path of accommodation. Just as he will not allow the believers to accept the claim that the emperor is a benefactor and mediator of divine favor (ch. 13), so he will not allow them to view even feigned participation in the machine that legitimates the emperor's rule as advantageous. The seven oracles strongly reinforce this appeal through their use of praise and censure (components of each of the oracles). By issuing commendations and condemnations from the mouth of the glorified Christ, John affirms for the hearers what behaviors are honorable and what are shameful in the eyes of the group. Prominent among the causes for censure before him who "searches minds and hearts" (2:23) is compromising one's separation from idolatrous worship (2:14-15, 20). This finds its complement in the praise of those who "hold fast to my name" and "do not deny" Jesus' name (2:3, 13; 3:8).

The social pressure to deny the name is great, extending even to the point of the lynching of Antipas, who remained loyal to his patron even unto death (2:13). Nevertheless John argues by means of his visions that the path to safe coexistence with the dominant culture becomes the path to danger and dishonor before the court of God, the court that ascribes the eternal verdict. As idolaters in general are targeted specifically as objects of God's wrath and judgments (9:20-21; 16:9, 11), so those who fail to resist society's pressure to offer honor to those who stand opposed to God tread the path to eternal dishonor. Those whose names are "not found written in the book of life"—identified earlier as those who participate in the universal cult of the emperor (13:8)—are thrown "into the lake of fire" (20:15). Those who are "cowardly" and "faithless" (21:8), who do not endure the pressures courageously out of loyalty to their divine patron, lead the list of those excluded from the New Jerusalem and found in "the lake burning with fire and sulfur, which is the second death" (cf. 21:8; 22:15). While not speaking in the idiom of an oration John nevertheless presents a refutation of his opponents' proposal of the path to advantage. Dishonor, disfavor, and destruction await those who show greater care for the demands of the dominant culture than for the honor of the One God and their debt of gratitude to the Lamb.

D. *"How honorable are those who die in the Lord from now on":*
The Path to Honor

What, then, is the path to honor in Revelation? What would the hearer of Revelation understand to be the truly advantageous course of action? Those who stand in God's favor (5:8; 8:3-4; 22:21) and under God's protection (11:18; 16:6-7; 18:20; 20:9) are regularly referred to in Revelation as *hagioi*, "saints" or "holy ones." This group is defined as "those keeping the commandments of God and the faith of Jesus" (14:12; cf. 12:17). Being identified as a "saint" gives one a claim to honor before God's court, and the hearer is immediately pointed to the importance of obedience to God's commands (the first of which, notably, prohibits the worship of other gods and the practice of idolatry) and steadfastness in one's commitment to Jesus.

The makarism that closes the episode of the three angels also points suggestively toward what is held out as "honorable" or as a sign of divine favor in Revelation:

> And I heard a voice from heaven saying, "Write this: Blessed are the dead who from now on die in the Lord." "Yes," says the Spirit, "they will rest from their labors, for their deeds follow them" (14:13 NRSV).

We recall our earlier discussion of K. C. Hanson's analysis of the meaning of "blessed" *(makarios)* in an honor culture: pronouncing an individual "blessed" for some attribute or behavior amounted to declaring that individual "honorable" and holding up that attribute or behavior as honorable as well. In this instance the most extreme experience of society's disapproval and censure, namely execution, is pronounced a mark of honor within the community and before the court of God.[25] When dying is a sign of being held in esteem by God and favored what pressures can the outside world bring to bear on one's commitment? Again the proximity of the Christian culture and philosophical culture impresses itself upon us: "The man over whom pleasure has no power, nor evil, nor fame, nor wealth, and who, whenever it seems good to him, can spit his whole paltry body into some oppressor's face and depart from this life—whose slave can he any longer be, whose subject?" (Epictetus, *Diss.* 3.24.71). In a similar fashion John arms the believer to yield up his or her life so as to remain a faithful witness to the divine patron, transforming society's ultimate expressions of shame into a claim to honor.

Readers of Revelation have noted that John preserves a set of seven makarisms strung throughout his visions. As we look to these, other elements of the "path to honor" emerge:

> Blessed is the one who reads aloud the words of the prophecy, and blessed are those who hear, and who keep what is written in it; for the time is near (1:3 NRSV).

> See, I am coming like a thief! Blessed is the one who stays awake and is clothed, not going about naked and exposed to shame (16:15 NRSV).

> And the angel said to me, "Write this: Blessed are those who are invited to the marriage supper of the Lamb" (19:9 NRSV).

> Blessed and holy are those who share in the first resurrection. Over these the second death has no power, but they will be priests of God and of Christ, and they will reign with him a thousand years (20:6 NRSV).

> See, I am coming soon! Blessed is the one who keeps the words of the prophecy of this book (22:7 NRSV).
>
> Blessed are those who wash their robes, so that they will have the right to the tree of life and may enter the city by the gates. Outside are the dogs and sorcerers and fornicators and murderers and idolaters, and everyone who loves and practices falsehood (22:14-15 NRSV).

Two makarisms (1:3; 22:7) label the one who "keeps" the words of Revelation "honorable" and "favored." These frame the whole of the book, pointing to the acceptance of the view of the world disclosed therein and the call to remain exclusively loyal to the Lamb and separate from the idolatry and luxury of the dominant culture as the way to stand honored in God's sight and to remain within God's favor. The makarism of 16:15 connects honor with eschatological readiness in a manner strikingly similar to Mark 13:32-36: readiness for Christ's return and preparation so as not to be "exposed" on that day of judgment make one honorable. The invitees to the Lamb's marriage feast are "favored." The literary context of this makarism, set at the close of the hymns celebrating the judgment of Babylon, reinforces John's call to remain separate from the Roman order, to remain "chaste" and "undefiled" through collusion with the idolatrous dominant culture. Such are those who are privileged to attend this eschatological banquet.

The remaining two makarisms (20:6; 22:14) also hold up as honorable and favored those who have experienced society's verdict of "dishonorable" on account of their loyalty to Jesus. The first of these makarisms appears at the close of the vision of those who "had been beheaded for their testimony to Jesus and for the word of God," who had not "worshiped the beast or its image" (20:4 NRSV). These whom society most marginalized and execrated (through execution) God most favors, for these share Christ's thousand-year reign, are consecrated as priests to God and Christ, and are preserved from divine punishment (the "second death"). Those who "wash their robes" had been encountered earlier in Revelation at 7:14, and the hearers' understanding of this image may be even further refined by the commendation of those who "did not soil their clothes" (3:4). The cleansing or soiling of garments takes the hearer into the language of purity, of boundaries that are to be observed, and hence again of keeping oneself "pure" in commitment to the One God and the Lamb and "undefiled" in terms of collusion with the world that rebels against the One God. Those who "wash their robes" come through the "great ordeal" (7:14), having suffered not the plagues of God but the pressures of society.

These seven makarisms are part of John's larger program of outlining for the members of the seven churches the path to honor before God's court. John speaks of the believer's honor in terms of their appointment to priesthood (1:6; 5:9) and frequently refers to God's loyal clients (those who would receive approval and reward rather than punishment and disgrace at God's judgment) as "saints" *(hagioi)*, a term common to early Christian texts. In Revelation, however, these terms, which resonate with conceptions of "holiness," "consecration," and "separation" from the profane, further reinforce John's equation of the community's maintenance of high boundaries between church and society with the honor of the believer.[26]

The seven oracles that preface the main body of the apocalypse, as we noted earlier, contain extensive sections of praise and censure, further delineating for the hearers what gives them honor in God's sight and what detracts from their honor. Perseverance in Christian witness and investment within the believing community are chief causes for commendation (2:2a, 3, 19; 3:8b), and John is careful frequently to transform the experience of marginalization at the hands of the representatives of the dominant culture into a claim to honor within the group (which is recognized by the glorified Christ, the coming Judge of all). The Smyrnaean believers' endurance of censure (2:9-10) and the Pergamene believers' loyalty even in the wake of the lynching of Antipas (2:13), measurements of the disrepute in which the larger society holds such deviants, receive Jesus' affirmation—an acknowledgment of honor witnessed by the churches throughout the province. The poverty of the Smyrnaean believers, a sign of their lack of patronage networks and marginalization within the economy of the city, becomes a sign of their true wealth in Jesus' eyes (2:9a); the Laodicean Christians, who claim honor on the basis of their wealth (3:17a), find their claim rejected by Jesus and instead receive censure for their failure to be useful to him (3:15-16).

In each of these seven oracles the believers are called to "overcome" or to "conquer." The possibility of victory lies before them, and great promises are made "to the one who overcomes" to stimulate the hearers' ambition to seek these honors (2:7, 11, 17, 26-28; 3:5, 12, 21). Those who "overcome" will be affirmed by Jesus before the court of God: the Lamb will bear witness to their loyalty and honorable character (3:5); those who resist the enticements to ally themselves with Rome's rule will receive a share in Christ's rule (2:26-28a; 3:21). John does not allow believers to see themselves as victims of society but gives them an active role in their encounter with the dominant culture. Accommodation will mean defeat and shame; treading the path of fidelity to God will constitute honorable victory over the world. What is "overcoming" in Revelation? John will clarify the behaviors that constitute "victory" as his visions unfold.

The first model of "overcoming" is the "Lion from the tribe of Judah" whose victory won for him the unique privilege and honor of opening the sealed scroll by which God's judgments are enacted. The acclamation of the Lamb, however, locates this victory in his redemptive death: his endurance of execution (slaughter, 5:9). A second type of conquering appears in the hymn of 12:10-12 where Satan's defeat is attributed not to the prowess of "Michael and his angels" (12:7) but to those who "did not cling to life even in the face of death" (12:11 NRSV). Holding fast to the "word of their testimony" and the "blood of the Lamb" even to the point of death is not a mark of defeat at the hands of Satan's agents but of victory over the Dragon.[27] This pattern of "overcoming" is reinforced in 15:2 where "those who conquer the beast and its image and the number of its name" gather before the throne of God to celebrate God's justice and their deliverance. Conquering the beast and its image, however, means resisting the pressures to worship the beast (cf. 13:15-17) even if it entails accepting execution (cf. 20:4-5). The path to honor—to the enjoyment of victory and its rewards before God's court—is the path of separation from the dominant culture and resistance to its efforts to "reform" the Christians. It is not honor in the eyes of the idolatrous society that matters, but honor before God and the holy angels. John urges the addressees so to live here that when "their deeds follow them" to God's court they shall be found loyal clients who have held the honor of God most dear.

CONCLUSION

Through visionary rhetoric John deals rather directly with the topics of "eternal honor and safety" as opposed to "temporary honor and safety." The seven oracles to the churches invite the believers to seek the greater honor Jesus has prepared for the faithful. The visions consistently move the hearers to identify with (and thus seek to embody the behaviors of) those who are honored before God's court, and to avoid those courses of action that, while they will lessen the tension between themselves and society, will ultimately lead to open and lasting disgrace before God and the holy angels. At stake quite explicitly in Revelation is the honor of God and the honor of Christ, and a strong message of the vision is that the believer's honor is only secure insofar as that believer honors God and God's Messiah even when the cost is high and temporary disgrace in the world's eyes ensues. In Revelation, as in other early Christian texts, marginalization and disgrace at the hands of society on account of commitment to the divine patron become a source of honor and assurance of favor within the Christian culture. The visionary rhetoric allows the believer to consider his or her choices and investments more directly in light of eternity, and in so doing clarifies for the believer the necessity of commitment to do as the Spirit directs.[28]

Once again it has been impossible to fully exploit the potential of the investigation of honor discourse as outlined in the first chapter. We have been able only to highlight the broader contours of John's use of honor discourse, hopefully raising the possibilities of the reader's developing this investigation further. The connections between the exploration of honor discourse and the larger exegetical task are already becoming apparent. Sensitivity to the cultural cues of honor refines our thinking about key lexical terms such as the meanings and, perhaps more importantly, the impact upon the hearers of such terms as "blessed." We learn more about what it means to "fear" God in Revelation, namely nurturing respect for God's honor and caution about affronting God and failing in one's obligations to one's divine benefactor. We come to understand God's "wrath" not as a psychological deficiency but as a culturally-contextualized expression of God's honor. Awareness of honor scripts helps us to look at the broader literary context of a given passage in a new light. We are enabled, for example, to trace the development of "paths" to honor and dishonor, to discern the cumulative effect of each step along this path proposed by Revelation.

Of course investigation of honor discourse relates directly to the rhetorical analysis of the text, opening up new avenues for the exploration of Revelation's impact on the hearers, the directions in which John seeks to move them, and the means by which he seeks to motivate them. Finally, our investigation links up with the study of the social setting of the group in its historical context. It helps us, for example, to delineate its relationship to other groups more precisely. When death is a sign of favor and honor in the sight of the counterculture the dominant culture's mechanisms of social control will be powerless, being viewed not as an ascription of dishonor but as the path to honor to be courageously endured, through which one can "overcome," achieve the "crown of life," and be invested with authority and a position on a throne. The increasing number of martyrs throughout the second and third centuries, and the veneration of such figures, testifies to the importance and pervasiveness of such "social engineering" strategies within the early Church.

NOTES: CHAPTER 7

[1] For an earlier attempt to analyze the strategy of John's visionary rhetoric see David A. deSilva, "The Construction and Social Function of a Counter-Cosmos in the Revelation of John," *Forum* 9:1-2 (1993) 47–61.

[2] For detailed discussions of authorship and date and support for the positions taken here see Adela Yarbro Collins, "Dating the Apocalypse of John," *Biblical Research* 26 (1981) 33–45; eadem, *Crisis and Catharsis: The Power of the Apocalypse* (Philadelphia: Westminster, 1984) 25–83; David A. deSilva, "The Social Setting of the Apocalypse of John: Conflicts Within, Fears Without," *Westminster Theological Journal* 54 (1992) 273–302; David E. Aune, "The Social Matrix of the Apocalypse of John," *Biblical Research* 26 (1981) 16–32; Robert H. Mounce, *The Book of Revelation* (rev. ed. Grand Rapids: Eerdmans, 1998) 15–21; Leonard L. Thompson, *The Book of Revelation: Apocalypse and Empire* (Oxford: Oxford University Press, 1990) 12–17.

[3] Landmark works in this area include W. M. Ramsey, *The Letters to the Seven Churches in Asia* (updated ed. Peabody, Mass.: Hendrickson, 1994); Colin J. Hemer, *The Letters to the Seven Churches of Asia in Their Local Setting* (Sheffield: JSOT Press, 1986); Helmut Koester, ed., *Ephesos: Metropolis of Asia* (Valley Forge, Pa.: Trinity Press International, 1995).

[4] See especially Leonard L. Thompson, *The Book of Revelation* 96–132, 171–185; Adela Yarbro Collins, *Crisis and Catharsis* 84–110; David L. Barr, "The Apocalypse as Symbolic Transformation of the World," *Interpretation* 38 (1984) 39–50; Charles H. Talbert, *The Apocalypse: A Reading of the Revelation of John* (Louisville: Westminster/John Knox, 1994) 24–25. Thompson and Collins forcefully argue against the likelihood that Revelation was written in response to a new persecution of Christians; all four show how apocalyptic rhetoric may function in a setting not marked by a rise in incidence of persecution.

[5] Cf. S.R.F. Price, *Rituals and Power: The Roman Imperial Cult in Asia Minor* (Cambridge: Cambridge University Press, 1984); G. W. Bowersock, "The Imperial Cult: Perceptions and Persistence," in Ben F. Meyer and E. P. Sanders, eds., *Jewish and Christian Self-Definition* (Philadelphia: Fortress, 1982) 3.170–182; Donald C. Earl, *The Age of Augustus* (New York: Exeter, 1968) 166–176; Leonard L. Thompson, *The Book of Revelation* 95–170; David A. deSilva, "The 'Image of the Beast' and the Christians in Asia Minor: Escalation of Sectarian Tension in Revelation 13," *Trinity Journal* n.s. 12 (1991) 185–208.

⁶ The author of 1 Peter, for example, speaks of the origin of the society's hostility in the unbelievers' surprise that their former colleagues no longer join them in their accustomed rituals and practices (4:3-5). While 1 Peter censures these activities as "excesses of dissipation" they included the "lawless idolatry" (4:3) that was the foundation of civic loyalty and solidarity. A view from the "other side" comes from Pliny the Younger (*Ep.* X.96), who sees the renewed interest in traditional religious activity as the healthy result of his investigation of the deviant Christians, many of whom are now returning to fulfill their social and civic obligations.

⁷ This bilingual pun is noted by R. H. Charles, *A Critical and Exegetical Commentary on the Revelation of St. John* (Edinburgh: T & T Clark, 1920) 1.52; J. Massyngberde Ford, *Revelation* (New York: Doubleday, 1975) 391.

⁸ Robert H. Mounce, *Revelation* 81; A. LeGrys, "Conflict and Vengeance in the Book of Revelation," *Expository Times* 104 (1992) 76–80; Charles Talbert, *The Apocalypse* 19; J. M. Ford, *Revelation* 291; G. B. Caird, *The Revelation of St. John* (London: A & C Black, 1966) 39: "The sum total of the Nicolaitans' offense, then, is that they took a laxer attitude than John to pagan society and religion."

⁹ While Mounce (*Revelation* 81) and Jürgen Roloff (*The Revelation of John* [Minneapolis: Fortress, 1993] 52) hold that the Nicolaitans deviated from the group's sexual norms, Caird (*Revelation* 39) insightfully notes that "in every other case except one in which he uses the verb *porneuein* or the noun *porneia* he uses them metaphorically." Given the allusiveness of John's language and his compounding of resonances from the Jewish Scriptures a metaphorical sense seems most appropriate here.

¹⁰ On the social and economic dangers facing the Christian who avoided all contact with idolatrous settings see Ford, *Revelation* 406; Charles, *Revelation* 1.69–70; Mounce, *Revelation* 85–86. David Aune ("Social Matrix" 28) presents the intriguing opinion that Jezebel is in fact the "chair" of the Nicolaitan circle of prophets, which has gained substantial ground in Pergamum and Thyatira, but been successfully blocked in Ephesus. According to this view she is John's primary rival among the seven churches.

¹¹ Adela Yarbro Collins, *Crisis and Catharsis* 132–133.

¹² For fuller discussion of how Revelation as "apocalypse" works to interpret everyday realities and choices in terms of a larger world construction see deSilva, "Counter-Cosmos," and Barr, "Symbolic Transformation."

¹³ A simple tally of words for honor and honoring in Revelation will demonstrate this: (*timē*: 4:9, 11; 5:12, 13; 7:12; 21:26; *doxa*: 1:6; 4:9, 11; 5:12, 13; 7:12; 11:13; 14:7; 15:8; 16:9; 18:1; 19:1, 7; 21:11, 23, 24, 26; *doxazō*: 15:4; 18:7).

¹⁴ See, e.g., Adela Yarbro Collins, "The Revelation of John: An Apocalyptic Response to a Social Crisis," *Currents in Theology and Mission* 8 (1981) 4–12.

[15] John thus bases his rhetorical strategy in central topics of "justice," specifically "piety" ("justice" toward the divine; see Aristotle, *Virt.* 5.2; *Rhet. ad Her.* 3.3.4; *Rhet. ad Alex.* 1421b. 36–40).

[16] C. G. Jung (*Answer to Job* [London: Routledge & Paul, 1954] 125), for example, thinks that Revelation "contradicts all ideas of Christian humility, tolerance, and love of your neighbor and enemies, and makes nonsense of a loving father in heaven and rescuer of [hu]mankind." It contains "a veritable orgy of hatred, wrath, vindictiveness, and blind destructive fury." D. H. Lawrence (*Apocalypse* [Harmondsworth: Penguin, 1974] 18) is more complete in his denunciation of the theology and ethics of Revelation: "Judas had to betray Jesus to the powers that be . . . and in the same way, Revelation had to be included in the New Testament, to give the death kiss to the Gospels."

[17] This is a well-known topic of "justice" in the Greco-Roman world. Aristotle (*Nic. Eth.* 1163b15-18), for example, had written that "requital in accordance with desert is in fact sometimes impossible, for instance in honouring the gods, or one's parents: no one could ever render them the honour they deserve, and a man is deemed virtuous if he pays them all the regard he can." Where John departs from this shared ethic is in his determination of what god deserves this response of gratitude, loyalty, and obedience. In reminding his Christian readers of God's claim on their gratitude and loyalty, particularly in cultivating a willingness to endure loss for the sake of this commitment to God, John comes strikingly close to the logic of 4 Macc 16:18-19, where the mother of the seven martyred brothers says: "Remember that it is through God that you have had a share in the world and have enjoyed life, and therefore you ought to endure any suffering for the sake of God."

[18] Cf. F. G. Downing, "Pliny's Prosecutions of Christians: Revelation and 1 Peter," *JSNT* 34 (1988) 105–123.

[19] Pliny, *Ep.* X.96; Justin, *Apol.* 1, 3–12.

[20] On John's ideological opposition to the emperor cult see further Ethelbert Stauffer, *Christ and the Caesars: Historical Sketches,* trans. K. and R. Gregor Smith (Philadelphia: Westminster, 1955); Dominique Cuss, *Imperial Cult and Honorary Terms in the New Testament* (Fribourg: Fribourg University Press, 1974); deSilva, "The 'Image of the Beast.'"

[21] Such propaganda appears in Virgil's fourth *Eclogue* and his *Aeneid* (see especially 1.234–37; 4.231–32; also Plutarch, *Mor.* 317A). Coins bearing the iconographic representation of Rome as a beneficent goddess show John's "unveiling" of this figure to be all the more striking and subversive. See Richard Bauckham, "The Economic Critique of Rome in Revelation 18," in *The Climax of Prophecy: Studies on the Book of Revelation* (Edinburgh: T & T Clark, 1993) 338–383, at 343–350.

[22] A similar critique of Roman power is placed on the lips of the British chieftain Calgacus by Tacitus: "Robbery, savagery, and rape they call 'government'; they make a wasteland and call it 'peace'" (*Agr.* 30).

²³ See Dio, *Or.* 14.18.

²⁴ One might here go on profitably to explore the connection between remaining "unsoiled" and receiving approval and praise from God and Jesus throughout Revelation (cf. 3:4-5; 7:14; 14:1-5; 21:27).

²⁵ While this verse has been used effectively as a text for funeral anthems, thus being applied to those who may not have experienced a violent death on account of their Christian commitment, the context of Rev 13:1–14:13, together with such other expressions of violent death as 20:4-6, suggests that John has this primarily in mind in the makarism of 14:13.

²⁶ On John's interest in heightening sectarian tension and group boundaries see further deSilva, "The 'Image of the Beast,'" 207–208; idem, "Social Setting of the Revelation," 296–302.

²⁷ On this transformation of the meaning of "conquest" see further Barr, "Apocalypse as Symbolic Transformation," 41–42.

²⁸ Revelation thus allows a critique of the dominant culture and the necessity of yielding to the demands of that culture by viewing the machinery of society *sub specie aeternitatis* (cf. Peter L. Berger, *The Sacred Canopy* [New York: Doubleday, 1967] 97 on the de-alienating potential of religion).

Conclusion: Honor Discourse, Exegesis, and the Church

In the preceding chapters we have seen how analysis of honor discourse in a New Testament text contributes to our understanding of the rhetorical strategy and purpose of a given text *and* to the social formation of the group that received and read the text. Our study of the rhetorical handbooks revealed that hearers made a decision based on their perception of advantage, and that this advantage was conceived in terms of honor and safety (with honor being primary for both Quintilian and the author of the *Rhetorica ad Herennium*). As we examine how the author of a text prescribes the path to (greater) advantage and warns against a certain course as disadvantageous we uncover the essence of the text's purpose and rhetorical goal, and the backbone of its rhetorical strategy for persuading the addressees. Our analysis of epistles, which show themselves to be immediately accessible to classical rhetorical analysis, and of the gospels and Revelation, which have been less accessible to rhetorical criticism, has supported our claim that since deliberation rests on showing the path to honor, by looking for these clues in a text we find the heart of its rhetorical strategy, deliberative purpose, and author's intent.

Integral to such analysis has been the investigation of the questions, "in whose eyes does honor matter?" and "in what terms can advantage be construed?" These questions are directly related to the worldview of a group and the maintenance of the group's constituency. Setting apart fellow group members (and relevant supra-social entities) as those who are best able to assess one's true honor is an essential aspect of sustaining the life of the group and keeping group members' ambitions in line with the survival of the group, the maintenance of its values, beliefs, and *ethos*. The rhetorical strategy of a text depends not only on appeals to the mind (or to the hearers' emotions, or the perception of the speaker's credibility), but also on providing the social framework for the reinforcement of the course of action advocated within the text.

HONOR DISCOURSE AND THE EXEGETICAL ENTERPRISE

No summary of the method will be attempted here. The reader, now armed with several models of the method at work, is invited rather to return to the first chapter and reconsider the theoretical basis for these inquiries. Instead we will reflect on the interconnections between analysis of honor discourse and the traditional disciplines of biblical exegesis. In our several forays into sample New Testament texts we have found that attention to honor discourse enhances our engagement in many traditional avenues of investigation. Permit me to stress the word "enhances" in the preceding sentence: honor investigations can never claim to be the "be-all and end-all" of exegesis, but rather interact with other avenues of investigation in enlightening ways.

First, this series of investigations has provided a new context for considering the meaning and impact of words themselves: terms like "glory," "fear," "anger," "grace" take on an added dimension and begin to be understood within their native context rather than our modern context (which frequently has difficulty finding a place for "fear" or "anger" in theology). Second, we have seen how attention to honor discourse in one passage leads to a fruitful examination of the broader literary context of a whole text, suggesting new ways in which the parts reinforce and develop one another (not only to expand on a theme, but also to create a cumulative and strategic impact on the hearers). Third, we have seen how the use of honor discourse within the New Testament opens up new avenues for the exploration of the philosophical context of these writings. The early Church exhibits connections with, for example, the Stoa not only where key terms like *logos* or *autarcheia* are used, but also where strategies for negating the opinion of non-initiates appear. Fourth, our future analyses of a New Testament author's use of earlier traditions and authoritative texts within a composition will take on an added dimension as we consider, for example, how these are used to cast praise or censure on a particular course of action or to support the claim that honor or dishonor will follow upon a certain choice.

Analysis of honor discourse remains most closely bound to rhetorical criticism and social-scientific investigations of a text. We have seen throughout this volume (and at length in the first chapter) how classical rhetorical handbooks prescribe the strategic use of considerations of honor to drive both deliberations and epideictic speeches, making us more sensitive to the purpose of epideictic passages or orations as well as to the ways in which honor language fed into all three types of appeal in deliberative orations *(logos, pathos,* and *ethos)*. We have also seen how an analysis of the way a text constructs a "court of reputation" for its hearers and weighs the opinion of different segments of the population tells us much about how the author would orient the audience toward group members and toward the outside world.

Part of the difficulty in any discussion of "exegesis" is, of course, the diversity of methods of biblical interpretation and the lack of an integrated conception of exegesis. In two recent volumes[1] Vernon Robbins has attempted to provide such a conception. His "socio-rhetorical interpretation" is not merely another method for reading texts: it coordinates multiple approaches to reading a text into an integrated method. The method begins with the understanding that texts speak within contexts. As one discovers the contexts within which the text was written and read and adds these dimensions to the reading of the text one approaches ever more closely the full meaning and impact of the text within a particular setting (in the exegetical enterprise usually the setting of the first hearers and readers). Robbins has codified contexts for reading under four categories: inner-texture, inter-texture, social and cultural texture, and ideological texture. Within each of these one will find recognizable aspects of other exegetical disciplines. The poetry of the method is, again, in the integration and dialogue created between these approaches.

Inner-texture takes the interpreter into areas regularly associated with literary and rhetorical analysis. One looks for clues within the text itself for units of narrative or thought (opening-middle-closing texture), repetition of specific words or morphemes within the passage (repetitive texture), movement within a story or argument (progressive texture), and the way in which a passage seeks to be persuasive (argumentative texture). This can be further expanded through attention to the evocative power of a text in a number of arenas usually missed by those who are focused on intellectual content alone (aesthetic or sensory texture).

Inter-texture calls the reader to look for other "texts" that are at work in the primary text. Most readers of the New Testament will be accustomed to investigating "oral-scribal" texture (looking for quotations or allusions within a New Testament text referring to a passage from the Hebrew Scriptures). The interpreter is called to explore the full range of

Jewish and Greco-Roman texts that might be in dialogue with the passage or book under investigation. But written "texts" are not the only meaningful source of inter-texture. Our exploration of the biblical text is enriched as we explore the cultural inter-texture—the allusions to or echoes of cultural phenomena such as the messages of Stoic and Cynic preachers, Roman imperial ideology, Greco-Roman theorists on education—and the social inter-texture—the social roles, codes, and institutions that make up the everyday context of the readers (e.g., honor, patronage, army, athletic competitions, et cetera). Finally, historical inter-texture enters the investigation as the interpreter looks for references or allusions to the fabric of historical events and data.

Social and cultural texture lead the investigator to focus on the social world of the readers of a particular text and how that text locates them in and moves them to respond to that world. Here Robbins finds it helpful to consider the work of sociologists such as Bryan Wilson, who has classified the types of responses of a sect to the larger society (conversionist, introversionist, reformist, etc.), and to determine what types of response to the society are present in, or motivated by, a text. Within this texture one is also invited to explore the "cultural location" of an author by examining the relationship of the values prioritized by that author to the values of other groups and of the dominant culture. Here again the cultural scripts of the first-century Mediterranean world appear as the interpreter is asked to explore how honor, purity, kinship, and patronage codes are operative in the text and how these scripts contribute to the shaping of the readers'/hearers' responses in the world.

The fourth texture, the ideological, asks the investigator first to look at his or her own convictions and commitments concerning the text and the world, and then to uncover the ideology of the author. How does the author develop his or her authority to instruct the readers/hearers? How does the author lead the addressees to move in the direction favored by the author? This calls the interpreter to read the author as shaping reality rather than merely mirroring reality, and to inquire into the interests that motivate and the effects that follow such shaping. In the investigation of each texture, it is imperative that the image of the tapestry (textures intertwined, braided, woven together) not be lost. In practice one must pursue dialogue between the textures, always returning to consider, for example, the inner-texture of argumentation after the inter-texture of social and cultural scripts has been explored, or to ponder social and ideological textures in light of discoveries made within the study of inter-texture (e.g., how does the author select traditions on which to build, and how does this selection reveal his interests for the community's self-understanding and response to the world?). If practiced in this mutually-informing way attention to the various textures will result in a finely nuanced reading of the text.

With this highly-developed scheme as a backdrop one can begin to fathom both the promise and the limitations of investigations of honor discourse. Honor discourse, of course, enters in most prominently at the level of argumentative texture (inner-texture) where we might explore, for example, appeals to *logos*, demonstrating that a certain path leads to honor (or dishonor, or greater honor), to *ethos*, promoting the character of the speaker as honorable, and to *pathos* stimulated by considerations of honor. It appears again as one considers social and cultural inter-texture, noting how honor or patronage scripts are at work within the text (which in turn acts back upon argumentative texture). Our analysis of a text's orientation of the readers or hearers toward their world is highly informative for the exploration of social texture: for example, the nature of a group's response to the world and the social engineering at work within the group. Finally, attention to honor discourse reveals much of what Robbins classifies as ideological texture: how an author motivates the audience to respond as that author would wish, how an author furthers the interests of the group, and the like. Robbins' scheme is equally useful, however, for the avenues of exploration it includes, but to which investigation of honor discourse has little or nothing to contribute, reminding us ever that no one approach can recover the full spectrum of meanings within Scripture.

HONOR DISCOURSE AND THE CONTEMPORARY CHURCH

Paying attention to how New Testament authors use the language of honor and dishonor opens up what was for the first hearers an important part of what made the texts persuasive. An author's appeal to the audience's desire for honor and fear of disgrace caught their interest and engaged them deeply. Looking closely at how an author focused the audience on the opinion of one another and of God, disqualified the opinion outsiders held of them, turned society's attempts at correction into badges of honor within the group, and the like allows modern readers to see how these New Testament writings preserved the Church in a frequently unsupportive environment. We enter into a flesh-and-blood community struggling with issues of how to keep their self-respect, how to remain committed to their newfound faith and hope in the midst of real social pressures.

As we grow in our awareness of this struggle we find that the texts may offer much meat for reflection for those who find themselves within believing communities in the modern world. The importance for these first-century authors of the body of believers—the "court of reputation" or group of significant others—for the commitment and growth of each individual believer challenges the Western emphasis on individualism and the privatization of religion in America and Western Europe. The writers of the texts included in the New Testament were engaged in forming a community based on values and an ideology wholly other from that of the society. Those who are responsible for the formation of believing communities in this age may learn a great deal from their first-century counterparts concerning how to create effective, energizing, supportive congregations that enable individuals to remain faithful to the life and witness to which God has called them. Equally valuable are the insights that can be gained concerning how to defuse the messages believers receive that dissuade them from wholehearted commitment to discipleship and seduce them into having a care first for the things of this life.

This is especially insidious in twentieth-century American society, where the dominant culture frequently speaks in the idiom of Christianity and where many churches function as proponents of a religion wholly adapted to the needs of the dominant culture. Our investigations of the early Christian texts suggest that contemporary pastors and lay leaders need to grow in their analysis of the dominant culture and their awareness of the early Church's techniques of group formation if they wish to see vital communities of disciples following the call of Jesus and not the call of society. While America would not be described as an "honor" culture individual Americans still seek to find their self-respect in achieving those indicators that the society sets forth as marks of "success." We still are raised to seek approval of our "peers" and to act so as to gain recognition. In some circles people are taught to value themselves in socioeconomic terms (position within the professional class, wealth, and ownership of prestige items) and to show their approval or disapproval of others based on similar values. In other circles people lay claim to honor within the group based on physical strength or sexual conquest.

The challenge facing the shapers of the first-century churches still faces leaders in the Church. "Success," the modern American counterpart to "honor," calls for redefinition in terms of the fulfillment of the ideals, behaviors, and attitudes set forward in the Christian Scriptures. Can the voices within the Church help the whole body of believers to measure their "success" wholly against the plumb line of Jesus' teachings? Where this causes believers to move contrary to the values and interests of the dominant culture the Church will need to develop a system of support such that encouragement and affirmation within the group outweighs discouragement from outside the group. These sorts of questions need to be explored in each church's cultural context: attention to honor discourse in the New Testament texts, however, opens up the possibility that these texts will inform not only theology and individual piety, but also the social formation of Christian communities and the development of vital congregations of disciples.

NOTES: CONCLUSION

[1] Vernon K. Robbins, *Exploring the Texture of Texts: A Guide to Socio-Rhetorical Interpretation* (Valley Forge, Pa.: Trinity Press International, 1996); idem, *The Tapestry of Early Christian Discourse: Rhetoric, Society and Ideology* (London: Routledge, 1996).

Bibliography of Modern Authors

Adkins, Arthur W. H. *Merit and Responsibility: A Study in Greek Values.* Oxford: Oxford University Press, 1960.

Attridge, Harold W. *The Epistle to the Hebrews.* Hermeneia. Philadelphia: Fortress, 1989.

Aune, David E. "The Social Matrix of the Apocalypse of John," *Biblical Research* 26 (1981) 16–32.

Barnett, Paul. *The Second Epistle to the Corinthians.* NICNT. Grand Rapids: Eerdmans, 1997.

Barr, David L. "The Apocalypse as Symbolic Transformation of the World," *Interpretation* 38 (1984) 39–50.

Barrett, C. K. *The Gospel According to St John.* London: SPCK, 1960.

Bassler, Jouette M. "The Enigmatic Sign: 2 Thessalonians 1:5," *CBQ* 46 (1984) 496–510.

Bauckham, Richard. *The Climax of Prophecy: Studies on the Book of Revelation.* Edinburgh: T & T Clark, 1993.

_____. *The Gospel for All Christians: Rethinking the Gospel Audiences.* Grand Rapids: Eerdmans, 1998.

Beasley-Murray, G. R. *John.* WBC. Dallas: Word Books, 1987.

Berger, Peter L. *The Sacred Canopy.* Garden City, N.Y.: Doubleday, 1967.

_____. *A Rumor of Angels.* Garden City, N.Y.: Doubleday, 1970.

Berger, Peter L., and Thomas Luckmann. *The Social Construction of Reality.* Garden City, N.Y.: Doubleday, 1967.

Boissevain, Jeremy. *Friends of Friends: Networks, Manipulators and Coalitions.* New York: St. Martin's, 1974.

Bowersock, G. W. "The Imperial Cult: Perceptions and Persistence" in Ben F. Meyer and E. P. Sanders, eds., *Jewish and Christian Self-Definition.* 3 vols. Philadelphia: Fortress, 1980–1982, 3.170–182.

Brown, Raymond E. *The Gospel According to John.* 2 vols. AB 29, 29A. Garden City, N.Y.: Doubleday, 1966.

Bultmann, Rudolf. "Αἰδώς" in Gerhard Kittel and Gerhard Friedrichs, eds., *Theological Dictionary of the New Testament.* Translated by Geoffrey Bromiley. Grand Rapids: Eerdmans, 1964, 1:169–171.

Caird, G. B. *The Revelation of St. John.* London: A & C Black, 1966.

Chapa, Juan. "Is First Thessalonians a Letter of Consolation?" *NTS* 40 (1994) 150–160.

Charles, R. H. *A Critical and Exegetical Commentary on the Revelation of St. John.* 2 vols. ICC. Edinburgh: T & T Clark, 1920.

Collins, Adela Yarbro. "Dating the Apocalypse of John," *Biblical Research* 26 (1981) 33–45.

———. *Crisis and Catharsis: The Power of the Apocalypse.* Philadelphia: Westminster, 1984.

———. "The Revelation of John: An Apocalyptic Response to a Social Crisis," *Currents in Theology and Mission* 8 (1981) 4–12.

Collins, Raymond F. *The Birth of the New Testament.* New York: Crossroad, 1993.

Cuss, Dominique. *Imperial Cult and Honorary Terms in the New Testament.* Fribourg: Fribourg University Press, 1974.

Danker, Frederick W. *Benefactor: Epigraphic Study of a Graeco-Roman and New Testament Semantic Field.* St. Louis: Clayton Publishing House, 1982.

deSilva, David A. "The 'Image of the Beast' and the Christians in Asia Minor: Escalation of Sectarian Tension in Revelation 13," *Trinity Journal* n.s. 12 (1991) 185–208.

———. "The Social Setting of the Apocalypse of John: Conflicts Within, Fears Without," *Westminster Theological Journal* 54 (1992) 273–302.

———. "The Construction and Social Function of a Counter-Cosmos in the Revelation of John," *Forum* 9:1-2 (1993) 47–61.

———. "Measuring Penultimate Against Ultimate Reality: An Investigation of the Integrity and Argumentation of 2 Corinthians," *JSNT* 52 (1993) 41–70.

———. "Recasting the Moment of Decision: 2 Corinthians 6:14–7:1 in Its Literary Context," Andrews University Seminary Studies 31 (1993) 3–16.

———. *Despising Shame: Honor Discourse and Community Maintenance in the Epistle to the Hebrews.* SBL.DS 152. Atlanta: Scholars, 1995.

———. *4 Maccabees.* Guides to the Apocrypha and Pseudepigrapha. Sheffield: Sheffield Academic Press, 1998.

_____. *The Credentials of an Apostle: Paul's Gospel in 2 Corinthians 1–7.* North Richland Hills, Tex.: BIBAL Press, 1998.

_____. "Exchanging Favor for Wrath: Apostasy in Hebrews and Patron-Client Relations," *JBL* 115 (1996) 91–116.

_____. "Meeting the Exigency of a Complex Rhetorical Situation: Paul's Strategy in 2 Corinthians 1 through 7," Andrews University Seminary Studies 34 (1996) 5–22.

Dodds, Eric R. *The Greeks and the Irrational.* Berkeley: University of California Press, 1966.

Downing, F. G. "Pliny's Prosecutions of Christians: Revelation and 1 Peter," *JSNT* 34 (1988) 105–123.

Earl, Donald C. *The Age of Augustus.* New York: Exeter, 1968.

Edson, Charles. "Macedonia, II. State Cults in Thessalonica," *Harvard Studies in Classical Philology* 51 (1940) 127–136.

_____. "Macedonia, III. Cults of Thessalonica," *HThR* 41 (1948) 105–204.

Fitzgerald, J. T. *Cracks in an Earthen Vessel.* SBL.DS. Atlanta: Scholars, 1988.

Ford, J. Massyngberde. *Revelation.* AB 38. Garden City, N.Y.: Doubleday, 1975.

Furnish, Victor P. *II Corinthians.* AB 32A. Garden City, N.Y.: Doubleday, 1984.

Gager, John. *The Origins of Anti-Semitism: Attitudes Toward Judaism in Pagan and Christian Antiquity.* New York and Oxford: Oxford University Press, 1983.

Hagner, Donald A. "The *Sitz im Leben* of the Gospel of Matthew" in David R. Bauer and Mark Alan Powell, eds., *Treasures New and Old: Recent Contributions to Matthean Studies.* Atlanta: Scholars, 1996, 27–68.

Hanson, K. C. "How Honorable! How Shameful! A Cultural Analysis of Matthew's Makarisms and Reproaches," *Semeia* 68 (1996) 81–111.

Hemer, Colin J. *The Letters to the Seven Churches of Asia in Their Local Setting.* Sheffield: JSOT Press, 1986.

Hendrix, Holland. *Thessalonicans Honor Romans.* Th.D. thesis. Harvard University, 1984.

Hengel, Martin. *Crucifixion in the Ancient World and the Folly of the Message of the Cross.* Philadelphia: Fortress, 1977.

Hock, Ronald. *The Social Context of Paul's Ministry: Tentmaking and Apostleship.* Philadelphia: Fortress, 1980.

Jewett, Robert. *The Thessalonian Correspondence: Pauline Rhetoric and Millenarian Piety.* Philadelphia: Fortress, 1986.

Johanson, Bruce. *To All the Brethren. A Text-Linguistic and Rhetorical Approach to 1 Thessalonians.* Uppsala: Almqvist & Wiksell, 1987.

Johnson, Luke T. "On Finding the Lukan Community: A Cautious, Cautionary Essay," *SBLSP* 1 (1979) 87–100.

Jung, C. G. *Answer to Job.* London: Routledge & Paul, 1954.

Kennedy, George A. *New Testament Interpretation through Rhetorical Criticism.* Chapel Hill: University of North Carolina Press, 1984.

Koester, Helmut, ed. *Ephesos: Metropolis of Asia.* Valley Forge, Pa.: Trinity Press International, 1995.

Lane, William L. *Hebrews 1–8.* WBC. Dallas: Word Books, 1991.

_____. *Hebrews 9–13.* WBC. Dallas: Word Books, 1991.

Lawrence, D. H. *Apocalypse.* Harmondsworth: Penguin, 1974.

LeGrys, A. "Conflict and Vengeance in the Book of Revelation," *Expository Times* 104 (1992) 76–80.

Leon, Harry. *The Jews of Ancient Rome.* Reprint Peabody, Mass.: Hendrickson, 1994.

Mack, Burton L. *Rhetoric and the New Testament.* Minneapolis: Augsburg Fortress, 1990.

Mack, Burton L., and Vernon K. Robbins. *Patterns of Persuasion in the Gospels.* Sonoma, Calif.: Polebridge Press, 1989.

MacMullen, Ramsay. *Paganism in the Roman Empire.* New Haven: Yale University Press, 1981.

Malherbe, Abraham. *Paul and the Thessalonians: The Philosophic Tradition of Pastoral Care.* Philadelphia: Fortress, 1987.

Malina, Bruce J. *The New Testament World: Insights from Cultural Anthropology.* Revised ed. Louisville: Westminster/John Knox, 1993.

Malina, Bruce J., and Richard Rohrbaugh. *Social-Science Commentary on the Synoptic Gospels.* Minneapolis: Fortress, 1992.

Markus, Robert A. *Christianity in the Roman World.* London: Thames and Hudson, 1974.

Marshall, I. Howard. *1 and 2 Thessalonians: Based on the Revised Standard Version.* NCBC. Grand Rapids: Eerdmans, 1983.

Marshall, Peter. *Enmity at Corinth: Social Conventions in Paul's Relations with the Corinthians.* Tübingen: J.C.B. Mohr, 1987.

Martin, Ralph P. *2 Corinthians.* WBC. Waco, Tex.: Word Books, 1986.

Meeks, Wayne. "The Social Function of Apocalyptic Language in Pauline Christianity" in David Hellholm, ed., *Apocalypticism in the Mediterranean World and the Near East.* Tübingen: J.C.B. Mohr, 1983, 687–705.

Morris, Leon. *The First and Second Epistles to the Thessalonians.* NICNT. Grand Rapids: Eerdmans, 1991.

Mounce, Robert H. *The Book of Revelation.* NICNT. Revised ed. Grand Rapids: Eerdmans, 1998.

Moxnes, Halvor. "Honor and Shame: A Reader's Guide," *BTB* 23 (1993) 167–176.

_____. "Honor, Shame, and the Outside World in Paul's Letter to the Romans" in Jacob Neusner, Peder Borgen, Ernest S. Frerichs, and Richard Horsley, eds., *The Social World of Formative Christianity and Judaism: Essays in Tribute to Howard Clark Kee.* Philadelphia: Fortress, 1988.

_____. "Honour and Righteousness in Romans," *JSNT* 32 (1988) 61–77.

Neil, William. *The Epistle of Paul to the Thessalonians.* Naperville: Alec R. Allenson, 1957.

Neyrey, Jerome H. "Despising the Shame of the Cross: Honor and Shame in the Johannine Passion Narrative," *Semeia* 68 (1996) 113–137.

Neyrey, Jerome H., ed. *The Social World of Luke-Acts: Models for Interpretation.* Peabody, Mass.: Hendrickson, 1991.

Peristiany, Jean G., ed. *Honour and Shame: The Values of Mediterranean Society.* Chicago: University of Chicago Press, 1966.

Pfitzner, Victor C. *Paul and the Agon Motif: Traditional Athletic Imagery in the Pauline Literature.* Leiden: E. J. Brill, 1967.

Pitt-Rivers, Julian. "Honour and Social Status" in Jean G. Peristiany, ed., *Honour and Shame: The Values of Mediterranean Society.* London: Weidenfeld and Nicolson, 1965.

Pogoloff, Stephen M. *Logos and Sophia: The Rhetorical Situation of 1 Corinthians.* SBL.DS. Atlanta: Scholars, 1992.

Price, S.R.F. *Rituals and Power: The Roman Imperial Cult in Asia Minor.* Cambridge: Cambridge University Press, 1984.

Ramsey, William M. *The Letters to the Seven Churches in Asia.* Updated ed. Peabody, Mass.: Hendrickson, 1994.

Richard, Earl J. *First and Second Thessalonians.* SP 11. Collegeville: The Liturgical Press, 1995.

Robbins, Vernon K. *The Tapestry of Early Christian Discourse: Rhetoric, Society and Ideology.* London: Routledge, 1996.

_____. *Exploring the Texture of Texts.* Valley Forge, Pa.: Trinity Press International, 1996.

Roloff, Jürgen. *The Revelation of John.* Minneapolis: Fortress, 1993.

Saller, R. P. *Personal Patronage under the Early Empire.* Cambridge: Cambridge University Press, 1982.

Seely, David. *The Noble Death. Graeco-Roman Martyrology and Paul's Concept of Salvation.* JSNT.S Sheffield: Sheffield Academic Press, 1990.
Spicq, Ceslaus. *L'Epître aux Hébreux.* 2 vols. Paris: Gabalda, 1952.
Stanton, Graham N. *A Gospel for a New People.* Louisville: Westminster/John Knox, 1993.
Stauffer, Ethelbert. *Christus und die Caesaren.* Hamburg: Friedrich Wittig, 1952.
Stowers, Stanley K. *Letter Writing in Greco-Roman Antiquity.* Library of Early Christianity. Philadelphia: Westminster, 1986.
_____. "*Peri Men Gar* and the Integrity of 2 Cor. 8 and 9," *NovT* 32 (1990) 340–349.
Talbert, Charles H. *The Apocalypse: A Reading of the Revelation of John.* Louisville: Westminster/John Knox, 1994.
Theissen, Gerd. *The Social Setting of Pauline Christianity: Essays on Corinth.* Philadelphia: Fortress, 1982.
Thompson, Leonard L. *The Book of Revelation: Apocalypse and Empire.* Oxford: Oxford University Press, 1990.
Thrall, Margaret E. *The Second Epistle to the Corinthians.* ICC. Edinburgh: T & T Clark, 1994.
Wanamaker, Charles A. *The Epistles to the Thessalonians: A Commentary on the Greek Text.* NIGTC. Grand Rapids: Eerdmans, 1990.
Weima, Jeffrey A. D. "What Has Aristotle To Do With Paul," *Calvin Theological Journal* 32 (1997) 458–68.
Williams, Bernard. *Shame and Necessity.* Berkeley: University of California Press, 1993.
Witherington, Ben III. *John's Wisdom: A Commentary on the Fourth Gospel.* Louisville: Westminster/John Knox, 1995.
_____. *Conflict and Community in Corinth: A Socio-Rhetorical Commentary on 1 and 2 Corinthians.* Grand Rapids: Eerdmans, 1995.
Yee, Gale A. *Jewish Feasts and the Gospel of John.* Wilmington, Del.: Michael Glazier, 1989.

Index of Texts Cited

1. Classical Authors

Anaximenes
Rhetorica ad Alexandrum
1421b23-27	32
1421b36-40	31, 201

Aristotle
Nicomachean Ethics
2.3.7	31
3.1.7	78
3.1.11	31
3.6.10	67
3.8.1-3	xvi
8.14.7	201

Rhetoric
1.2.4	20
1.2.5	32
1.3.5	15
1.5.5	40
1.7	183
1.9.1	20
1.9.35-36	15
1.9.38-39	152
2.1.8-9	32
2.2.1-8	158
2.2.1	21, 189
2.2.3	21, 189
2.2.8	21, 23, 54, 86, 189
2.5.1	21, 22, 161
2.5.3	21, 161
2.5.5	21, 161
2.5.12	33
2.6.2	23
2.6.12	23
2.6.14-15	165
2.9	32
2.9.11	32
2.11.1	24, 44

Virtues and Vices
1.1-2	32
5.2	201

Aulus Gellius
Attic Nights
7.14.2-4	161

Cicero
Nat. D. 1.4   175

Dio Chrysostom
Orations
8.9	119
8.15-16	30
14.18	202
29	30
31	3, 31, 116
31.14	32, 161
31.37	11
31.65	160
31.100	23
32.39	142
44.1	177
44.6	166
48.5-6	2
48.5	19
48.15-16	19
55.1, 3, 5	135
66.15	177
77/78.21, 25	141
73	176
74	176

Diodorus of Sicily
Bib. Hist.
34.1-4	29, 115
40.3-4	29, 114

Epictetus
Dissertations
1.18.21	30
1.24.1-2	30
1.29.50-54	29, 69, 141, 177
1.30.1	29
2.19.24	142
3.22.56	30
3.22.63-65	177
3.24.71	194
4.1.91-98	153
4.5.22	69, 141

Index of Texts Cited

Fronto
Ad M. Caes.
5.34, 37   176

Isocrates
Ad Demonicam
13   175

Juvenal
Satires 14.100-
104   29, 114

Lucian
My Native
Land 8   165
Peregrinus 14   175

Plato
Crito
44C   29
46C-47A   29

Gorgias
526D-527D   29
508D   45

Pliny
Epistulae
10   31
10.96   114, 175, 200, 201

Plutarch
Vit. Per. 3   25
Moralia
317A   201
544D   33
607A   166
1057E   142
1125D-E   175

Pseudo-Cicero
Rhetorica
ad Herennium
3.2.3   8, 16

3.3.4   16, 31, 33, 201
3.3.5   17, 33
3.3.5-9   31
3.5.8-9   16
3.8.15   32

Quintilian
Institutio Oratoria
3.4.16   32
3.7.28   15
3.8.1   31
3.8.12   32
3.8.13   32
3.8.33   183
3.10.12   41
3.10.17   47

Seneca
De beneficiis
1.4.2   2, 30
2.22.1   31, 156
2.24.2   31, 156

De constantia sapientis
11.2   141
13.2   29, 69, 141, 165
13.5   29, 69, 141
16.3   45, 141

Epistulae Morales
81.27   12, 139

Sophocles
Antigone   188

Oed. Tyr.   30

Tacitus
Agricola
30   201
33-34   177

Annales 15.44   175

Historia 5.5   29, 114

Thucydides
History
2.35-46   67
2.35-42   2, 30
2.35   24
2.35.2   24
2.43.1-4   25
2.45.2   31

Virgil
Aeneid
1.234-37   201
4.231-32   201

2. Scriptural texts

Old Testament

Exodus
17:1-7   157

Numbers
13:31–14:4   158
14   158
14:3   158
14:4   158
14:31   158
20:2-13   157
25:1-3   180
31:16   181

Esther (with the Additions)
1:14   152
3:1   152
13:4-5   93
14:1   68
15:1-6   142
15:6   68
15:13   68

2 Maccabees
7   50, 115, 168

Psalms			4:26	190	
2	151		5:21	190	
9:5	12				
29:2	12		*New Testament*		
34:3	12				
88:51-52	167		**Matthew**		
110	151		1:5	37	
110:1	152		1:21	41, 46	
118:22-23	44		1:24-25	40	

Psalms
2 — 151
9:5 — 12
29:2 — 12
34:3 — 12
88:51-52 — 167
110 — 151
110:1 — 152
118:22-23 — 44

Proverbs
6:32-33 — 2

Wisdom
2–5 — 115
3:5 — 8
13:1-9 — 97
14:22-27 — 97

Ben Sira
4:11 — 176
23:18-19 — 29
26:10-18 — 31
42:9-14 — 31
44:1–50:24 — 18, 30
44:20 — 25
45:1-3 — 152
45:24 — 25
46:10-12 — 25
47:20-21 — 25
49:4-5 — 25

Isaiah
29:18-19 — 43
35:5-6 — 43
52:5 — 12
53:4 — 43
61:1 — 43

Jeremiah
31:32 (LXX 38:32) — 176

Daniel
2:21 — 190

4:26 — 190
5:21 — 190

New Testament

Matthew
1:5 — 37
1:21 — 41, 46
1:24-25 — 40
2:1-12 — 37
2:5-6 — 41
3:7-9 — 51
3:11-12 — 50
3:17 — 42, 56
4:23-25 — 42
5:3-12 — 60
5:10-12 — 60, 61
5:11-12 — 64
5:11 — 175
5:16 — 65
5:17-20 — 48, 58
5:21-48 — 58
5:45 — 58, 160
6:1-18 — 54
6:9-15 — 61
6:9 — 12
7:13-14 — 55
7:21-23 — 58
7:28-29 — 49
8:1-17 — 42
8:2 — 43
8:5-13 — 37
8:17 — 43
8:23-27 — 67
8:28–9:1 — 42
9:1-8 — 43, 47
9:8 — 42, 43, 49
9:10-13 — 47, 68
9:14-17 — 47

9:18-33 — 42
9:18 — 43
9:26 — 42
9:31 — 42
9:33 — 40, 42, 49
9:34 — 39, 51
10:5-6 — 37
10:17-18 — 64
10:23 — 37
10:24-39 — 59
10:24-26 — 59
10:24-25 — 55, 64
10:24 — 83
10:25 — 39
10:26 — 55
10:28 — 56
10:32-34 — 59
10:32-33 — 56
10:37-38 — 59
10:40 — 41
11:2-6 — 47
11:2-3 — 43
11:4-5 — 43
11:6 — 60, 61
11:20-24 — 37, 53
11:27 — 41
11:28-30 — 48
12:1-8 — 47, 68
12:24-42 — 47
12:9-14 — 47, 68
12:21 — 37
12:22 — 40
12:23 — 49
12:24 — 39, 51
12:27 — 39
12:38 — 53
12:41-42 — 53
12:48-50 — 56
13:14 — 61
13:16-17 — 60, 61

Index of Texts Cited

13:38	37	20:28	46	25:1-13	63
13:41-43	64	20:30-31	40	25:14-30	63
13:54-58	68	21–23	49	25:31-46	63
14:28-33	67	21:9	40	26:3-5	44
15:1-20	47, 51, 68	21:11-14	61	26:14-16	44
15:1-2	37	21:15-17	47, 68	26:18	46
15:3-9	51	21:15	40	26:21	46
15:3	51	21:23-25	47	26:27-28	46
15:8-9	51	21:28-32	47, 67	26:31-32	46
15:14	52	21:33-46	47, 68	26:39	46
15:21-28	37, 47	21:33-43	37	26:42	46
15:24	37	21:33-36	67	26:45	46
15:29-31	42, 49	21:42	44	26:52-53	46
15:31	43	22:1-10	37	26:59-61	44
16:1-4	47, 68	22:5-8	54	26:64	50
16:4	53	22:8	37	26:65-68	45
16:5-12	48, 51	22:15-22	48	26:65	50
16:16-19	60	22:16	35, 50	27:2	45
16:16	61	22:22	49	27:18	44
16:21-23	46	22:23-33	48, 68	27:19	44
16:24-27	59	22:33	49	27:25	37
16:27	50	22:34-40	48	27:26	45
17:1-8	49	22:41-46	48, 67, 68	27:27-31	45
17:5	56	22:44	56	27:35	45
17:9-12	46	22:46	49	27:39-44	46
17:14-21	42	23:1-39	37	27:43	47
17:22-23	46	23:1-36	49, 51	27:54	37, 45
17:24-27	56	23:4	37	27:63-64	39
18	56	23:5	37	28:18-20	37, 47, 50
18:4	59	23:11-12	59		
18:10-14	57	23:17	56	Mark	
18:15-18	57	23:16	56	13:32-36	195
18:23-35	58, 61	23:19	56	Luke	
18:32-35	62	23:24	56	14:7-11	152
19:3-9	47, 68	24:9-10	64	23:2, 5, 14	39
20:17-19	46	24:14	37	John	
20:18-20	66	24:30-31	50, 56, 64	1:8-9	71
20:24-28	55, 59	24:45–25:46	62	1:10-11	83, 85
20:25-28	85	24:45-51	62	1:10	82
				1:12-13	84

1:14	74, 82, 86	6:14	76	12:26	85
		6:33-35	76	12:28	79
1:17	75, 82	6:38	76	12:32	78
1:16-18	74, 86	6:42	76	12:42-43	81
1:20	71	6:63	85	12:42	72
1:26	82	6:65	83	12:46	82
1:29	79	6:71	78	13:11	78
1:30	71	7:6	78	13:14-16	85
1:32-34	76	7:8	78	13:18-19	78
1:49	77	7:16-18	77	13:20	85
1:41	77	7:18	75, 81	13:21-30	78
1:46	74	7:24	82	13:31-32	80
2:4	78	7:30	78	13:34	83
2:11	76	7:31	76	14:6-7	75
2:16	75	7:33-36	78	14:29	78
3:2	76	8:12	82	15:1-17	86
3:5-6	85	8:15	82	15:8	86
3:13	76	8:20	78	15:12-13	83
3:14	78, 79	8:21-29	78	15:18-21	83
3:16	79	8:23	75	15:27	73
3:17	79	8:34-36	85	16:1	74, 84
3:17-19	83	8:45	83	16:2	72
3:18-19	82	8:49-50	75	16:3	84
3:19-21	81	8:54-55	77	16:4	84
3:28	71	8:54	75	16:33	84
3:30	71	9:22	72, 81	17:1	79
3:31-32	82	9:30-33	76	17:4-5	80
3:33-36	86	10:10	79	17:5	80
3:31	75	10:11	79	17:18	73
3:33	86	10:15	79	17:22	85, 86
3:36	75	10:17-18	78	17:24	80
4:42	76, 79	10:25-27	83	18:6	79
4:54	76	10:41	71	18:8	79
5:22-23	75, 80, 86	11:4	76	18:9	89
		11:27	77	18:11	75, 79
5:23	75, 80	11:40	76	18:12	77
5:27	75, 80	11:51-52	79	18:22	77
5:31-47	77	11:52	79	18:24	77
5:41-42	82	12:23	78, 79	18:37	83
5:41	75	12:25	85	19:1-3	77
5:44	81				

19:2	11	5:1-11	122	13:4-5	128
19:17	77	5:1-6	137	15:3	44
19:18	77	5:1-2	138	15:31	141
19:23-24	77	5:6	138, 141	15:43	135
19:30	78	5:11	137		
19:38	81	6:1-7	124, 138	2 Corinthians	
20:31	73, 74	6:4	124	1–9	140
21:19	84, 86	6:5	138	1:3-9	131
21:29	80	6:9-11	124, 125	1:3-7	130
		6:12-20	125	1:5	131
Romans		6:19-20	125	1:6	131
1:18-32	97	7:29-31	135	1:7	131
2:24	12	7:32	136	1:8-9	130, 132, 135
3:21-31	115	7:34	136	1:12	130, 141
1 Corinthians		8–9	138	1:14	141
1–4	120	8	120	1:22	125
1:17-25	134	8:1-13	128	2:3-11	122
1:17	128	8:1	120	2:15-16	129, 141
1:18-29	122	8:1-2	128	2:15	131
1:18	123, 129	9	128	3:1-6	125, 135
1:22-24	115	9:15-23	128	3:7-18	125, 141
1:23	43	9:15	141	3:9	141
1:26-31	124, 136	9:16	141	3:10-11	126
1:29	141	10:14-21	139, 184	3:10	125
1:31	141	10:19-20	187	3:16	134
2:1-5	128, 135	11:1	128	3:18	126
2:1-2	134	11:2-16	138	4:1-6	123
2:2	123	11:5	138	4:7-18	134
2:4-5	129	11:7	138	4:7	129, 130, 131, 135
2:8	123	11:15	138	4:8-9	127, 31
2:9-10	127	11:16	138	4:10-14	127
2:14-15	124	11:17-31	138	4:10-12	130
3:1-4	138	11:17	138	4:10	131
3:18-20	123, 138	11:21	136	4:12	131
3:21-23	127	11:22	120, 138	4:14	130, 131, 132
3:21	141	12–14	128, 138	4:15	131
4:3	136	12:4-11	127	4:16–5:8	126
4:5	136	12:23-26	120, 136	4:16-18	139
4:6-7	127	12:31	128	4:16	126
4:7	125, 127, 141	13:3	141		

4:17-18	132	11:18	141	1:5	99, 100, 105
4:17	127	11:21-23	143		
4:18	127	11:22-28	132	1:6-10	102
		11:21–12:10	133	1:6-9	113
5:1-8	135	11:23–12:10	143	1:6	92, 98, 101, 102, 105, 116
5:1-4	135	11:23-29	143		
5:5	125	11:23-27	133		
5:10	136	11:23	133		
5:11-13	126	11:30	133, 141, 143	1:9-10	102, 103
5:12	130, 141			1:9	93
5:15	44, 139	11:32-33	143	1:10	95, 115
5:21	141	12:1	141	2	91
6:3	130	12:5	141, 143	2:1-12	100
6:4-10	132	12:6	141	2:1-2	102, 105
6:4-5	132	12:7-10	132	2:2	103
6:6-7	132	12:9-10	143	2:3	100
6:8-10	132	12:9	133, 141	2:4	98, 105
6:14–7:1	140	12:10	134	2:7-12	115
7:4	141	12:11	143	2:11-12	103
7:14	141			2:11-14	105
		13:4	132, 134	2:12	101, 112
8:1-7	137, 138	13:5-6	126	2:13-16	94
8:24	137, 138, 141	Galatians		2:13-14	101
		3:26-26	115	2:14	92, 96, 102
9:1-4	137, 138	5:11	44		
9:2	141			2:14-16	96, 113, 115
9:3	141	Ephesians			
9:11-14	138, 139	4:17-20	97	2:15-16	96, 115
		4:18-19	97	2:15	96
10–13	130			2:17–3:1	115
10:8	141	Philippians		2:17-18	94
10:12-16	136, 143	2:6-11	164	2:17	94
10:13	141	Colossians		2:19-20	99, 104, 105
10:15	141	1:16	185		
10:16	141	3:11	115	3:1-5	94
10:17-18	125			3:2-5	95
10:17	141	1 Thessalonians		3:3-5	100, 115
		1:2-3	98, 105, 113	3:3-4	92, 102
11:5-6	143			3:3	95
11:10	141	1:3-10	105	3:5	95, 96, 105
11:12	141	1:3	101		
11:15	141	1:4-5	99, 105	3:6-10	115
11:16	141	1:4	101		
11:17	141				

Index of Texts Cited 223

3:10	95, 105, 111	5:15	104	3:14	107
3:12-13	103, 105	5:23	104	3:17	112
3:12	99, 104, 105, 106, 115	2 Thessalonians		2 Timothy	
		1:3-4	109	1:16	175
		1:3	107, 109, 111	Hebrews	
3:13	99, 105, 112	1:4	92, 107	1:1-6	154
		1:5	92, 109, 116	1:2	154
4–5	91			1:3	152, 155
4:1-5	115	1:6-10	110	1:4-14	154
4:1-4	105	1:6	92, 111	1:5-14	151
4:1	96, 98, 100, 101, 105	1:8	115	1:5	151
		1:8-9	115	1:6	152
		1:11-12	101, 111, 112	1:9	152
4:3-6	96	1:11	106, 111	1:13	13, 22, 152, 169
4:3	97	1:12	111		
4:4-5	115			2:1-4	144, 159, 176
4:4	100	2	91	2:1	148
4:5	97, 100	2:1-12	107	2:3-4	145
4:9-10	99, 101, 105, 111	2:2	112	2:3	148, 149
		2:3	107, 108	2:5-7	164
4:11	111	2:7	107	2:7-9	152
4:12	104, 106	2:9-12	111, 112	2:8	152, 169
4:13-18	98	2:9-10	108	2:9-18	18
4:13	98, 105	2:10-12	115	2:9	153
4:18	99, 105	2:10	108	2:10	110, 164, 170
		2:11-12	106, 115		
5:3-8	96, 97, 105, 112	2:11	108	2:14-15	153
		2:12	106, 108	2:16	153
5:4	103, 106	2:13-15	108, 112	2:17	152, 155
5:8-9	112	2:13	111	2:18	153, 164
5:9	99, 104, 105	2:14	101, 110, 111	3:1-6	23, 151, 154, 161
5:10-14	105	2:15	111	3:1	152, 170, 172
5:10	99				
5:11	99, 101, 106	3	91	3:6	17, 149, 153
		3:1-2	108		
5:12-13	100, 105	3:2	108, 115	3:7–4:13	144, 157–59
5:13	99, 106, 115	3:5	110		
		3:6-15	111	3:7–4:11	17
5:14	99, 111, 116	3:6	107, 116	3:9	157
		3:14-15	107		

3:10	158	10:3	155	11:13-16	17		
3:11	151, 158	10:12	152, 155	11:16	166		
3:12-13	172	10:13	22, 169	11:13	166		
3:12	148, 149, 159	10:19-22	156	11:14	155		
		10:19-21	18	11:24-26	167		
3:14	149, 170, 172	10:21	17	11:24	167		
		10:22	168	11:25-27	17		
3:18-19	158	10:23	18, 148	11:25-26	161		
		10:24-31	18	11:25	167, 173		
4:1-11	158	10:24-25	168, 172	11:26	167		
4:1	159, 161	10:24	169	11:27	167		
4:11	148	10:25	148, 149, 159	11:35-38	168		
4:14-16	18, 156			11:38	168		
4:14	151, 152	10:26-31	17, 22, 144, 159, 160	11:39	163		
4:16	156						
5:4-5	152			12:1-4	150, 171		
5:8-10	170	10:26	23, 160, 162	12:1-3	18, 150, 164		
5:8	164						
5:9	153	10:27	161	12:1-2	17, 25		
5:11-14	24, 172	10:29	149, 151	12:1	171		
		10:31	161	12:2	150, 152, 164–65, 171		
6:2-3	145	10:32–12:3	150, 162–69				
6:6	151						
6:4-8	18, 144, 159			12:3	149		
		10:32-35	168	12:4-12	8, 110		
6:4-6	149, 160	10:32-34	17, 115, 146–48, 159, 162, 164, 166, 169, 170, 172, 173	12:4	171		
6:4-5	160			12:5-11	170		
6:9-10	172			12:5-13	150		
6:12	148, 150			12:7	17		
6:15	17			12:8	170		
6:20	152, 155			12:15	159, 172		
		10:32	150	12:16-17	17		
7:1–10:18	154	10:33-34	167, 169	12:16	149		
		10:35	162	12:17	176		
8:1	152	10:35-38	159	12:24	154		
8:6	154	10:36-39	18, 163	12:25	144, 176		
9:1-3	155	10:36	149	12:28	18, 156		
9:6-7	155	10:38-39	165				
9:7	155	10:39	160	13	172		
9:9	155			13:1	17, 172		
9:12	155	11:1–12:3	18	13:2	18, 173		
9:15	154	11:2	163	13:3	17, 159, 167, 169, 173		
9:26	155	11:4	163				
		11:5	163				
10:1-4	155	11:8-22	165				

Index of Texts Cited

13:4-6	17	3:8	193, 196	13:11-18	186
13:4	18	3:12	8, 196	13:14	188
13:11	164	3:15-16	196	13:15-17	192, 197
13:12-14	18	3:17	180, 196		
13:14	155, 166, 167	3:21	8, 196	14:1-5	202
		4–5	184–86	14:6-13	183
13:15-16	173	4:1	183	14:6-7	184, 186
13:17	173	4:11	185	14:7	185
				14:8	190
1 Peter		5:8	193	14:9-11	19, 191–92
4:1-4	97, 115	5:9-10	185		
4:3-5	114, 200	5:9	196, 197	14:12	193
4:14-16	175	5:13	185	14:13	194, 202
		6:9-11	190	15:2	8, 197
Revelation		6:15-17	187	15:3-4	186, 189
1:3	194, 195				
1:5	191	7:9-12	186	16:5-7	190
1:6	196	7:9	186	16:6-7	193
1:12-20	184	7:14	195, 202	16:9	188, 193
				16:11	188, 193
2:1–3:22	178, 179–82	8:3-4	193	16:15	194, 195
2:2	196	9:20-21	187, 188, 193	16:21	188
2:3	193, 196			17:2	191
2:7	8, 196	11:3-13	188	17:4	191
2:8-11	179	11:9-10	188	17:6	190
2:9-10	196	11:12	188	17:18	190
2:9	196	11:13	189		
2:11	8, 196	11:15-18	189	18:3	190, 191
2:13	193, 196	11:18	186, 193	18:4	191
2:14-15	193			18:7	190
2:14	180, 188	12:7	197	18:20	190, 193
2:17	8, 196	12:9	187	18:23	191
2:19	196	12:10-12	197	18:24	190
2:20	180, 188, 193	12:11	8, 197		
		12:17	193	19:1-8	189
2:23	193	13–14	202	19:2	191
2:26-28	196	13	192	19:9	194
2:26	8	13:1	187		
		13:4	184, 186, 187, 188	20:4-6	192, 202
3:1	180			20:4-5	197
3:4-5	202	13:5-6	187	20:4	192, 195
3:4	195	13:7	192	20:6	194, 195
3:5	8, 196	13:8	186, 193	20:9	193
3:7-13	179			20:15	193

21:8	190, 193
21:27	202
22:3-4	189
22:7	195
22:14-15	195
22:15	193
22:21	193

3. Extra-biblical Jewish literature

2 Esdras
16:70-73	175

3 Maccabees
3:3-7	93
4:16	69

4 Maccabees
6:9-10	30
6:28-30	67
8–9	168
11:20	30
13:17	29
14:11–17:6	31
15:30	90
16:16	30
16:18-23	18
16:18-19	201
17:11-16	30
17:20-22	67
18:6-9	30

4Q521	43

b. Sanhedrin
43a	39
107b	39

Josephus
Ap.
2.121	29, 114
2.258	29

Bell.
4.149	152
4.164	152
4.168	175

Philo
Flacc.
5	175
53-57	175
53-55	177
72	175

Omn. prob. lib. 26-27 30

Spec. leg.
1.142	152

Vit. Mos. 152

Testament of Levi
2–5	185
16:3	39

4. Extra-biblical Christian literature

Gregory of Nyssa 177

Ignatius
Smyrn. 10 175

John Chrysostom 147, 176, 177

Justin
Dial. 69 39
Apol. 1, 3-12 201

Melito of Sardis 175

Origen
C. Celsum
1.6	39
8.75	177

Exhortatio
3.7.11-14 177

Index of Modern Authors

Adkins, A. W., xiv, xvi, 47
Attridge, H. W., 175
Aune, D. E., 199, 200

Barnett, P., 140, 141, 142
Barr, D. L., 199, 200, 202
Barrett, C. K., 72, 73, 88, 89
Bassler, J. M., 116
Bauckham, R. J., 33, 36, 66, 67, 72, 88, 89, 201
Beasley-Murray, G. R., 71, 72, 73, 74, 88, 89
Berger, P. L., 115, 141, 202
Bowersock, G. W., 114, 199
Brown, R. E., 71, 88, 89
Bultmann, R., 176

Caird, G. B., 200
Chapa, J., 114
Charles, R. H., 200
Collins, A. Y., 199, 200
Collins, R., 114
Cuss, D., 201

Danker, F. W., 30, 176
deSilva, D. A., 28, 30, 67, 68, 114, 140, 141, 175, 199, 200, 201, 202
Dodds, E. R., xiv, xvi
Downing, F. G., 201

Earl, D., 199
Edson, C., 114

Fitzgerald, J. T., 143
Ford, J. M., 200
Furnish, V. P., 128, 141, 142, 143

Gager, J., 29

Hagner, D. A., 37, 38, 67, 68, 72, 88
Hanson, K. C., 51, 60, 68, 194
Hemer, C. J., 199
Hendrix, H., 114
Hengel, M., 67, 89
Hock, R., 116

Jewett, R., 113
Johanson, B., 115
Johnson, L. T., 66
Jung, C. G., 201

Kennedy, G. A., 31
Koester, H., 199

Lane, W. L., 176
Lawrence, D. H., 201
Leon, H., 29
Luckmann, T., 141

Mack, B. L., 31, 66

MacMullen, R., 175
Malherbe, A. J., 114
Malina, B. J., xiv, xvi, xvii, 30, 31, 66, 67, 143
Markus, R. A., 114
Marshall, I. H., 116
Marshall, P., 128, 142
Martin, R. P., 140
Meeks, W. A., 66, 117, 140
Morris, L., 113, 114
Mounce, R. H., 199, 200
Moxnes, H., xvii

Neil, W., 113
Neyrey, J. H., xiv, xvi, xvii, 30, 31, 66, 67, 77, 80, 89, 90, 143, 176

Pfitzner, V. C., 29
Pitt-Rivers, J., xiv, xvi, 10, 28, 30, 31, 47
Pogoloff, S., 119, 140
Price, S.R.F., 114, 116, 199

Ramsey, W. M., 199
Richard, E. J., 113, 116, 117

Robbins, V. K., xvii, 29, 66, 205, 206, 207, 209
Rohrbaugh, R., xvi
Roloff, J., 200

Saller, R. P., 30, 176
Seely, D., 67
Spicq, C., 175
Stanton, G. N., 67, 68
Stauffer, E., 201
Stowers, S. K., 113, 140

Talbert, C. H., 199, 200
Theissen, G., 140, 141
Thompson, L. L., 114, 199
Thrall, M. E., 140

Wanamaker, C. A., 113, 114, 116
Weima, J.A.D., 142
Williams, B., xiv, xvi, 176
Witherington III, B., 33, 72, 73, 88, 89, 90, 140, 141, 142

Yee, G. A., 88

www.ingramcontent.com/pod-product-compliance
Lightning Source LLC
Chambersburg PA
CBHW062016220426
43662CB00010B/1354